WORSHIP IS THE ROAD TO REVIVAL:
CONVERSING WITH DR. ROBERT E. WEBBER

Worship Is the Road to Revival

CONVERSING WITH DR. ROBERT E. WEBBER

ROBERT E. WEBBER

EDITED BY
Keith Call

CASCADE *Books* · Eugene, Oregon

WORSHIP IS THE ROAD TO REVIVAL
Conversing with Dr. Robert E. Webber

Copyright © 2024 Wipf and Stock. All rights reserved. Except for brief quotations in critical publications or reviews, no part of this book may be reproduced in any manner without prior written permission from the publisher. Write: Permissions, Wipf and Stock Publishers, 199 W. 8th Ave., Suite 3, Eugene, OR 97401.

Cascade Books
An Imprint of Wipf and Stock Publishers
199 W. 8th Ave., Suite 3
Eugene, OR 97401

www.wipfandstock.com

PAPERBACK ISBN: 978-1-6667-8946-1
HARDCOVER ISBN: 978-1-6667-8947-8
EBOOK ISBN: 978-1-6667-8948-5

Cataloguing-in-Publication data:

Names: Webber, Robert E., author. | Call, Keith, editor.

Title: Worship is the road to revival : conversing with Dr. Robert E. Webber / Keith Call, editor.

Description: Eugene, OR: Cascade Books, 2024 | Includes bibliographical references.

Identifiers: ISBN 978-1-6667-8946-1 (paperback) | ISBN 978-1-6667-8947-8 (hardcover) | ISBN 978-1-6667-8948-5 (ebook)

Subjects: LCSH: Webber, Robert E., 1933–2007. | Public worship. | Historical theology. | Evangelicalism.

Classification: BV15 W685 2024 (print) | BV15 (ebook)

To the magnificent
Dr. J. Oliver Buswell, warrior, preacher,
theologian, pastor, and president,
who deserves, and will receive,
so much better

Table of Contents

Introduction by Rodney Clapp | ix
1. What Younger Evangelicals Want—and Are Getting! | 1
2. In Honor of Robert Webber: An Interview | 13
3. Together in the Jesus Story: Robert E. Webber Interview by David Neff | 16
4. Don't Get Hung up on Style: A Conversation | 21
5. "Orthodoxy, Catholicism, Protestantism" 1–10 | 26

Bibliography | 203

Introduction

by Rodney Clapp

WHO OR WHAT, EXACTLY, was Robert E. Webber? The scion of Baptist missionaries, he was born and lived the first seven years of his life in the Belgian Congo. As a burgeoning academic, he was educated at conservative evangelical universities, seminaries, and graduate schools. He began his studies focusing on the New Testament, but shifted to biblical and historical theology after being introduced to the early church fathers. He spent most of his career teaching at Wheaton College, where he introduced legions of young evangelicals to his beloved early fathers, and where a train of students followed him into the Episcopal Church (I am one).

Beyond this glancing biography, Bob was charismatic, energetic, peripatetic, passionate, and winsome. Most of all, he was captivated by what he called "God's story," that the creator God of Israel was incarnate in Jesus of Nazareth, by whose life, death, and resurrection the entire creation was rescued, recreated, and restored. The novelist David Foster Wallace has said that all people worship something or someone, and that worship determines our lives. Bob would have agreed, and would have instantly added that the God met in Jesus Christ is alone worthy of worship and the entirety of our allegiance.

In the interviews culled by archivist Keith Call for the present volume, Bob's singular regard for worship shines through. For instance: "Worship involves us in the story of God's saving deeds and our relationship with God—which is established by God's activity on our behalf. The content of worship is essentially the gospel—the narrative from creation to re-creation. It is telling and enacting the story of the living and the dying and the rising of Jesus Christ, and everything that implies for us."

And as he says in one of the lectures found here: "The church is primarily a worshipping commune. This does not mean that is all the church is. The church is more than that. But primarily the most basic calling and function of the church is to be a community that worships and adores God in Jesus Christ."

Bob was tireless in spreading this message. Sitting with the yellow legal pads on which he drafted his publications, he wrote more than forty books centered on worship alone. He traveled the far points of North America in particular, preaching, lecturing, holding seminars. Late in his career he founded the Robert E. Webber Institute for Worship Studies, in Jacksonville, Florida, which still today grants graduate degrees in liturgy. His influence also continues institutionally at the Robert E. Webber Center for an Ancient Evangelical Future, based at the Evangelical Anglican Trinity School for Ministry.

Readers of this book will get a sense of what made Bob so prolifically tick: the centrality of worship in the life and mission of the church. More importantly, they will especially in the lectures that comprise the second half of the book get Bob's argument for why all Christians—Catholic, Orthodox, and Protestant—should agree with him. For his call was for a return to and revisiting of the theologians especially of the first three centuries, the "common roots" of all subsequent theology and church life. Furthermore, he noticed how analogous those centuries are to the present-day circumstances of the church, when we are immersed in hyper-pluralism and adrift in a waning Christendom. "The opportunity," as Bob puts it in one the interviews reproduced here, "is that postmodern culture is so much like that of the early church (Roman era) in pluralism, relativism and pagan religions, that we can look at how the church thought and ministered in that ancient culture as a model for how we minister today in this post-Christian, neo-pagan culture."

Those who never had the privilege of studying under Bob here, thanks to the gift given by Keith Call in the second half of this book, have the chance to get a taste—an entire repast, really—of what a course with Webber was like. He was always on the lookout for how Protestants, Catholics, and the Orthodox were alike and different. He constantly compared and contrasted. His lectures included close, verbatim readings and commentary on biblical texts, creeds, catechisms, early theologians such as Irenaeus, Tertullian, and Athanasius, and Reformers such as Luther. And there were frequent punctuations of humor. For instance: "I think that there are many [people with muddled theologies] running around in the Protestant church, they just do not know it, because they have really never thought about their theology. Our churches are full of tritheists and ditheists. But that does not mean they are heretics, and it does not mean they will go to hell. Just purgatory, the Protestant purgatory. There is a special one for Protestant people. It is not quite as severe. You do not need indulgences. You just need to learn your theology. I will be there teaching. That will be purgatory. You are going through it now."

I hope I have said enough to whet interest and indicate why Bob Webber's work remains worthy of continued attention. The ancient, commonly revered faith he recovered so vividly is relevant and alive yet. And worship, profoundly understood, really is at the center of the church's life. That is Keith Call's conviction and hope in bringing you this book, and I join him enthusiastically in that conviction and hope.

So, who or what was Bob Webber? He was actually and centrally an evangelist. He purveyed and pointed to the gospel, the good news that God in Christ is alive and well and all about bringing heaven to earth and saving his precious but fallen creation. With Bob now resting in the communion of the saints above, I am confident he would want no higher designation.

1

What Younger Evangelicals Want —and Are Getting![1]

Robert E. Webber is the William R. and Geraldyn B. Myers Professor of Ministry at Northern Seminary in Lombard, Illinois, one of the only seminaries in the country that offers a Master's and a Doctorate in worship and which has intentional studies that integrate worship and spirituality into the program. He is also the President of the Institute for Worship Studies which offers MWS (Master of Worship Studies) and a DWS (Doctor of Worship Studies). He is also Professor of Theology Emeritus at Wheaton College, Wheaton, Illinois. Dr. Webber has lectured on worship in nearly every denomination and fellowship, and has authored or edited more than forty books on worship including the eight-volume work, *The Complete Library of Christian Worship*. His most recent books include: *Planning Blended Worship* (Abingdon, 1998), *Ancient-Future Faith* (Baker, 1999), and *Journey to Jesus* (Abingdon, 2001). His latest book, *The Younger Evangelicals* (Baker, 2002), is attracting broad attention and interest because of its incisive look at new emerging leadership in the church, while at the same time pausing to look at the leadership models of the twentieth-century church.

Dr. Webber was scheduled to speak at a conference in Grand Rapids, Michigan, on Radical Orthodoxy, where Homiletics was to meet up with him for this interview. But he called a few days before the conference to say that he had had back surgery and wouldn't be there. So we met with him in his home in Wheaton, where in the kitchen, and in a straight-back

1. Originally published in *Homiletics Online*, January–February 2004. Used by permission.

chair, he gladly and graciously discussed his observations about a church that is in the midst of change and the Younger Evangelicals who are leading the way.

Homiletics: To start, we should probably clarify the categories you develop for Evangelicals in the twentieth century and the early twenty-first century. You identify Traditional, Pragmatic and Younger Evangelicals. What defines these groups?

Webber: The underlying idea of these three groups is that Evangelicalism seems to follow the curvature of culture and reflects culture. And if you look back over the last fifty to sixty years, culture has actually gone through three very distinct groupings: Boomers, Gen-Xers, and now Millennials. It seems to me that as Evangelicalism encounters each cultural shift [and]that each cultural shift as they integrate with it gives a different shape and form, not so much to the message, but to the way in which the message itself is communicated. So if you go back to Traditional Evangelicalism, I see it shaped by World War II and post-World War II. And then the Pragmatics, who emerged in the eighties or so under the leadership of Bill Hybels and others are essentially shaped by the sixties and the revolution that the sixties introduced—even though they didn't begin until the late seventies and eighties, they are really children of the sixties. Now things are changing again. The rise of the Millennials (who have been born since 1982 and these are not hard and fast dates) have been shaped by postmodernity, and as a result of their cultural interaction with postmodernity, they're beginning to reflect in a different way on what Evangelical Christianity looks like.

Homiletics: Does this mean that in subsequent generations, we can expect to see a different expression of the church?

Webber: Probably we will. If you look back over history, cycles took a long time. But since the 1950s, studies of sociologists like Strauss and Howe, in particular—two people on whom I lean for sociological analysis—show how rapidly the cycles are now occurring. So what used to take, good grief, 400 or 500 years or more, is now occurring within one or two generations.

Homiletics: So then, the Traditional Evangelicals function within a modern worldview that is rationalistic and propositional?

Webber: That probably is the most distinguishing feature of the Traditionalists. They've been shaped by the Enlightenment. So they work with modern philosophy, a modern understanding of science, history, sociology. They're modernists, and so they interpret the Christian faith through these modern categories. And what's very interesting about Traditional Evangelicals is that the categories through which they interpret the Christian faith are almost regarded as sacred, almost as sacred as the Christian faith itself. So if you say, "Well, I don't believe in evidential apologetics," there's something wrong with you. Another way to look at these groupings is to look through a communication lens. So, for example, Traditionalists are given to print communication, are much more verbal. The Pragmatists, emerging in the eighties and nineties, they're much more given to the communications revolution that took place in the sixties and seventies, which is oriented around television and broadcast. So their churches are broadcast churches, and they want to show the gospel and present the gospel and entertain people with the gospel. So they're very much shaped by a broadcast model of communication. Now a third group, that I call the Younger Evangelicals, or the Millennials, they're shaped more by the internet. Therefore, their approach to worship and the church is going to be much more oriented around the interaction of the internet.

Homiletics: So the Pragmatists are plugged in, the younger Evangelicals are unplugged, i.e., wireless, the internet . . .

Webber: Yes, that's a good image.

Homiletics: Why do you use the word "pragmatic" to describe the Boomer church?

Webber: I use the word "pragmatic" because they're really shaped by the business model, the market model, the advertising model. Just as all the market and business and advertising began to emerge in the late seventies and eighties—and that's observable to anybody who looks at magazines and television and notes how consumerism began to develop. It seems to me that they've created a consumerist church. The product is Jesus and the good life. It's therapeutic Christianity. And they're out to sell that. So they've asked themselves the question: "What's the best way to sell Jesus and get people into the life of the church?"

Homiletics: And they're very successful at it.

Webber: Very successful. In jest, I call them the Walmart churches. There's something for everyone. You walk in that door and no matter who you are, they've got something for you. I'm not saying that's entirely wrong. I'm saying that's a reflection of the culture, and the result of the Christianity they've promoted—and my judgment is that Christianity accommodated itself so much to the culture, it has come to look like the culture. Christianity has been catechized by the culture as opposed to Christianity catechizing the culture itself.

Homiletics: Is this the Constantinian model of the church, or is that linked more to Traditional Evangelicals?

Webber: The Constantinian model is more oriented to the Traditional church. But then what I see is that this Pragmatic model is caught between the Constantinian model and the performance model. It still seems to be the tail end of the Constantinian model, although the Traditional church is probably more rooted in the church serving the cultural, serving the nation, a much more civil religion would be found in the Traditional church, although there's plenty of it in the Pragmatic church as well. This is where the Younger Evangelicals are breaking with the past. They do not see the church as an accommodation to the culture. They don't see it in terms of a civil religion. They see the church in a very countercultural way.

Homiletics: So they embrace more of a pre-Constantinian model?

Webber: Yes.

Homiletics: And by that you mean that they embrace what kind of core values?

Webber: I think they would all sense that the church is functioning in a pagan America. The notion that this is a Christian nation, or ever has been, or should be, is a notion that is really foreign to the new way of thinking. This is more of a missional model; it is a church that exists within the context of a post-Christian, a post-Constantinian, postmodern era. This era is essentially pagan in similar ways in which the church grew up or was early formed in a pagan culture. So my argument has been that if you want to know what the church should look like in today's pagan American or pagan world, then we need to go back to the first three centuries in particular and take a look at what the church did at that particular period of history and translate that into our postmodern, post-Constantinian, post-Christian world.

Homiletics: Why do you use the comparative form of the word "young"?

Webber: For a couple of reasons: One is, the word does reflect the leadership of the young people. Second, it's younger in the sense that it's new movement, and therefore expresses a younger spirit within the context of the Evangelical world, but it draws upon the experience of older people as well.

Homiletics: Have Hybels, or Warren, or others responded to the book *The Younger Evangelical*?

Webber: Traditionalists have by and large pooh-poohed it. "He doesn't know what he's talking about. He's made up a lot of this stuff." The book is at the cutting edge of the movement, and there are a lot of people who just don't believe this is happening. Let me give you an example. I was talking to a professor at Biola in California. He said that he'd read the book, and liked it, but he said, "You know, I just don't see it." Two weeks later I got an email from some students at Biola who said exactly the very things we're saying in *The Younger Evangelicals*. Pragmatists have completely ignored the book. *The Younger Evangelicals*, and primarily websites like The Ooze and Emergent Village, have raved about the book. They've basically said, "It's me. I could have written this book. This is my life. This is the way I think; I thought I was the only person who thinks this way. I thought I was nuts. I thought we were the only group who thinks this way, and now all of a sudden someone is telling us that this type of thing is going on all over the world."

Homiletics: What alerted you to the presence of this emerging new group of younger leaders?

Webber: I've been doing workshops on worship all over the country since about 1994. I've gone to virtually every city in the United States and many of them twice to do workshops on worship. I suppose the first alert was when I was in California and a young woman stood up who was on the InterVarsity staff, and she said, "Finally, I've come to a conference where somebody understands my age group." I started thinking about that. I kept meeting young people who kept coming up to me to tell me what they were thinking. In Albany I met with a couple of kids from the Salvation Army. They wanted to have coffee with me afterward. I sat there for about three hours and listened to them. I had nothing to say. Just listened to them. I was so impressed with the books they were reading. All the connections started to fall into place. When I got home, I sent a book proposal to Baker and forgot about it until later, my wife called me while I was on the road and said there's a contract in the mail!

Homiletics: Let's talk about the Younger Evangelicals in terms of different rubrics. How do they, for example, approach apologetics?

Webber: The underlying shift is away from Christianity as an idea to Christianity as a life. If Christianity is an idea, then you have to defend it. You have to marshal all the arguments you can to make it look good. One of the things I like about the Radical Orthodoxy movement and John Milbank is that he claims that in bringing all the disciplines in support of Christianity, we've actually marginalized the Christian faith. And so the Christian faith needs to stand on its own and interpret the world instead of the other way around. So the shift is from the Big Idea to the real, authentic life. This is exactly what attracts younger people. They are saying that the very best approach to the Christian faith and to expressing it is to live the life. So they're very attracted to St. Francis, who is reported to have said, "Everywhere you go preach the gospel, and if necessary, use words."

Homiletics: Worship?

Webber: Their approach to worship is an embodied reality. My sense is that they're still pretty much all over the map in terms of worship. But one of the things that they're really trying to do in worship is create a sense of transcendence. If you look at worship over the last thirty years, the movement has been primarily the nearness of God, the immanence of God, the friendship of Jesus, the relationship and even a lot of romantic terminology in contemporary music about a relationship with God. The Younger Evangelicals are sick of that stuff. They just think it's shallow, not really real—all this romantic stuff about their relationship with Jesus. And they're beginning to see God more on the side of God's holiness, God's otherness, God's transcendence. They're trying to create an atmosphere that allows for that. What are big with Younger Evangelicals are candles, icons—they will either use real icons, or they will flash icons on the walls of the church. There's a recovery of hymnology, there's a recovery of liturgy. I'll give you an example that's just a week old. The chaplain from my Institute for Worship Studies, which is down in Florida, called me with this story. The staff of a well-known contemporary gospel singer and writer called him and asked him to come every two weeks to do liturgy with them and be on staff to counsel anyone who needs counseling. So they sat him down and said, "Even though we write contemporary stuff, we hate it. When you do chapel, no contemporary songs, please. We don't know what you're going to do, but no contemporary stuff." The Institute is very much rooted in ancient traditions, so he translated what we do in our chapel, and did the first liturgy with them last week. He did the passing of the peace, some ancient hymnology, and even on the prayers, they would pray, and they would sing together [he sings] "Lord have mercy." He said, "Blew them away." That's the kind of thing the younger person is attracted to, and some older people, too. They're so sick of wearing your relationship with Jesus on your sleeve.

Homiletics: Sounds like Evangelicals are thirsting for what has traditionally been an integral part of the typical mainline worship service.

Webber: There's some truth to that. I think that there is almost like, "What the other person does is better than what we're doing. We're getting a little tired of what we're doing." But I've found, on the other hand, that mainline churches are going for the Evangelical praise stuff, and it lasts for a little while, and then it peters out.

Homiletics: So is praise music dead?

Webber: No, I don't think it's dead. But many of the people who are into praise music have never learned any of the hymns or any of the ancient parts of the mass, or things of that sort. So what is going to happen is that it will become integrated into the whole, and get lost as a movement in and of itself.

Homiletics: So do we have a problem with the word "contemporary"?

Webber: It's a dead word.

Homiletics: Not a useful word.

Webber: No, people aren't attracted to that. The words that are used more frequently are "authentic," and "genuine." The term I've used is "ancient/future." There's a longing for roots and connection, something from the past to give meaning to the present. Whereas the Pragmatists hate the past. They basically said it's no good. Let's start this Christian thing all over again. Of course that was the spirit of the sixties. The children of the parents of the sixties see the poverty of what the sixties revolution produced in every way.

Homiletics: Youth ministry?

Webber: Youth ministry is moving away from parties, picnics, *Fear Factor* kinds of things, to much more serious Bible study, prayer and things of that sort. I was at a Methodist conference in Pittsburgh, and the speaker was talking about youth ministry. He said he had tried everything in the book to get youth to come to the church: pizza parties, retreats, the whole thing. One day, he said, it was like God spoke to him: "You know, these kids have plenty of parties connected with school and so on." So he shut the whole thing down and just started a Friday night prayer meeting and Bible study. He said, "I've no room for all the kids that are coming." That's a phenomenon that other people speak of. Howe and Strauss talk about this. There is a new seriousness about young people, millennial people. They don't want to be entertained. They want to be challenged. They want a faith that is challenging as opposed to a Christianity that is entertaining.

Homiletics: What does the Younger Evangelical pastor look like?

Webber: This pastor is just the opposite of the Pragmatist, CEO model, the Standard Oil CEO operation, running a big business, which is exactly what the megachurch has become. It's become a big business. The concept of the pastor for the Younger Evangelical is to go back to being the shepherd. They don't like big churches. They don't want big churches. They want small churches. There's a church here in Wheaton. One of the younger pastors decided he was called to go down into Chicago to start a series of neighborhood churches. So he talked to the church about this, and the church decided to support him. They encouraged some of their families to actually move into this Chicago area where they're going. And they did. They started a church that is essentially a neighborhood church. Their goal is to have 100 neighborhood churches in this area in Chicago, and they would come together once in a while to have worship—more like the New Testament model, the house church. I find this going on all over the United States. They don't want to be known. This church I just referred to was mentioned in my book, but they only agreed to let me use their example on the condition that I wouldn't identify them or say where the church is located. They said, "We don't want to get known." They want to be known in our community, but [their] goal is not to get known. This is very different from the goal of the Pragmatists. So you find a servanthood model, a shepherd model. You also find a team model in the new emerging church. As opposed to having, say, a senior pastor. No one would use that term. No one would stand up and say, "I am the Senior Pastor." They would only say, "I'm one of the pastors." The other thing, too, is that a lot of these younger people are willing to work, to be school teachers, or trades people. They want to go to the city. There's a tremendous interest in rebuilding the city. So they'll work during the week and pastor the church on the weekend.

Homiletics: But don't you agree that while there are the Traditionals and Pragmatics, and the Younger Evangelicals, they all in a sense resonate with certain elements of the culture and that together they provide a holistic approach, and no one model is going to work for everyone? Certainly the approach of the Younger Evangelicals is not going to connect with everyone.

Webber: The diversity lends itself to the unity of the church. But, frankly, I think the Younger Evangelicals with their small group fit the biblical model better than others.

Homiletics: Would you have said this twenty years ago when the Seeker-Sensitive approach was acclaimed as the New Big Idea?

Webber: I thought from the beginning that it was shaped more by culture than by biblical principle. Now I don't deny that a lot of people have been very much helped by this. I was at a conference one time, and someone asked me what I would say to Bill Hybels if I sat down with him. I know what I would say to him: "Thank you for all the people you have helped, because you've helped some of my former students who have fallen astray." So obviously I want to affirm the good that has been done and acknowledge it, but at the same time say that this approach to the Christian faith has been shaped by the culture. Granted, we always interact with culture one way or another, but I see the Younger Evangelicals as interacting toward a countercultural model that reflects more of what was going on in the first three centuries. I mean, I can't discount Constantinian religion, or the medieval church, or the Eastern church, or the Reformation. Here's a history of the church. The Christian church began as a mission in Jerusalem, it moved to Rome and became an institution, it moved to Europe and became a culture, it moved across the ocean and became a big business. [Laughter all around.] That's the history of Christianity in four easy steps. But it does speak some truth in terms of the way Christianity is so flexible. It does speak to cultures in different ways. But now we're facing new cultural issues, and I don't think the Pragmatic model is going to survive in the long run. It may have a long history yet of twenty-five or fifty years. The Millennials are bringing a new type of leadership. My book is not a historical book, but a projection of where the church may go, based on sociological studies out there, and based on my study of Younger Evangelicals who are already moving in this direction.

Homiletics: Are these postmodern kids reacting against postmodernity in the attempt to recover what was a part of the pre-Constantinian ethos or are they apart from the postmodernism? Have they stepped outside postmodernism to critique postmodernism?

Webber: Actually, most of the Younger Evangelicals are very well informed about postmodernity, and see themselves as a counter-cultural movement.

Homiletics: But do they see themselves as within postmodernity?

Webber: Oh yes, definitely.

Homiletics: So they see themselves as postmoderns, but it seems as though they're speaking out against postmodernity?

Webber: Yes, well in the same way that Radical Orthodoxy is, too. We live in a postmodern world. Is there an alternative to postmodernity? And what they're saying is that Christianity is an alternative to the relativism of postmodernity. What I do is say, "Okay, the relationship of the church to the culture is always countercultural, but always affirms the culture." So the countercultural shape is that the Younger Evangelicals are not going to go with ethical relativism, spiritual relativism, and religious relativism. They're not going to allow Christianity to be shaped by that. So they will affirm, as they do, that there are absolutes, that spirituality is not just New Age stuff. They are affirming even more clearly than ever the uniqueness of Christ, that he is the Way, the Truth and the Life. But they're cultural in the sense that they will address globalization issues, technology, environmental concerns, because they have a better grasp of creation and re-creation than their predecessors.

Homiletics: How does a Younger Evangelical pastor preach?

Webber: Since the Younger Evangelical likes a smaller community, the Younger Evangelical is much more of an interactive preacher. There are two different ways to do the interaction. If you're with a small group in a house church, you might get up and begin with a question, or you might begin with a passage of Scripture, make comments on it and answer questions about it in the same way that the rabbi did. They are very Bible-oriented and much more exegetical than the Pragmatics, who are more oriented around topics, topics that may pertain to having a better life, winning the race, having a better spouse. Younger Evangelicals don't seem to be interested in that. The other approach is what I call a "Talk Back Sermon." A person delivers a sermon, and at the end of the sermon, would say, "We have a couple of minutes to turn to each other and ask, 'What did God say to you through the reading of Scripture and the sermon?'" And then if it's a small group they may take a Q and A time. It's much more interactive, as is the whole service. The prayer time is interactive. Everything is interactive in their worship.

Homiletics: Do they not like to use technological aids in their worship?

Webber: No, they don't. They hate it. They do not like PowerPoint. They don't like outlined sermons. The only way they will use PowerPoint is to flash icons on the walls. They want it to create atmosphere, but they don't like it for sermon purposes. They don't like video clips.

Homiletics: And why do you suppose this is? Bored with it?

Webber: I'm not sure. I think the answer is that they want authenticity, and they don't regard PowerPoint and outlines as authentic. They see them more as entertainment.

Homiletics: What do you think the landscape of the church will look like in ten years?

Webber: I think all three of these will survive. It's not that one will supplant the other. The Traditional church may experience a resurgence because the Traditional church is actually a bit closer to where younger people are today. The dean of a college where I gave some recent lectures told me that he read my book, and he said, "I've got this phenomenon going on in my own home. In my church, we do a contemporary worship service, and we do a traditional service. I go to the contemporary service. My twenty-year-old son hates it and goes to the traditional service." So I say to the Traditional churches, "Don't go contemporary, but go more liturgical." I would say to almost every church, "Go higher, higher, and higher in your liturgy. But integrate the more immanent side." God is both transcendent and immanent, and we tend to emphasize one side or the other. The Traditional church has typically emphasized the transcendence of God. But there's this caveat: The Traditional church has expressed the transcendence of God through dry, intellectual, boring preaching. That's not transcendence; that's just bad communication.

Homiletics: Made God utterly inaccessible.

Webber: Utterly inaccessible. Then we shifted to immanence with this Pragmatic group. And the immanence of God has been spoiled by the romantic relationship with God that has come out of our choruses. So maybe we have the opportunity to bring together true transcendence and true immanence.

2

In Honor of Robert Webber: An Interview[1]

Robert Webber, a man who encouraged Christians to reclaim the Great Tradition and to learn from the ancient church in matters of worship, died on Friday after a serious illness. In honor of Dr. Webber and his tireless efforts to call Evangelicals back to a God-centered worship, I am posting an interview I had with Dr. Webber last year.

Dr. Robert Webber was one of Evangelicalism's foremost authorities on worship renewal. He founded the Institute of Worship Studies in 1995 and spent the last ten years conducting seminars across the United States. He authored more than forty books, including *Worship Old and New*, *Evangelicals on the Canterbury Trail*, the *Ancient-Future* Series, and *The Younger Evangelicals*.

Dr. Webber did extensive research on the younger generation of Evangelicals (of which I am part). So I was thankful that Dr. Webber agreed to answer some questions I had for him after reading many of his works.

Trevin Wax: Who are the younger Evangelicals?

Robert Webber: The younger Evangelicals are characterized by three commitments: 1) To deconstruct the reliance of Evangelicalism on modernity, especially the empirical method and on culture, especially its anti-historical attitude, its pragmatism, and narcissism. 2) To return to the sources of the Christian faith, especially in the ancient church, and 3) To build a church in the postmodern culture that reflects the two previous commitments. However, let me add, there is no uniformity in the

---

1. Originally published by the *Gospel Coalition*, April 28, 2007. Used by permission.

movement yet. So my answers to your questions will reflect my own challenge for Evangelicals to recover an "Ancient-Future faith."

Trevin Wax: What are the major distinctives of the younger Evangelicals, in comparison to the previous generations?

Robert Webber: My distinctive is that Evangelical ministry be re-situated in the divine narrative. Scientific theology based on reason and science has resulted in a compartmentalization of theology from practice. For example, worship separated from the divine story is free to "free float." In this state it has been shaped by pragmatism and narcissism. Worship returned to the divine narrative "tells and enacts God's story for the life of the world."

Trevin Wax: Do you see postmodernism as more of a threat to historic Christianity or as a window of opportunity?

Robert Webber: I see postmodernism as an opportunity and threat. The threat is in the temptation to adapt faith and practice to postmodern philosophy. To do this is what moderns did with science and reason. We don't want to go there.

The opportunity is that postmodernism culture is so much like that of the early church (Roman era) in pluralism, relativism and pagan religions, that we can look at how the church thought and ministered in that ancient culture as a model for how we minister today in this post Christian, neo-pagan culture.

Trevin Wax: In a postmodern society, how are the younger Evangelicals treating the role of apologetics in the task of evangelism?

Robert Webber: Here is a good case in point. In the ancient church, the primary apologetic was the "embodied community." Tertullian writes that the pagans say "look at how they [Christians] love each other." We aren't there yet, but it is a goal.

Trevin Wax: How can the churches of younger Evangelicals become transgenerational, avoiding the trap of generation-isolation in order to effectively minister to all age groups?

Robert Webber: Generational studies and divisions primarily arose out of the "consumer mentality." It has some value, of course, but it is the "slick trick of marketing." We need to deconstruct our reliance on marketing and return to the authentic life of the New Testament and early church community.

Trevin Wax: What lies at the heart of younger Evangelical worship services? And why is there such a hunger among this generation for liturgy and ritual?

Robert Webber: Traditional (1950s) worship is based on reason and verbal communication. Today's young (older too) live in a culture of mystery and symbol. Words remain important, of course, but communication must also be embodied. Today people want to worship with their bodies. Again this was true in the ancient church. The models are there, we don't need to create new models, but adapt ancient models to our life in this world. Worship that continues to be verbal only, simply does not engage the whole person.

Trevin Wax: What view do younger Evangelicals have of the church?

Robert Webber: There is a growing sense that the church is an incarnational continuation of the presence of Christ in and to the world. This lies behind the new ecumenism in which the barriers with Catholic and Orthodox Christians are breaking down.

Trevin Wax: What dangers lie ahead for younger Evangelicals? Where are we most likely to become captive to culture?

Robert Webber: The primary danger is to remain disconnected from God's story and theological reflection on that story. Until we re-situate faith and practice into God's story through serious study of the activity of the Triune God in creating, becoming incarnate to re-create, and calling the church and its worship to "re-present" and to "live out" God's action in history moving toward the restoration of all things in the New Heavens and the New Earth, our ministries will continue to be shaped by new forms of pragmatism and narcissism.

3

Together in the Jesus Story: Robert E. Webber Interview by David Neff[1]

Northern Seminary's Bob Webber likes to tell this story. One day during his tenure at Wheaton College, a colleague remarked, "Webber, you act like there never was a Reformation."

Bob recalls saying, "You act like there never was an ancient church."

The trick for Protestants, of course, is to hold these two sources of our historical identity together, frequently returning to both periods to rediscover the wellsprings of our beliefs and our worship.

Without forsaking the achievements of the Reformation, Webber has long been known for calling our attention to the rich deposit of the ancient church's faith. Almost thirty years ago, he and a group of colleagues produced "The Chicago Call: An Appeal to Evangelicals." The document addressed a variety of ills by prescribing a healthy dose of historical consciousness: "We cannot be fully Evangelical without recognizing our need to learn from other times and movements concerning the whole meaning of [the] gospel."

At the time, *CT*'s Donald Tinder called the group "an ad hoc group of 46 comparatively unknown Christians . . . more or less identified with Evangelical institutions or views." But despite the authors' relative obscurity, "The Chicago Call" made waves. *CT* published its text in full, and the editorial page cautiously commended it. *Newsweek* devoted its entire religion section to "The Chicago Call." And since 1977, Evangelicals have been paying increasing attention to the early church.

---

1. Originally published in *Christianity Today*, September 2006. Used by permission.

Now comes another call with Bob Webber's fingerprints all over it. This one addresses different ills, but it retains some of the same historically minded prescriptions. The challenges addressed in "A Call to an Ancient Evangelical Future" are external ("the current cultural milieu, and the resurgence of religious and political ideologies") and internal ("Evangelicals' accommodation to civil religion, rationalism, privatism, and pragmatism").

Whereas the 1977 call addressed modern ills, this 2006 document focuses on issues in the emergent and postmodern discussions. But it does so from a very un-postmodern stance: Whereas postmoderns tend to fight against any "metanarrative," any grand, overarching story that claims to explain the meaning of history and existence, this call commends "God's story" as the single interpretive narrative by which the church must live.

The call says, "Today, as in the ancient era, a pressing issue is who narrates the world." What does that mean?

There are a lot of proposed narratives of the world. Some people say, "Let's narrate the world by Communism." (They're still with us.) Others say, "Let's narrate the world by Islamic fundamentalism" or "Let's narrate the world by democracy." These are the three leading contenders. But God's kingdom is what narrates the world for Christians.

What do those stories say?

The Communist story arises out of an atheistic view and says we have to bring workers and management together to create a communal world. The Islamic fundamentalist story is that Allah will rule over the world through Muslims. One way to implement that is to get rid of all the infidels. The story of democracy says freedom is the most important thing.

All three stories are political. In a contest between Communism, Islam, and democracy, I'll go with democracy. But as Christians, we're about the politics of Jesus and about the politics of the kingdom. Our primary belongingness is to that realm, as opposed to any other political realm. So we're at odds with all earthly politics.

All of those stories see a glorious future.

Absolutely. And so does the Christian story.

Most of the "calls" and "covenants" issued by Evangelical groups are created in some face-to-face meeting. But this call was crafted by e-mail and on the Web. How did that work?

It worked rather well, but it was very difficult, very time-consuming. I started off by just making a list of concerns. At various times, there were 36, 39, even up to 41 different items. We emailed them out broadly and said respond to this, and about 300 people responded. We read everything that came through. There wasn't a single response that wasn't seriously considered.

The way the call was developed dovetailed nicely with how the Web works. Once you put something out there, you really don't have control. We had people recommend the working document to other people, so then we would send them a copy of it.

And then one day, the current scheme just fell into place. Bang, it was there. In the end, there were four people who were emailing back and forth two or three times a week. And those are the four people who are called the theological editors.

So you and Phil Kenyon were conveners, and there were four theological editors, a 25-person board of reference, and a long list of participants.

And now we're sending it out for signatures. Soon we'll probably have 500 or 600 people.

Why did you take on this arduous process?

One of the things that drove me to put this together is the enormous diversity among Evangelicals. There is no longer a common set of convictions around which Evangelicalism evolves. One of the things I wanted to accomplish was to say that the items in this call are the fundamentals.

You sound like a fundamentalist.

God's story is no myth. It constitutes the fundamentals of the faith that are applicable to the life of the church in a postmodern world. I do not think that it's any different from any historic document that attempts to unite people, but it is articulated differently. The story-formed consciousness of the document is a new kind of hermeneutic; we're calling people into a united grasp of the Christian faith that restores the biblical narrative as the primary one from which all ministry derives.

The big problem is that we have compartmentalized the story, and we have tried to analyze each piece of the story and even prove it. In doing that, we've lost the story. We need to regain the fullness of the story and resituate all ministry within the story's fullness; modern Evangelicals, by creating a faith of propositions, have divorced theological reflection from ministry. I hope to see that corrected.

Another key element in this document is a consciousness of the church. Why is it important always to think about the gospel in the context of the church?

God has always been about the business of creating a people to witness to himself. God calls a family into being with Abraham, calls a nation into being with Moses. And now God has called a universal body of people, the church, to be a continuation of the presence of Jesus in the world and thus a witness to the reality of God and to God's story.

I'm asking people to see all of history through the story of God. God's story is the substance of the church, its worship, its spirituality, and its life in the world.

What difference would this make in pastoral ministry?

We would get away from a lot of our counseling techniques and go back to confession. A lot of what we do is sin, and we need forgiveness for that sin. And confession will help us to deal with that, rather than trying to analyze ourselves into some way of feeling better about ourselves.

How else would it affect ministry?

Primarily in worship. Currently, worship seems to be divorced from the story. It is programmatic and narcissistic. If we resituate worship in the story, then worship tells and enacts the story of God. And God is the *subject* of that worship rather than the *object* that we worship. The *subject* acts on us in worship and forms us into Christ's likeness and thus affects our spirituality.

And today, spirituality, like worship, is divorced from the story. Spirituality is shaped by psychology, shaped by focusing on the self. It's very narcissistic instead of being our continual embodiment of the story. Spirituality is ultimately not having some sort of esoteric experience, but becoming what God created us to be and making the world what God created it to be, a place of his glory.

Hans Urs Von Balthasar said that we need to take a passage of Scripture and so internalize it that we become it. If somebody asks where's Matthew 25, we should be able to say, "Oh, it's walking over there."

The call says some harsh things about "separatist ecclesiologies." But can a separatist ecclesiology be a temporary expedient?

Just today I picked up one of my favorite books—*The Principle of Protestantism,* by Philip Schaff. Schaff does say that there is a principle of separation to bring about a correction. When that correction has been achieved, we ought quickly to unite again with the group from which we separated. He was using that with regard to the whole Protestant world and saying the Protestant world left the Catholic church for a correction. Once that correction has been made, he said, we should reunite again with the Catholic church.

We'll have a hard time agreeing with each other on when that should happen.

Right.

4

Don't Get Hung up on Style: A Conversation[1]

Editor Emily Brink met with Robert Webber one afternoon last fall on the campus of Wheaton College in Illinois, where he has taught in the theology department for the past twenty-eight years. We spoke together in his office in the Billy Graham Center, an impressive museum and office complex.

Recently, Webber has been on the road almost every weekend, leading "Renew Your Worship!" workshops and introducing Renew! Songs and Hymns for Blended Worship *(Hope, 1995). He has committed the next several years to leading workshops across North America with ideas for renewing worship on the congregational level.*

He begins his message of renewal by tapping into the rich biblical and historical traditions that bind all Christians together. He then offers ways to give expression to that heritage in contemporary terms, amid the growing diversity in North American congregations.

Robert Webber teaches in the theology department at Wheaton College. Emily Brink recently met with him there to discuss his views on worship.

Brink: It used to be that when we entered a church in a particular denomination, we knew pretty much what to expect in worship, and we could assume that most of the members grew up in that denomination. Not anymore. What accounts for all the changes?

---

1. Originally published in *Reformed Worship*, March 1996. Used by permission.

Webber: For one thing, we are living in a postmodern world. And pluralism is one distinct feature of postmodernism. There is an extraordinary amount of crossover in members and in worship patterns among different churches today.

Considering the kinds of changes that have taken place in the world since 1950, it is not surprising that we would have a breakdown of denominations and a crossover from one denomination to another. In a sense, the communications revolution and the concept of the world as a global village have contributed to the collapse of those little denominational "ghettos" that we used to live in. The breakdown of the Berlin Wall is symbolic of the breakdown of many walls that we built around ourselves.

Can this pluralistic mix of different traditions strengthen worship in a given congregation?

I think so. Our approach to worship can be strengthened by opening ourselves up to different historical and cultural traditions. For example, drawing from African American, Asian, and from different contemporary worshiping communities—these all can strengthen our approach to and our experience within worship.

But some traditions have different structures, and certainly different styles. How can a church borrow from another tradition and still remain faithful to its own heritage?

The convergence discussions are taking place mainly in the area of style. And changes in style are disturbing to a lot of people. What I suggest is that in thinking about worship, we don't begin with style. That will come, but let's put the issues out there in the order in which they really ought to be discussed.

There are three things we need to distinguish: content, structure, and style. A lot of churches who talk about style first don't think enough about content, and that is why they may be too influenced by a market-driven style.

So we need to begin by asking about the content of our worship. And from a biblical point of view I would argue, in brief, that the content of worship is "the gospel in motion." Worship involves us in the story of God's saving deeds and our relationship with God—which is established by God's activity on our behalf. The content of worship is essentially the gospel—the narrative from creation to re-creation. It is telling and enacting the story of the living and the dying and the rising of Jesus Christ, and everything that that implies for us.

You mention content first and then structure as the second issue that must be settled before dealing with style issues. What do you mean by structure?

To state it very simply, you gather the people, you tell them the story, you break bread, and you go home to love and serve the Lord. This basic fourfold structure is analogous to what we do when we entertain people in our homes or have any kind of meeting. And so it is when we gather to worship together. It is a meeting with God, and therefore we need to think about—well, how do we gather the people? How do we tell the story that is central to Christian worship—the Word, reading the Word, and preaching the Word? How do we respond to the story with thanksgiving, eating together, fellowshipping together—in a way that allows relationships to be repaired, transformed, and established? And then how do we send people forth?

Churches in the Evangelical and Reformed traditions may agree on content, but they are certainly diverse in structure. I'm thinking, for example, of services with the sermon at the very end, with little, if any, place for a corporate response to what we have heard.

I think everybody—those involved in praise and worship, charismatic, and liturgical worship styles—will agree that content is not negotiable. We must tell the story. But how do we do it? Is there anything in the biblical and historical tradition that would give us a shape for worship? I am arguing that there is. It is a simple shape of gathering, hearing, celebrating, and going forth. Now, in saying that I am in good company, because all the churches today that have been studying the field of worship are either keeping or going back to that fourfold pattern. The Catholic church did; the Episcopal Church has; the Lutherans have; the Presbyterians have; the Methodists have. And I think Evangelicals are rediscovering the fourfold shape of worship as well.

What about the Reformed tradition?

Protestants who come out of neither the liturgical tradition nor the Praise and Worship tradition, but are in the middle, like many Reformed and Evangelical churches—these are the churches that have the most work to do. They have to learn about worship from both the liturgical and contemporary renewal movements, and that takes education. They need examples and models.

But what about those style issues that churches struggle the most with?

Only when you have the structural issues settled can you talk about style. The style issue has to come third, after content and structure. When that order is followed, style is up for grabs. You could do jazz, you could do African American, you could do Asian, you could do liturgical, you could do charismatic—the style is really up to the group. And, because of the crisscrossing of people that you mentioned earlier, I think most churches are somewhat eclectic in their choices.

They recognize that just forcing a particular style on their congregation is probably a great mistake.

It's also true that many different styles work well for that fourfold structure of gathering, hearing, celebrating, and sending. The style could look very liturgical, or very Pentecostal, or very charismatic and still follow the fourfold structure.

You speak often as well about blended worship, or about a "convergence" model. Is blended worship a matter of style?

Yes, what I am suggesting is the blending of hymns and choruses, the blending of organ and contemporary instruments, all within the context of a content that is the gospel in motion structured by our fourfold pattern.

Each congregation needs to work out its own style mix. A traditional—let's say liturgical—church might achieve a blend by adding contemporary choruses and music in the gathering or during the reception of bread and wine. A Pentecostal church might blend their style of singing into the fourfold pattern, so that they would also be drawing from historic elements of worship such as the Eucharist, with its prayer of thanksgiving.

If a common content and structure characterized all of the churches, what would be unique to each particular congregation would be its specific style. For example, African Americans would use drums and spirituals with a call-and-response style of singing, charismatic worship would include a lot of raising of hands and anointing of oil. Liturgical worship would continue to be more ordered. So blended worship doesn't destroy the style of a particular congregation—it preserves it, but adds to it by drawing from the richness of other styles.

In your seminars you spend a lot of time helping congregations start working out their own "style mix" within a fourfold structure. Could you conclude by suggesting a few practical steps to making changes in structure or style?

Remember that worship is not a program, a series of isolated and unconnected acts. It's a narrative, a rehearsal of our relationship to God. I think the first thing a congregation needs to do is to work on its shape of worship—to move worship from a program to a narrative. Then it should work on the flow of acts that gather the people into the intimate presence of God—acts that tell the story and instruct the congregation in the faith, acts of response (such as communion), which give thanks to God by remembering the work of the Son and celebrating his saving and healing presence, and acts that send people forth with a commission to serve God in all of life. Bathe these changes in prayer so that the leadership of worship is not rote but energized by the sense that the congregation is in the presence of God, standing on holy ground.

5

Orthodoxy, Catholicism, Protestantism[1]

SESSION #1, DECEMBER 5, 1978

Webber: What I am going to talk about for the next thirty minutes or so is really going to be directed mainly towards those of you who have no background in theology at all, and my apologies to those of you who do. Next week we will get into some of the heavier stuff, although we have to go through things so quickly that none of it is going to be as heavy as what I would like to make it, but nevertheless let's do a few things. First of all, I want to mention very briefly the branches of theology and simply designate the branch from which I am coming, so that you have some understanding of the approach I am going to be taking for the subjects of theology in this course.

We generally think in terms of several branches: biblical theology, historical theology, systematic theology, and philosophical theology. Let me try to define each one of these and then tell you where my preferences lie, so that you will know where you can beat me up and get angry and say, "You're really off the wall at that particular point, because I come from another perspective," which is very fine.

Biblical theology, of course, has to do with the putting together, the systematizing of the biblical revelation of the biblical data. When we talk about biblical theology, we try to get back to the biblical roots of Christian teaching. There are several approaches of biblical theology. One

---

[1]. Class lectures originally delivered for the Institute of Slavic Studies. Used by permission.

would be a dispensational approach, and I noticed that some of you come from this particular background, and [another] would be a covenantal approach. Sometimes these two are wed together, maybe in some of your educational experiences they have been, I do not know.

But my own personal preference in biblical theology falls in the line with a covenantal approach, that God in history has made a series of covenantal agreements. These covenantal agreements that God has made in history I would see as all related to the single Covenant of Grace. Maybe we can put it that way, that God in Christ is reconciling the world to himself, and that in reconciling the world to himself, there have been a series of revelatory actions of God within history by which he is expressing his work of redemption, his work of salvation, to his people. For example, there is the Abrahamic Covenant, the Mosaic Covenant, the Davidic Covenant, and these are all kind of fulfilled and expressed in the Covenant of Jesus Christ, which is known as the New and the Better Covenant.

I do not like to think in terms of New and Old in this sense. There are certain problems with that. Rather, I would think in terms of New Covenant as being the New Covenant that stretches across all of history, that is to say, all of biblical theology, everything from Genesis through the book of Revelation, as having to do with the New Covenant identified with Christ. Christ is the New Covenant. So that from the persuasion of biblical theology there really is only one way in which man comes to God, and that is through Jesus Christ. That does not mean to say that there is not some historical differences between the Old Testament and the New Testament. I would see some historical differences here. Obviously, the ceremony of the Old Testament no longer exists in the New Testament. There is a kind of fulfillment of everything that has been foreshadowed in the New Testament in Jesus Christ. So Christ is the single covenant. There are not two ways of salvation, the way it works in the Old Testament, and now the way of grace. That grace in Jesus Christ extends throughout all of history.

So if Adam is saved, he is saved by grace through Jesus Christ; and if you are saved, you are saved by grace through Jesus Christ. Therefore this means that I would tend not to make a distinction between—to some extent I would, but not a heavy distinction—between Israel and the church. Some people would tend to think that Israel is God's earthly people and the church is God's heavenly people. Rather, I would identify the people of God simply by that designation, the people of God. I think at bottom that is what we are, whether we are Old Testament people or New Testament people, we are people of God. We want to stress this notion of God. It is God who initiates salvation. It is God who brings us to himself as God. It is God who sustains us. It is God who creates the people. It is God who is involved in the history of those people who move toward the eschaton, or the conclusion, of what he has in mind for the human race and his created order. Central to biblical theology is Christ. In addition to that, it seems to me—we will take this up more when we get into the question of Scripture—that coming out of this whole biblical theology, there is a kind of framework of theology. This framework of theology—it's always hot in this room, right?—coming out of biblical theology, is what I like to think of as being the root of historical theology, that is to say, that biblical theology begins to express itself in summaries. These summaries are sometimes called rules of faith. That is one designation. Another designation that we give to these is creeds, for example the Apostles' Creed, as a basic summary of biblical theology. The Apostles' Creed as being a basic expression of historical theology is the biblical, let's call it the biblical frame of reference from which theological thinking is done.

Do you follow what I am doing here? You are thinking, "Webber is crazier than I thought." See where I am going? I want to make sure you see where I am going. You are sitting there staring at me, as if to say, "When is this going to be over?" Biblical theology. The framework of biblical theology in historical theology. Got it? The Apostles' Creed.

Okay, now let's take a step from that because I want to make sure that you know what I am saying. I am going to beat you over the head about this idea for the whole quarter. If the Apostles' Creed is a summary of biblical theology, then the Apostles' Creed is at bottom, in the most essential sense, a summary of Christian truth. Systematic theology is human thinking about the basic framework of biblical Christianity. I do not want to rush through this stuff. I do not want everybody to walk out and say, "Did you get what that character said?"

Okay. Let's draw a tree. Biblical theology is basically expressed in historical theology, in the trunk to the Apostles' Creed or any one of the creeds, and then you could go into a number of creeds, which attempt to summarize the roots and summarize the basics. As you go up that tree, you build branches. The branches I would like to describe as systematic theology, that is to say, they are attempts to explicate, to understand, to expand and to develop the creed. So our tree is like this: biblical theology, then creedal summary.

Let's take a look here at systematics, where you could have a Lutheran interpretation, or a Calvinistic interpretation, or an Arminian interpretation. I do not think there are very many Arminians in this class. These are interpretations that you are familiar with, okay? Systematic theology is a particularization of the general theology of the creed.

The second point I am going to make is that systematic theology becomes historical theology the moment it is written. Systematic theology grows old, because systematic theology is related to philosophical theology in the sense that all systematic theology attempts to communicate basic Christian teaching through a particular philosophical and cultural grid. Let me give you some examples. You would have some philosophical theology, like in the ancient church. If you are discussing some of the ancient Christian theology, you would describe it as a Platonic theology. It attempts to take the basic creedal statements, and the grid through which those creedal statements are understood would be a Platonic structure of reality. If you come into the medieval period, you take the basic creedal structure of the Christian faith, and you attempt to explain that through an Aristotelian grid. That is the genius of Aquinas. If you come, for example, into the Enlightenment you have a Newtonian physics, the Newtonian worldview, an attempt to relate the basic biblical framework through that particular worldview. You come, for example, into the twentieth century, and you are interested in the New Physics and the Whiteheadian approach to reality, seeing reality not as something static, as from a Newtonian physics perspective, but seeing things more around quantum theory and relativity. You would see the universe as dynamic and interrelated, rather than as a static block. And so you interpret your theological point of view in respect to that particular worldview. Thus we make the distinction between theology and theologies. We will see more of that when we talk about the whole business of Scripture, tradition, and authority. Any questions or feedback on this particular introductory point of view here? Do you feel baffled, confused, angry?

Student: Is the Aristotelian perspective theological?

Webber: The Aristotelian is more just a philosophical point of view, apart from any scientific considerations.

Student: So it would be speculative rather than empirical?

Webber: Speculative rather than empirical, that would be a good way to put it. Whereas the Newtonian physics is really built on the vertical, so-called empirical evidence. During the Copernican Revolution they began to discover universal laws, for example, and discovered the law of gravity. People began looking for laws in every area of life. For example, they began to look for laws in religion. Deism is an example, an attempt to interpret the Christian religion within the framework of a Newtonian world machine perspective. I do not know that it is terribly important for you to grasp all the details of that at this particular point. Just simply get the notion that when we are talking about theology, we are really talking about the variety of different ways of talking about God.

Student: If systematic theology is human thinking about the rule of faith, are not the creeds human thinking about biblical theology? I am trying to make a distinction between historical theology and systematic theology. I know you said that systematic theology becomes historical theology, but weren't the creeds systematic?

Webber: Not really. Not in the strict sense. Here I am talking about the rule of faith, the Apostles' Creed. The Apostles' Creed derives from the rule of faith, the Old Roman Symbol, and various other developments. But these are not so much analytic or systematic attempts to develop theology, as much as they are just pure statements of the biblical truth. Let's take the Apostles' Creed for a moment.

> I believe in God, the Father Almighty, Creator of Heaven and earth; and in Jesus Christ, His only Son Our Lord, who was conceived by the Holy Spirit, born of the Virgin Mary, suffered under Pontius Pilate, was crucified, died, and was buried. He descended into hell; the third day He rose again from the dead; He ascended into Heaven, and sits at the right hand of God, the Father almighty; from thence He shall come to judge the living and the dead.

First, you find no theory of creation there, other than the brute statement that God created. You do not find a long-day theory, evolutionary theory, a gap theory or all these other millions of theories that people come up with. You do not find any theory of the Virgin Birth. How do you explain John 1:14, "The word was made flesh"? Did he assume flesh? Was it metamorphized into flesh? In other words, all of those things are attempts to explain raw data. The Apostles' Creed is almost raw data from the Bible itself.

Student: I can understand that, but it is a considerable step up from the first knowledge about God, from the knowledge before the creeds were written, and the controversy that went on for the writing of the creeds, involved a great deal of arguments about what pertained to the systematics.

Webber: No, you are thinking of Nicene Creed and the Chalcedonian Definition. I am not thinking of those two creeds at all. I will do this more in "Scripture, Tradition, and Authority," so there is not much I can do in two hours. But I could develop for you, at least to my own satisfaction, I do not know it would be to yours or not. But I think that Christian scholarship can demonstrate that these elements that are to be found in the Apostles' Creed have always been in what I would call the primitive church, that is to say, the church was born believing in the Triune God. The word *Trinity* does not appear until Tertullian. *Trinity* is not a New Testament word. But the church in her liturgy, in her worship, always thought in terms of Father, Son, and Holy Spirit. She always thought in terms of the second coming of Christ. She always thought in terms of the literal bodily resurrection of Christ, or the Virgin Birth, or the death of Christ as the means by which the sin is destroyed, and we come into a new creation. All of those things, I really think I could demonstrate, are not the result of theological battle. See, the theological battles all result from the question of how do you interpret creedal statements?

Good grief, we have got those theological battles going on today about the age of the world, but some of them are ridiculous, one of which is the whole question of creation. Six days and one Sunday. Well, six working and one resting. Days, long periods of time, evolution. The real point of Scripture is that he [God] did it. Sometimes we battle over how long it took him to do it and we miss the point that he did it. And then we do not garner the implications of creation by God, and therefore the importance and significance of being alive. We are living. It's fun! That is the essence, to affirm life. The real meaning of creation is not rooted in how many days it took God to do it, but it is rooted in the fact that *he* did it, and that because he did it, it is significant. So we look for the religious meaning of certain things rather than the scientific meaning. The scientific search for a lot of this stuff is Enlightenment and comes out in the seventeenth and eighteenth centuries.

Student: When I read this human thinking about it, the implication that I get is that you are saying that the creeds—I know you did not say that—but the implication is that the creeds are inspired, which I do not think you meant. I wonder if we could say that people gathered to write the creeds, and usually when scholars write systematic theologies, do they more or less mean that?

Webber: Well, to a certain extent, except that I did want to say that I give the creeds much more significance than do [Henry Clarence] Thiessen's *Systematic Theology* or [Louis] Berkhof's *Manual of Christian Doctrine*, simply because—we are back to this argument again, which I think is missed by an awful lot of Christians—the raw data of the Apostles' Creed could all be lifted right out of Scripture. In that sense, it is in fact inspired. Any truth, wherever it is to be found that is true to the Scripture, is inspired truth. You could find something in Berkhof that is inspired truth. The creeds have a significant place in the life of the church. But anyway, I was simply trying to define the various fields of theology for you, to say that my sympathies—but you have already seen my sympathies, haven't you? I cannot hide it—my sympathies really belong to a biblical and historical theology. I regard my theology with many grains of salt, and I regard philosophical theology as being interesting probes into creative approaches to theology, which are valuable. I think the task of the church is always to be thinking and relating and communicating the faith to the world in which she finds herself. This means that the raw data may be communicated one way in the West and another way in the East. For practical implications for where we are at in this class and what you are planning to do, that means that you need to be very, very careful that you do not take a Western way of doing theology into the Eastern world and say, "Hey, baby, you've got to have it the way I've got it." You do not usually do that with theology anyway, but you know what I am saying. Let's not implant the Western theological perspective in an Eastern worldview. That means that part of the problem that you are going to be involved in here is the problem of cross-cultural communication. If you, as a Westerner, go to the Eastern world, how do you communicate truth within the Eastern framework? You do not want to have confrontation of frameworks, because what you want to do is to enter into that framework and speak through that framework for the expression of Jesus Christ.

Student: In your overview of history, or Western history, you seem to be implying that the theological understanding throughout history is always conditioned upon the scientific understanding that man has in a particular age. I am just wondering what is your basis for assuming this? This smacks to me of the dialectical sort of interpretation of history, and I am not quite sure that that is entirely appropriate. Do you see what I am saying?

Webber: Yeah. I do not know that I really meant to leave that impression, because I would see a continuity of truth throughout history. But I would say that that truth is interpreted often in keeping with a particular framework in which a person finds himself.

Student: Okay. I guess my question is, what I interpret you as saying is that theological understanding always follows on the heels of scientific understanding and achieves its progress thereby. And like I said, I think this is just a little bit too dialectical, maybe even Marxist or whatever approach to interpreting history, and it is communistic and it is against the law!

Webber: I hear what you are saying, and I want to say right away that I am not, I would not for one moment, want to say that I see that in the progress of theology.

Student: Okay, fine.

Webber: But I see the process of theology, not the progress, because it does seem to me that what we have gotten ourselves into in twentieth-century American Evangelicalism, by and large, is a kind of reductionistic Christianity. We have simplified, then simplified, and then we have simplified it a little bit more simple, and then we simplified the simplification and then simplified the simplification to simplify the simplification, and we have gotten it down to *The Four Spiritual Laws*. [Laughter.] You all laughed. Why did you do that? Because it is too true. See, *The Four Spiritual Laws* are okay. I think that basically they are true. I do not know that I would want to begin with God loves you. I think that the basic essence of the man as fallen, Christ is Redeemer, and all of that. But I think that to reduce Christian faith to such a simplistic term and leave it there, because that is what I think has happened in evangelistic practices, what we have added to that is just a lot of garbage, the baggage of "you too can be successful." *The Four Spiritual Laws* will lead you to the means of success. God will make you successful in your marriage, in your family. I will own a big Cadillac, nice blue suit, red tie, if I do these things. There is that kind of success syndrome that has permeated Western American Christianity.

What is that? Western American Christianity become enculturated with the American Dream, which is two cars in the garage and a chicken in every pot. And now we tie that into the Christian religion and the best way to achieve the American dream the quickest way. That is bad news, but we deliver it as good news. Somehow we have twisted the good news all the way around to something which it is not. And we have done that because we have allowed the individualistic and pioneering spirit connected with the industrial revolution and the technological revolution to shape the values of the American West. We have allowed that to shape our Christian message. And if you were referring to the dialectical approach....

Student: No. I was just a little bit concerned that you were taking an approach that our theological understanding can only increase our scientific understanding.

Webber: As a matter of fact, I think the theological understanding of the ancient church is superior in its theological understanding than most of Western Protestantism. I think that if we want to get into depth, we need to go back to gain perspective.

Student: I sort of get this feeling that, at the end of twentieth century, the church in the countries under Communism, a lot of this type of depth is being furrowed out, and it probably won't be revealed until later on in history.

Webber: I think it is there in the tradition. I think it is there in the liturgy.

Student: I wasn't necessarily speaking so much of that, but I mean the church, the so-called underground church, even though they deny that such a thing exists, the church which finds itself in open hostility with the authorities, and they are just doing a lot of this activity. We sometimes just get this picture that God is saving America in order to evangelize the world and that everything revolves around, well, America's historical mission and so forth, right?

Webber: If anything, we need missionaries to America. My guess is that the Third World is sending its missionaries. It is a stronger Christianity in the Third World than here, and I think it is because they are grappling with issues much more realistically than we are. We think that we have it all together, and we do not need to grapple with these issues. So, you feel like we finally worked that through, and you have got a general idea about what we are doing?

Student: How should we communicate the message?

Webber: My own feeling is that the communication ought to follow the same pattern that God's communication to the human race followed in the Scriptures. That is to say, it did begin with something very basic and simple, but it did become more complex and finally expressed itself in the flesh of God in the incarnation, and that our communication needs to follow that same pattern, and that ultimately a communication that will communicate is an incarnate communication.... The church should not simply give information about God. It is a tremendous mistake to start at the most complex point. What you need is essentially just a clear description from Scripture of creation and redemption.

Now the second thing I want to talk about here is to say just a few things about the various periods of historical theology. Well, this is my last point, ten minutes or so, and then we will go. Let's talk about these periods.... Generally we think in terms of the ancient period that goes up to AD 600 or so. We think of the medieval era up to 1500. The Reformation up to 1600. The modern period up to 1900. And the contemporary. The ancient period is generally known as the development of classical theology. Have you ever heard that term? Classical theology. It was a tremendously productive period of theological development, a period of creeds, a period of controversies, Trinitarian, christological, soteriological, origins of ecclesiology, Scripture, sacraments, and various things of that sort.

So by the time you come up to about AD 430, say, at the time of Augustine, the first 300 years after AD 100, classical Christianity has its shape. You have the roots of both Eastern and Western Christianity in the in this classical period. I think it is important for us to realize that. Let's say that you have certain centers of the Christian faith. If you can picture a map, you have Constantinople. You have Antioch. Jerusalem. Alexandria in Egypt. Carthage in North Africa. And then Rome. These are the major centers of Christianity in the ancient period. Alexandria and Jerusalem and Constantinople really sort of constitute the Eastern division of Christianity, whereas Rome and Carthage and Antioch are sort of the center for Western Christianity. Now it is Western Christianity that we know of as medieval Christianity. As a matter of fact, practically everything that we are talking about happened in the Western world. Eastern Christianity remains relatively untouched by a lot of this. So Eastern Orthodoxy shifts from Constantinople to Moscow after the fall of Constantinople . . . . So we are basically untouched by this whole thing here. Western Christianity becomes somewhat reshaped by the Aristotelian notions, and Aquinas would be your great example of that. We may refer to Aquinas a couple of times this quarter and see what he has to say about some things. But as we move up into the medieval period, you can say that Western Catholicism becomes fixed at the Council of Trent in 1563. At that point, Western Catholicism basically remains the same until you get up to 1963, which is the Vatican Council II. Are most of you familiar with the documents of Vatican II? Since that time, Catholicism has really been opening up, as I think all of you are aware. As far as Protestant Christianity is concerned, it was at the Reformation that we broke away from the Western trends. So in this sense, Protestant Christianity is Western and not Eastern. I know that is very basic, but nevertheless that is something you need to understand as we work through the differences between Eastern and Western Protestant Christianity. So Protestant Christianity breaks off into the Lutheran, the Anabaptist, the Reformed, and the Anglican. Then out of the Anglican reform comes a host of different points of view, and these from a host of different points of view on down to the twentieth century, and it just keeps proliferating. Then we are out here someplace. The question is when we look at the schema, how can we who are out here . . . ? Think in terms of a tree. Let's get back to trees, a tree laden with snow, Eastern and Western churches, the branches beginning to fill the air, and here we are, way up here, a little twig. How can we, the twig, get back down here to all these branches? That is what we are trying to do, seeing the differences, trying to get a view of the shape of that tree as it goes up and where the differences are. But also, we need to ask ourselves, is there in that trunk, that base down there in history, something that is in fact common to the whole tree, or do we have, in fact, different trees? We have the Orthodox tree. A Catholic tree. A Protestant tree. An Evangelical tree. Before we go, I want to get a few more commitments. How many of you would say there is only one tree with many branches?

Student: What do you mean by only one tree? Do you mean that truth is one, or do you mean that there are different standards?

Webber: The truth is one.

Student: Let's say church started strong and brave in the Lord, and as the years go on, they have children who do not believe, and more and more children, and they keep these children in the church, yet they are not believers. Can you say that the church is the tree that it once was, and that some other church that has begun has not taken over its place?

Webber: Let me answer. The church of Christ on earth, is it only purely subjective, or is there an objective aspect to the church, such as the Scripture, the sacraments . . . . ? I really should stop. I'll see you Thursday.

6

Orthodoxy, Catholicism, Protestantism

SESSION #2, DECEMBER 7, 1978

Webber: I want to discuss how all of this begins to come together in the Council of Nicaea and how this problem finally becomes solved. Now we move over to our friend, Origen, in the early third century, whose view of God looks somewhat similar to Tertullian's point of view. But there are some things that Origen said that are rather interesting that will help us to see the debate that occurred. So you have Father, Son, Spirit. These down here are souls. We shall talk about them sometime later. But basically what he is saying is that the Father is *authotheos*, that is to say, that the Father is God alone. And in respect to the Father, he says that the Father is "ingenerate." You have probably heard that term *ingenerate* used before, meaning that nobody made God. It is the kind of question that little kids ask, "Who made God?" About the Son, Origen uses the term "eternal generation." You can see that that business of eternal generation is somewhat similar to Justin's idea. Remember Justin with the Logos leaping from the bosom of the Father, as fire from fire? There are two schools of thought that arose from Origen's analysis, which attempts to bring unity and diversity together. The one school of thought comes from this God alone approach, which emphasizes the distinction. The emphasis here is the distinction between the Father and the Son. I suppose we could put it this way. The distinction is between the Father and the Son, based on the notion that God alone is ingenerate.

The second school of thought, which is really based on this eternal generation concept, emphasizes the unity between the Father and the

Son based on eternal generation. These schools of thought were running around in the world, thrown out into the universe, prior to the AD 325 Nicene Creed, so we can say that these are ideas that existed at the eve of the creedal statement. And they are, as a matter of fact, the two notions that created the controversy that resulted in the Nicene Creed and the conclusion to the Trinitarian concept. In this particular school of thought, there were two points of view, the one that was taken by Eusebius—I do not know that you need to get his name there, that is not something I would ask you to remember—but the important thing to remember about Eusebius is that he would say that there is a similarity between the Son and the Father. He would see the distinction, but nevertheless he would say the Son is similar to the Father. The second comes from the school of Arius, and Arius makes an outright distinction between the Father and the Son, and he says that basically the Son is unlike the Father. Let me comment a little bit on Arius's position, because I think most of you are probably familiar to some extent with Arius, and what you need to recognize here is that this is the basic position of the Jehovah's Witnesses, which you might call a modern-day Arianism. The statement for which Arius is most famous says there was a time when he was not, "he" referring to the Son. There was a time when he was not. If you go all the way back, as far back as you can go, only God was there. Arius's argument is that Jesus is the first begotten of the Father. That is a biblical term too. That is to say, that the Son is the first creation of God. The Son is the first creation. When God decided to create, the first thing he created was the Son. That puts him pretty close to God. But he is not God. He is only the first creation of God. It is this first creation of God, the Son who became incarnate, who lived and died and was raised again for our justification, who is the savior of the world. The Jehovah's Witnesses, like Arianism, would say of John 1:1 that in the beginning was the Word, and the Word was *a* God. He is not God by sameness of substance—that is a Greek word—but he is God by divine appointment. That is to say, God made him and said, "My son, by divine favor I make you a god." So God did become incarnate, not God-God, but God the created god, Jesus, became incarnate, thereby affirming the singularity or the unity of the Godhead, but definitely denying the distinction.

Student: So this would be another form of adoptionism, correct?

Webber: Not really. Technically you could call this another form of adoptionism, because adoptionism would mean that because he did such a fine work in this world that God adopted him into the Godhead. That is what it usually means, and that is a monarchianism, whereas this is really quite different than adoptionism. It means to say that by creation and divine favor, he designated him as a god. The person that came along over here from this point of view, there were several, but the most important was Athanasius. Athanasius said that the Son is the same as the Father. Sounds a little bit like modalism, doesn't it? It is not quite modalism. It is not even near modalism, but on the surface, it sounds to be somewhat similar to modalism. I will just tell you this now and we will get into it in a moment: Athanasius's view has become the orthodox view of the way of talking about the Trinity. But I want to ask you, what do you suppose would be the arguments that Athanasius would level against Arius?

Student: That the Son coexisted eternally with the Father? Basically John 1:1.

Webber: That is a metaphysical argument, isn't it? I mean, how would you know that? How could you crawl back into the Godhead and know that before the creation?

Student: Assuming that by this time the authority of the Scripture had been established, and so it wasn't necessarily a metaphysical argument between the two theologians, or was it just a matter of what exactly did the Scripture mean?

Webber: Well, does the Scripture teach that clearly? I mean, can you determine that as a matter of fact from the Scripture?

Student: From John 1? That the Son coexisted eternally with the Father? Was that your question?

Webber: Well, the question is, can you determine from an interpretation of that passage of Scripture that the eternal preexistence of the Son with the Father was in such a way that you would say that he is the same as the Father?

Student: Athanasius would, of course, say yes. I am not really familiar with Arius's line of thinking. But yeah, obviously . . . .

Webber: Yes, that is true. But I guess what I am getting at here is that there is another way of arguing, and I think this is the key to the Trinity, which lies right at the heart of our Christianity. There is another way of talking about the sameness of the Son with the Father, and that is soteriological language. Do you understand what I mean when I talk about soteriological language? If you look, for example, in the Nicene Creed, the phrase is found, "For us and our salvation..." I will show you that in a minute when we get to the Nicene Creed. This is soteriological language. *Soteros* is the Greek word for salvation. Soteriological means "theology of salvation." Let me ask you this, because this is getting into the heart of Athanasius's argument. Could Jesus save the created order if he is part of the created order?

Student: But even when you say that, you are presupposing that the entire created order fell, aren't you?

Webber: I am presupposing, but you do not have to presuppose that. I do, yes, but I do not think you have to presuppose that for that particular argument.

Student: Well, you could be Arian and say that the Son was indeed created by the Father, but since the whole creation didn't fall, the Son did not fall, therefore he could still be the agent of salvation.

Webber: That is true, but the point is that God would not be the agent in salvation, the appointed Son of God . . . Yeah, that is right. God the Father would not be the agent of salvation. The appointed Son would be the agent of salvation.

Student: It seems to me that you could not base your Trinitarian concept upon soteriology, unless you had a totally fallen creation. In other words, the fall had extended itself to all aspects of creation.

Webber: Well, I . . .

Student: Let me throw something else out there. Was that not Aquinas's argument, that basically the entire creation was not fallen, but only certain aspects of man's understanding?

Webber: Yeah, but if you are going to look at early church theology, and particularly Recapitulation Theology, the argument is that the entire created order is in fact fallen, or that the entire created order is in fact affected.

Student: So you are saying that Athanasius was presupposing this while developing his Trinitarian conception?

Webber: What I am saying is that the Trinitarian doctrine, or the Trinitarian controversy, is basically a soteriological controversy having to do with the question of salvation, and the issue is, who saves you? If you answer this question by saying that—what I am going to call "Axiom One" of the early church, *only* God can save—then you answer the Trinitarian question from that perspective and say, "Okay, then, the Son must be the same as the Father."

Student: Why could not the logical corollary to that be that if only God can save, why does he need an agent?

Webber: Of course, that is the argument of Arius. The reason why that was rejected by Athanasius and others who came to regard the Athanasian position as the Orthodox position is because Jesus, as the agent of salvation in the New Testament, is presented to us as God. So it finally rests on a biblical teaching. But it rests on Christ as the agent of salvation being declared God, being understood as God, worshipped in the liturgy of the church as God.

So there were basically two arguments that Athanasius used here to argue for the sameness of Christ with God. The first argument was this soteriological argument, which I have put up here. The second argument that he used was the liturgical. The liturgical argument is that the church has always worshipped Jesus as God. It has always been that way. That connects with some of the information I was trying to give you in the beginning of the class, that the triadic understanding in the New Testament and in the liturgy of the church has always confessed that Jesus is God.

See, the Jehovah's Witnesses, or the Arian position, can come along and say, "Now wait a minute. You really have more than one God. What you have is a kind of tritheism." So how do you explain this? How do you get at this? On the other hand, you could take a look at the sameness position, which in Greek is known as the *homoousion* position of Athanasius, and say, "You don't really have any distinctions in the Godhead if the Son is the same as the Father." So how do you solve the problem of maintaining both the unity and the diversity of the Godhead?

Student: The direction it was basically taking us became a question of what does it mean to exist as a person, and it was settled something along the lines of the three-one God existing in three persons, and it became the question of what about translating Greek terms into the Latin term *persona*, right?

Webber: Yeah, that is all involved. Those are all sort of on the outside, though, of what was really happening in the inside. The church said, "Let's make a distinction between *ousia* and *hypostasis*," which they did in the Council of Alexandria in AD 360. And *ousia*, which means substance, and *hypostasis*, which means standing under. The literal interpretation of that, standing under, refers to the diversity. So you have one, three: one *ousia*, three *hypostases*. Later this term *hypostasis* was translated into the Latin *persona*, which I think is better, so that you have one *ousia*, three persons. So what does that tell you? What does that solve?

I think we have to go deeper than the mere external machinery by which they solved this problem to look at the internal struggle that was going on in terms of determining precisely how to understand the Trinity. There occurred a battle after AD 325, from 325 to 381, when this whole question was raised in the Roman world. Basically, I would like to suggest that what was occurring here was an issue having to do with what we can call coinherence. Let's try to define coinherence. What does that mean? The concept of coherence is a very difficult to define. The word itself is its own definition, but what I am going to try to do is illustrate the meaning of this word. It means that more than one can coinhere in a single unity. In other words, God can be three persons who coinhere in a single essence. This business of coherence becomes a major theme in early Christian theology, which is applicable not only to the concept of Trinity but is going to be applicable to the concept of Christology in other aspects. For example, how do two natures exist in a single person? They coinhere. How can you speak of the church as being the body of Christ? There is a coinherence between the church and the body of Christ. How can you speak of the wine being more than wine, and the bread being more than bread? It is a coinherence, that Christ is in fact actually present there.

Student: Could you give a strict definition?

Webber: Let me see if I can give you a strict literal meaning of coinherence. That is a tough one to give a strict little literal meaning to, because it is itself self-descriptive. I would go back to the definition I gave you earlier, that more than one can exist at the same, that plurality can exist at the same time in singularity. I suppose that is a way of putting it. Plurality can exist in singularity. Let me try to illustrate this for you with a picture. Let me use symbolic language for a moment. We think of God in this sense, do we not? Father, Son, Spirit. But we think of God as having to Father, Son and Spirit a common essence. This common essence, which would be common in glory, in power, in consciousness, speaks to us of the coinherence. So this descriptive symbol speaks to us of the coinherence. Yet, although Father, Son, and Spirit coinhere in a single essence, nevertheless we may speak of the distinctions of Father, Son, and Spirit as real persons. What have we come to here? Well, we have come to a paradox. That is where we started, right? But I want to try to describe this paradox for you. See, the Nicene Creed affirms the non-explained common faith that has always rested in the bosom of the church. What she affirms is the mystery, and she affirms it with the usage of Greek language in such a way that the language itself preserves the mystery. What has occurred here is a beautiful example of translation, or contextualization, if you want to use that word. The mystery of the Godhead, which cannot be rationally known, because it lies beyond language, lies beyond mere human comprehension, has in fact been preserved in the creed of the church. In a moment I am going to give you the creed. The creed of the church, therefore, basically writes negative theology. It tells you what it is not, but it cannot tell you what it is. But by telling you what it is not, it comes closer to giving you a sense of the mystery of what it is. Do you follow? Well, in technical terms it is apophatic theology, which means the theology of negation.

Let's take a look at the Creed, and then I think we better use the rest of the time to just sort of discuss this, so you feel like you have gone away with something. The Nicene Creed is actually the Constantinople Creed of AD 381. Let's take a look at how it treats this whole subject. *We believe in one God, the Father, all governing Creator of Heaven and Earth, and of all things, visible and invisible. We believe in one Lord Jesus Christ, the only begotten Son of God, begotten from the Father before all times.*

Note, describing how he is begotten, as light from light, true God from true God, begotten not created. When the Creed says begotten not created, what theology is it negating? Arianism. The Creed describes the relationship of the Son to the Father, of the same essence as the Father, *homoousion*, through whom all things came into being, *Creator, Who for us men and because of our salvation.* See, there you have the soteriological key. Only God can save. That is the first axiom of the early church. *He came down and was incarnate.* That is God who is incarnate, not something that God created, but actually God himself became incarnate, by the Holy Spirit, the Virgin Mary. This incarnate God was *crucified for us under Pontius Pilot, suffered, was buried, rose on the third day according to the Scriptures, ascended to heaven, sits on the right hand of the Father. He will come again with glory to judge the living and the dead. His Kingdom shall have no end. We also believe in the Holy Spirit, the Lord and Life Giver, who proceeds from the Father, who was worshipped and glorified together with the Father and Son, who is also God, who spoke through the prophets and in one, holy, catholic, and apostolic Church. We confess one baptism for the remission of sins. We looked forward to the resurrection of the dead and the life of the world to come. Amen.*

What does that tell you about the Trinity? Not very much in the sense of giving you a positive theology. No ropes. No eggs. No ice.

But what it gives you is a soteriological explanation, if you want to call it that, from the perspective of salvation, that Jesus must be the same as the Father, so that it is God and not something that he created, who saved, because the liturgy has always worshipped him as God, and because only God can save, and we meet Jesus in the New Testament as an agent of salvation. That brings us right back to the mystery. We are all such rationalists, we want to explain everything. We want to have the final and definitive answer to the Trinity, but the early church is saying, "Hey, wait a minute. The New Testament, in continuity with the Old Testament, has always witnessed that only God can save, so therefore Jesus must be God, and therefore we have a Trinity." Let me stop babbling . . . . What do you think?

Student: Hasn't the Orthodox church criticized the Western Church, both Protestantism and Catholicism, as too rationalistic?

Webber: Yes. What I have given you here is the early church's interpretation of the Trinity, which the Orthodox church would say it still stands in that point of view. You Roman Catholics have become considerably rationalistic via Aquinas. And you Protestants are worse. I mean, most of you Protestants reject the Trinity altogether, you stupid bunch of Protestants. Evangelicals do not reject the Trinity. The Orthodox would say you do not begin to understand the implications and the meaning and the significance of the Trinity.

Let me give you a couple of those implications. If you were to write an article, let's say on communication, where would you begin? Suppose you were to develop a Christian understanding of communication. Is there an ultimate and final reference point from which communication is to be understood? In the Trinity. There has always been in the Godhead communication between Father, Son, and Holy Spirit, so that when God creates his world, he imprints upon his world the ability to communicate. How do you explain the unity and the diversity of the world? Well, it can only be understood, analogically, in terms of the unity and diversity that exists in the Godhead, because the creation is an expression of God and therefore has unity and diversity in it, as God does. See, the church does not want to affirm that you have a monad as modalism or Sabellianism would affirm. Nor does it want to affirm that you have three gods kind of living side-by-side, a tritheism. But rather, it wants to affirm the mystery of coinherence, the mystery of three-in-one, which we can we can perceive in terms of analogical thinking, but we cannot perceive in terms of pure rational conception. The Orthodox would say that you do not understand the Trinity, but you can only approximate an understanding of the Trinity through faith. We believe in order to know. Well, it's time to quit.

7

Orthodoxy, Catholicism, Protestantism

SESSION #3, DECEMBER 14, 1978

Webber: The Eastern school of thought is what is called the Word-Flesh Christology. Let's try to define and understand the meaning of Word-Flesh. First, in reference to this Word-Flesh Christology, I want to point out that the philosophical grid through which Christology is understood in the East is the Platonic, or the Neoplatonic, philosophical grid. Let's look at it this way. The Platonic or Neoplatonic grid looks something like this. It would say that the real is in the upper story. That is where the really real exists. Therefore, that which we see here is the shadow of the real. For example, true mannish-ness—I am using the word generically—is something that exists outside of the created order. The mannish-ness, or the humanity that we possess, is therefore a shadow of the really real, which exists above and beyond us. This approach to things always puts down, to a certain extent, the ultimacy and the importance of the material. It sets spirit over flesh, or spirit over material. For example, you could say spirit here, and material over here.

We have a lot of this, I think, running around in our own Christian background. There is among us in our background a kind of denial of the importance of the material, is there not? Somehow, if we deny ourselves, we feel that we will attain spirit. So if we fast and deny ourselves food, we may gain spirit. If we deny ourselves bodily comfort, we may gain spirit. A lot of that is Christian, but a lot of that is also Christian filtered through a Platonic worldview. Alexandria is the seat of Platonism, and Origen and Clement come from Alexandria, and the whole Eastern Church is somewhat schooled by the Alexandrian school of thought. Therefore, the Eastern Church tends toward the mystical, and tends toward lifting the earthly up into the mystical, so that as the earthly, which is the shadow of the real, gathers up into the real, it finds its own reality. Let's apply this for a moment to the question of Jesus. In the broadest sense we would see immediately that what we are going to be talking about in terms of the relationship between the God-man is that for the humanity to really be significant, it must be united into divinity. That is one possible approach, and that is the more orthodox approach, the humanity must be united into divinity. Just looking at that on the surface, what would you say would be the tendency of error, if we are going to say that the truth is in the balance? Which way do you think this school of thought is going to tend? In Christology, in which direction is this going to move? It will overemphasize the divinity, that for the humanity to be real, it must be gathered up into the divinity. I want to introduce you at this point to an extreme answer that was given here, an extreme Word-Flesh Christology, which is not in any way Eastern Orthodox, but nevertheless I want you to see this. It is the view of Apollinaris.

I will give you an illustration that describes the Apollinarian point of view. A number of years ago I was in living in St. Louis, and I was asked to give a talk to an InterVarsity group at a local university. So I went over to the home where this was being held, and I gave my talk and raised a few controversial issues, and we got ourselves into a whole big discussion. I do not even remember how we got into the subject, but we got onto the subject of the relationship between the human and the divine in Jesus, and how could we talk about that. And so I threw it out to the audience—it was in my days when I was radical and brash and young, and now I am old and mellow and I do not do this kind of stuff anymore—so I just said, "All right, what do you think?" So I started getting all these answers, and this one guy in back who looked like a man of great wisdom put up his hand, and he said, "Well, this is the way I understand it. Jesus had a body. That body was somewhat like a shell, sort of empty, and the Logos came down from heaven or wherever and dwelt in the body, so that the way in which we talk about the union between the human and the divine is that the divine Logos enters and dwells in a body." How many of you think that he was right? I had a teacher who taught that. What is wrong with that point of view? It is not a very good conception of the incarnation, is it? It is really not an incarnation of the Word of God. It is simply the Word, the Logos, finding some place to live for a few years, "I'll choose that bod over there," and dwell in that body and do his thing. I did not take time to ask the man anything, and I did not burn him. I just pulled out my pistol and shot him, killed him right on the spot—to the glory of God, of course. We have not yet answered the reason why that is not good. It is fragmented, that is true.

Student: It's sort of suggesting that he is now something that he was not before, and that what he was before he no longer is. The reason that I really had difficulty with that is on the basis of this one passage, John 1:14.

Webber: Right. How many of you do not like either one of the terms? Well, let's erase it then. I am only erasing it because I need the board. I am not throwing the concept out, but we will come back to that. Let's go back again to the New Testament for just a moment and recognize that the common faith—do you remember anything that we did last week?—the common faith of the church in the New Testament is really that Jesus is both God and man. The God-man. Anybody object to that as sort of a persuasion of the New Testament? Okay.

Now you remember that last week we were talking about the theology of the church being born in the bosom of the church and the common faith being an unexplained faith. I asked you, didn't I, to speak to the bulletin giver-outer, and say, "Do you believe in the Trinity" and then meet him after church and ask for an explanation of the Trinity? Since you did such a good job on that last week, I will give you another assignment for this next week. Ask the bulletin giver-outer, "Do you believe that Jesus is both God and man?" And the bulletin giver-outer will say, "Yes." Then say, "Meet me after church, either the east wing or the west wing, depending on how you feel after this lecture, and *explain* it to me." Here is the problem. What we want to do in the church, in our understanding of Jesus, is to always affirm that he is the God-man. However, when we try to explain or talk about Jesus as the God-man, we are either going to overemphasize divinity or overemphasize humanity. So as the church is struggling to find a way to talk about Jesus Christ as the God-man, she goes through this process of overemphasizing one against the other.

If you look at the first page of your outline, you will see that the overemphasis on the humanity is in the Ebionism and the Dynamic Monarchianism. We spoke about the Dynamic Monarchians last week in terms of their Trinitarian point of view. When you come to the Christology of the Dynamic Monarchians, naturally, if they are going to be emphasizing, as they did, the unity—and you remember the Spirit came upon Jesus at the time of baptism, stayed upon him until the time of death, and left him and then he was adopted into the Godhead, from that point of view—Jesus is obviously seen as purely human, right? Human until the Spirit comes upon him, at which point he becomes the God-man, and then human again at the death. So there is an overemphasis on the human, and not a proper balance between the human and the divine.

By and large, however, in the first couple of centuries of the church, there were very few people who were really asking for an explanation of the relationship between the human and the divine. What you find running down that middle line is in the rule of faith in Irenaeus, in Tertullian, in most of the early church theologians, just simple basic expressions that Jesus is both God and man. . . . For example, with the rule of faith concerning Christ Jesus, the Son of God who became incarnate for our salvation, there is no attempt to give an explanation. It is simply an assertion. It is what you might call a fact of faith. Ignatius, for example, puts together the paradox. Notice how he does this. *There is one only physician, of flesh and of spirit, generate and ingenerate, God in man, true Life in death, Son of Mary and Son of God, first passible and then impassible, Jesus Christ our Lord.* If you go through all of those persons, Justin, Irenaeus, Hippolytus, and Tertullian, you will see that they offer no explanation whatsoever. They simply affirm it. When you get down to Origen and Malchion, you are getting into an explanation of the relationship between the human and the divine. And if you will notice Origen's statement—maybe we should read it.

> We believe that the very Logos of the father, the wisdom of God himself, was enclosed within the limits of that man who appeared in Judea, nay, more, that God's wisdom entered a woman's womb, was born as infant and wailed like crying children.

Note the comment. He defines the relationship of the two natures as an actual union, or commingling, resulting in the deification of the humanity, and not as a mere association. Let's stop and think about that for just a moment. If you go back to the picture that I had on the board a few minutes ago, in interpreting the John 1:14 phrase, where do you think that Origen would fit? Would he tend to say that God *became*, in the sense of transformed or turned into, or would you think that he would exegete that in the terms of assumed or became? Origen and Malchion, the follower of Origen, tend to overemphasize the divinity. Let me explain how. In Origen's sense, and Malchion's who follows him, it is as though the humanity is gathered up into the divinity, participates in the divinity, and therefore loses its identity as humanity, and we can speak of the humanity of Jesus or the person of Jesus in words that would almost sound like "divine flesh." Origen is an Eastern thinker, right? He is therefore going to influence the East, and the East is going to stand more in the tradition of Origen. Are there any questions about that before I try to develop this?

What I am trying to do is tell you stories of how these concepts of Christ developed. I just want you to see where Origen fits, and how we have one overemphasis on divinity, and one overemphasis on humanity, by the time you come up to, say, AD 325. Let's go into the period from 325 to 428 because this is a very, very important period of time. The doctrine of Christology has really not yet begun to take shape, but between 325 and 428 there emerge two schools of thought, which are going to be determinative for Eastern and Western conceptions of Christology.

First of all, the East. To begin with, we are going to look at some of the biblical references in regard to Christology. I am not planning to look these up because of the considerable amount of material that I need to go over with you to get ourselves up to the place where we begin to see the whole Eastern and Western concept of Christology. But I would like to mention several of these passages of Scripture and give you a little indication of the kind of things that we see here.

In the first place, you recognize from our discussion of Trinitarian thought last week that the church was born recognizing that there is a preexistence of Jesus, and the Trinitarian debate, which of course at heart was mainly a soteriological debate, centered around the question of the status of the preexistent Word with the Godhead. The way in which we concluded the Trinitarian debate was to recognize something that looked like this, that you have in the Trinity, the Father, the Son, and the Spirit, but that there is a coinherence between the Father and the Son and the Spirit, so that you can say that there is one single essence to the Godhead, although we can speak in terms of three persons, as the Latin Fathers used it later. They took the Greek *hypostasis* and translated that into *person*, so that we can speak in terms of one God, one *ousias*, one essence, three persons.

This is not a tritheism. The understanding of the Godhead is that there is only one God, but that there are relations in the Godhead, so that you can speak in terms of Father, Son, and Spirit. What we are facing, and the whole question of Christology, which is related to the Trinitarian question, is how do you talk about Jesus being the incarnate God? How do you find a language that can discuss the Son coming down to the earth? How can you discuss the Son coming down to the earth and uniting himself with humanity? This is the problem that we have here. We have the human and the divine united together in the single person of Jesus Christ. The question that we have to deal with is how do you find a language to talk about this, because it is unrelated to our experience. We cannot think of anything in terms of our experience that is like this. The biblical witness is, as I have indicated, that Jesus is the preexistent Word who is one with God. Then the Romans 1 passage indicates that in the incarnation we talked of this person Jesus as being of the Spirit and of the flesh. So we recognize immediately that "of the Spirit" could be connected with this whole concept of the divine, and "of the flesh," which may be connected with this idea of the human, after the spirit and after the flesh. It is John 1:14 that begins to give us a kind of interpretation of this, because John 1:14 says that the Word was made flesh, or became flesh, depending on the translation that you are using. Let's use, "was made flesh." So now you have a picture from John 1:14 that begins to interpret this data, the Word who is one with God is made flesh.

The problem here is finding a way to interpret the word "was made" or "became." How do you talk about that? What does it mean to make flesh? This is what I would call the exegetical problem, which is essential to the different positions that come out in the church. Let's take a look at this. How would you speak about this?

Well, you could say the Word was made flesh in the sense that the Word became or was metamorphosed. The idea here would be that the Word changed into flesh. Or you could say that when you think about the Word being made flesh, it means to say that the Word *assumed* flesh, as one puts on a cloak or a garment or something of that sort. I would like you to make some commitments today and tell me which of those two just on the surface.... We are not going to write this in the books of heaven. We are not going to burn any heretics after class. But just on the surface of things, which of these two interpretations of the statement "was made flesh" do you think most accurately represents this symbolic descent and movement into the earth of the incarnation? How many of you—let's start with hands—how many of you will take the "became" point of view? Up a little higher. Do I assume, therefore, that the rest of you shaking your heads are going to take the second position, so that means that Christ as God assumed flesh, assumed the human body? How many of you take that point of view?

Student: Is that language an accurate symbol?

Webber: Okay, maybe I did not mean the picture, but using this as a symbol of what happened may or may not be an accurate symbol. It is hard to symbolize a lot of this, but which do you think would be the most accurate? So we have some people committed to "the became" and we have some committed to "the assumed." Second question. Which of these positions would you say is closest to the Eastern Christology? How many of you would say that the "became" is closest to the Eastern theology? No idea? Okay. How many hands do I have on "became" is Eastern? Ah, one fledgling soul. How many hands do I have that "assumed" is Eastern? Well, then you assume that "became" is Western, right? Not necessarily? Nothing is neither. Right.

8

Protestantism, Orthodoxy, Catholicism

SESSION #4, DECEMBER 14, 1978

Webber: Do you remember the First Axiom? Anybody remember? The First Axiom is only God can save. The Second Axiom is only that which is assumed is healed. Do you remember that one? Do you understand that one? It is the christological axiom. You either understand it or you die. Let me say it again: only that which is assumed is healed. All right. Now let's apply that to this.

In Apollinarianism, what did God assume? . . . So therefore, if God assumed that body—though the assumption there is not even in the sense in which Orthodoxy understands it—but if God just simply kind of dwelt in a body there, at best the body would be saved. What about the mind? What about the intellect? What about the will? To clarify Apollinarianism for you a little bit more, Apollinarianism is saying that the interiority of the man Jesus was the Logos, but the external of the man Jesus was just the human. So the human and the divine are blended together by the divine being the interior, and the exterior being the human. . . .

Let's go one step beyond Apollinarianism into the West and see how the West was approaching this whole thing, because we are going to get into a Western, not necessarily a Roman, but at least a Western, point of view about this at that particular time. We do not see a correct view yet at all, do we? The West is what is called the Word-Man Christology. The Word-Man Christology really talks in terms of the Word joining man, whereas the emphasis over here is on the Word uniting [with man], with the exception of Apollinarianism, which is just simply way off the wall.

As this Eastern point of view in Alexandria is Platonic, so the Western point of view—which incidentally centers in Antioch—is Eastern, but always took a sort of Western point of view, the Western point of view is Aristotelian. All right, now let's take a moment to compare Aristotle's philosophy with Plato's philosophy about materiality. So the emphasis in Aristotelianism is always on the earthly. You do not have preexistence in Aristotelianism. Rather, the whole concept is that the created order is what is. For example, if we were to try to symbolize the Aristotelian point of view, it would look like this, as opposed to this. The really real—which obviously is not a very good term, but to pick it up from our friend Francis Schaeffer[1]—it is the really real is here. You do not have to look elsewhere. You do not have to go outside for the really real.

Student: Really?

Webber: Really, really, really! This means, then, that full humanity is present at birth. With this idea back here—I should have gone into it a little more extensively—the idea would be that you have a body and that the soul for that body—now this is not really a strict Orthodox position at all, this has been shifted and changed—but that the soul from that body comes from a preexistent bank of souls. Therefore, the soul of Christ would come from the preexistent Christ and dwell in that body as the human soul from the human bank of souls would come in that body and dwell in it. Now, in the Aristotelian point of view, body, soul, and spirit, which they did not use, but I am going to use anyway by way of illustration, is present immediately at conception, or birth, whichever one you want to choose, it does not matter to me. But it does not come from something outside. Therefore, in the Aristotelian point of view, the Antiochian school also believes in the preexistence of Jesus. So you can put your Trinity up here. The preexistent Word, then, comes down into the world and joins with the whole person that is already there. So what you have in the human and the divine is, you might say, a conjunction. How does that conjunction take place? When you look in the Old Testament, the Spirit of God would come upon people to do unusual things, right? The Spirit of God comes upon Gideon, lickety-split. Gideon does his thing. The Spirit of God comes upon us.

---

1. Francis Schaeffer (1912–1984) was a Presbyterian pastor, theologian, apologist, and author.

The school of thought in Antioch under Theodore of Mopsuestia described the relationship between the Word and Jesus the human in terms of the Spirit dwelling with the human, as the Spirit dwelt with Gideon, except always from birth through death. See where we are going? No, the heretic does not see. I wonder if there is a heretic-ess? Let's get the female aspect in there. I am trying to show you how this whole business of the God-man, in terms of explanation, when it is filtered through a Neoplatonic grid, is going to come out with one emphasis, which is going to be an emphasis on union, absorption.

At this point, let's kind of forget about Apollinarianism, because that is really the worst heretical notion in this that you could possibly get. So let's take Apollinarianism away, and what you get coming out of the Neoplatonic emphasis would be something that would look like this. There is the human Jesus. You see the human Jesus here. Now, upon the human Jesus, we put the divine Logos, so that the humanity is absorbed into the divinity, and we speak in terms, then, of the union of the two natures. On the other hand, in the Aristotelian point of view, here is Jesus the human, and the divine comes upon Jesus this way, so that have a conjunction of two natures.

Let's look for just a moment at the possibility of error. Maybe I should say of overemphasis, rather than error, the possibility of overemphasis in these two schools of thought. What is the possibility of overemphasis in the Eastern Platonic grid? It overemphasizes the divinity by so uniting the human and the divine that the human is absorbed into the divinity. That is the tendency. I am not saying that that is exactly what happened, but that is the tendency. So what we are looking for here are tendencies, because you are going to come out with different christological tendencies in the East and the West, which are going to be at bottom one of the basic differences between Eastern and Western Christianity. What, then, would be the tendency of the Antiochian school? To overemphasize the humanity, to so separate the divine from the human that the relationship of the divine to the human can be spoken of in terms of a sort of a dwelling of the Spirit.

All right, one more question. What does each of these positions do to the incarnation? Describe the incarnation under the Alexandrian school. How would you describe the incarnation? The Eastern school is really "the became." How many of you committed yourself to that Eastern position? Okay, so we have some Eastern Orthodox people here. How many of you committed yourself to the Western position? See, that is "the assumed." All right. Did God, in fact, turn into man? Did God, in fact, simply assume man?

Student: When you say "turned into man," does that mean he let go of divinity?

Webber: No, no. I always hesitate to do this, but I shall do this anyway because it is a way of getting at the problem. We will have to go inside of the womb of the Virgin Mary and see what was happening. What happened? Did the Logos enter into the womb of the Virgin Mary and turn into humanity? Or at the conception was a human conceived with whom the Logos entered into the womb and joined?

Student: I have had a hard time getting into the fact that when you believe Jesus was totally God and totally man, except for the nature of sin, and in the Western thought it looks like there that if that would be true, then Jesus would have a sinful nature, because he assumed all of man. And you cannot really side with either one of those, there is a medium.

Webber: Well, it does not have to, because Adam was a complete human without sin prior to the fall. The second Adam is compared to the first Adam, so that does not necessarily follow with the Antiochian school. God could join with humanity and that humanity be yet without sin, as Hebrews says. Okay, I am going to see a show of hands here, and then I am going to give you a break. How many Antiochians in the class at this point? How many Alexandrians in the class at this moment? How many heretics in the class at this moment? Oh, yes. I will put my hand down.

Student: I'm not sure how I meant my question....

Webber: Oh, then I do not mind taking it in the way in which you did not mean it! Let's take a break.

***

Webber: Okay, now in tracing the historical development of the doctrine of Christology, we move into the final period of conflict between the Antiochian and Alexandrian schools of thought, and this occurs between AD 428 and 451. Just as these two schools of thought, the Word-Flesh Christology, began to emerge in the period after Nicaea. So it is these two schools of thought that come into conflict in this crucial period from 428 to 451, at which time by 451 the problem becomes somewhat solved, not totally and completely, but somewhat solved. The debate, as it occurs, is between Cyril of Alexandria and Nestorius, who is of Constantinople. This is going to be confusing for a moment, because you are going to notice that both Alexandria and Constantinople are in the East. But I want to emphasize the fact that even though both of these schools of thought are in the East, you cannot say that each of them is Eastern Orthodox. The position of Cyril is going to be closer to Eastern Orthodoxy, and as a matter of fact, somewhat closer to Catholicism too, and I would say that maybe the Protestant point of view is a little bit closer to Nestorius. So I will just give that as a general introduction, and we will start looking at the conflict that occurred.

The conflict between these two schools of thought occurred around the use of the word *Theotokos*. Let me put the word up there. Who knows what the word Theotokos means? Mother of God. Right. Now the word Theotokos, just take a look at that. Which of these two groups do you assume would be the happiest with that term? The Cyrillian group or the Nestorian group? Cyril, right, because he is going to emphasize the word "flesh." So the Theotokos is the Cyrillian word. Mary is the mother of God. What do you suppose would be a word that Nestorius would prefer to use? *Christakos*. Mary is the mother of Christ, emphasizing that what Mary has given birth to is human—also divine, but in using the word Christakos emphasizes the conjunction, whereas Theotokos emphasizes the union. You see where we are going here? So that the whole concept that looks something like this is going to be coming out of Cyril, and the emphasis that looks like that, the human and the divine joined together, is going to be coming out of Nestorius . . . .

I want you to see the symbol of union in Ephesus AD 431. Have you found it? These two schools of thought, which had been denouncing each other as heretical, came together to Ephesus in 431 and wrote this symbol of union. I want to read through this symbol of union and show you that it is not at all a symbol of union. As a matter of fact, it is just putting Band Aids on the problem. So let's take a look at it. *We confess, therefore, our Lord Jesus Christ, the only begotten son of God, perfect God and perfect man, composed of a rational soul in a body*—incidentally, that statement "composed of a rational soul and body," is a rejection of Apollinarianism. Both Cyril and Nestorius reject Apollinarianism, which presupposes that Christ does not have a human, rational mind or soul, or will, or whatever you want to call it. *Now begotten before the ages from his father in respect of his divinity*—which simply says we believe that he is preexistent, and both your Alexandrian and Antiochian schools are going to affirm that. . . . *But likewise in these last days for us and our salvation*—now underscore that statement, "for us and our salvation," because it is a soteriological thing that we are dealing with here, the emphasis on soteriology. *From the Virgin Mary in respect of his divinity, and at the same time, consubstantial with us in respect of his manhood.* What I want you to notice is how this continues. For a *union* of two natures. Who would that be? The Cyrillian point of view. *For a union of two natures has been accomplished. Hence, we confess one Christ, one Son, one Lord.* Now, in virtue of this conception of a union without confusion—and note the statement "without confusion" is going to have to do here with a Nestorian point of view, because the Nestorian conjunction insists that there can be no confusion between the human and the divine. So they are calling it a union without confusion. So you are getting both the Alexandrian and the Nestorian position here. Let's see how it works out, because it gets worse. *In virtue of this conception of a union without confusion, we confess the Holy Virgin as Theotokos*—a Cyrillian word—*because the divine word became flesh*—Cyrillian—*and was made man*—Nestorian—*and from the very conception united*—Cyrillian—*to himself the temple*—Nestorian—taken from her. The idea is that the body is like a temple in which the divine resides. *Now as for the Evangelical and apostolic statements about the Lord, we recognize that theologians employ some indifferently in view of the unity of persons, but distinguish others in view of the duality of natures, applying the God befitting ones to Christ's divinity and the humble ones to his humanity.* Recognizing in this last sentence, then, the distinction between the human and the divine, so that you can say that when Jesus pleads ignorance about the second coming, you can say, "Oh, he is speaking out of his human nature." When he stills the water, you can say, "Oh, he is functioning out of his divine nature." So it kind of separates the human and the divine.

The Council of Ephesus, let's face it, did not work. You can see that this is no solving of the problem whatsoever. The problem still exists. Are we going to talk about the human and the divine in terms of union or in terms of conjunction? Putting the two words together simply does not solve the problem. If you look at the chart, you will notice that after the Council of Ephesus there is a Council of Antioch in 433. The Council of Antioch in 433 simply sort of affirms again what the Ephesus 431 council affirmed, and nothing was solved. At this point, however, I want you to notice that a person by the name of Eutychius—I suppose that is the best way to pronounce it—says, "Look, you guys can play your little games all you want, but as far as I am concerned, this is the way it is." And he says, "Before conception, I believe there were two natures, the divine, the human. After the conception, only one." How many natures are there in the person of Christ? The Nestorian has been insisting on human and divine, two natures. The Cyrillian has been insisting on human and divine, two natures. But the issue for them has been how do you talk about the relation of these two natures? Eutychius says one. This is what is called the monophysite position. The one nature position. A lot of Eastern churches are monophysite. Not all. Orthodoxy is not. But the monophysite—note where that comes from: *mono* = one, *phusus* = nature. So monophysite is one nature. The Coptic and the Armenian are Monophysite churches. Here began one of the largest splits, probably the earliest large split, in the Christian church, because the monophysites exist until today. I do not really know how many hundreds of thousands there are who are monophysite, but there are quite a few. Really, they are relatively small by comparison with the amount of people who call themselves Christian. Now getting the true monophysites out of the way, so to speak, it gave opportunity for those who came from a Cyrillian position and those who came from a Nestorian position, to examine once again, without the monophysites, who would really be stressing for the unity, gave them an opportunity to examine once again the whole question. In the meantime, there is some input from Pope Leo.

Finally they come to Chalcedon in AD 451, and they put together what is called the Chalcedonian Statement, which is an ecumenical statement. We will read it. *In agreement, therefore, with the holy fathers, we all unanimously teach that we should confess that our Lord Jesus Christ is one and the same Son, the same perfect in Godhead and the same perfect in manhood, truly God and truly man.* That sounds like Ignatius, doesn't it? Or the rule of faith. It sounds like one of the early fathers of the church. Sounds like the common faith. *The same of a rational soul and body, fully human, consubstantial with the Father and Godhead, and the same consubstantial with us in manhood, like us in all things except sin.* So what you have here is 100 percent God, 100 percent human. *Begotten from the Father before the ages as regard as Godhead and in the last days the same because of us and because of our salvation begotten from the Virgin Mary.* Theotokos, so this is retained. The Theotokos, but it is described here as regards his manhood. So in other words, the Theotokos undergoes change to emphasize the fact that Mary gave birth to the God-man. It would not say she is the mother of God; she is the mother of the God-man. *One and the same Christ, Son, Lord only begotten made known in two natures.*

Note the adverbs that come after this statement. *These two natures are without confusion, without change, without division, and without separation.* Those adverbs speak to the Cyrillian Christology, don't they? Because the adverbs are saying, "Okay, we can talk about a union between the God-man." But in this union it is of such a nature that there is no confusion. The problem that we are talking about is the communicatio idiomatum, which is an issue back here which I did not bring up, but need to discuss now. The communicatio idiomatum is to what extent does the divine communicate the divine to the human? To what extent does the human communicate the human to the divine? Communicatio idiomatum, literally translated, means "the communication of one's own." The communication of one's property. The argument in these adverbs, without confusion, without change, etc., etc., is that the union between the human and the divine takes place in such a way that the properties of the divine are fully and completely kept. He is no less divine. And the properties of the human are totally and completely kept. Christ is no less human. Nevertheless, the human and the divine are so united that we can speak of Jesus as being a single person.

What we have is something similar to the way in which we dealt with the Trinity. There is only one God, and yet in the essence of the one God, there is the relation of Father, Son, and Holy Spirit, so we do not have tritheism. We have only one God. In Christology, the same principle of coinherence is taking place.

Did I talk about the principle of coinherence last week? I did? Okay. I just wanted to check and make sure.

The same principle is occurring here. The human and the divine coinhere in a single person. Now in both instances we are dealing with paradox. For one is three and three is one. And one and one, which we would assume would make two, makes one. Because Jesus is no schizophrenic. He is a single person, yet with the human and divine nature so united that they do not destroy the property of each. Yet Jesus as subject always functions from the union between the human and the divine. Let's look at the rest of this statement and then I am going to talk about the implications, and the differences between Protestant, Catholic, and Orthodox at this point, because there are significant differences.

But the property of each nature being preserved and coalescing in one person and one hypostasis, not parted or divided into two persons, but one in the same Son, only begotten divine word, the Lord Jesus Christ as the prophets of old, and Jesus Christ himself have taught us about him and the creed of our fathers has handed down.

Okay. I have said all that to get to the final point of showing you the differences between these three schools of thought that we are studying. First, let's look at the East. . . . Chalcedon would look like this. Let's put it this way. The distinction of the human and the divine is united in the single person. The adverbs would discuss the fact of completely human, completely divine. The Eastern view really wants to stick to the Cyrillian point of view, which continues to look something like that. The Catholic point of view—and I will talk about the implications of this in a minute—wants to stay with the Chalcedonian. And it would appear that a Protestant view, while staying with the Chalcedonian Statement—incidentally, I should say the Chalcedonian Statement does stand behind all three of these views, the Eastern, the Catholic and the Protestant church all affirm the Chalcedonian Statement. It is only the Monophysite church that does not affirm this statement. But they have different ways of looking at the statement. The Protestant wants to look at it in, I would say, almost that way. All right. This does not mean anything to you yet, because you have to see the christological implications before it begins to mean anything. I think there are a number of places where I could give you christological implications, but I am not going to give you more than one today, because I think one is all that we should discuss at this point. As the course moves on, we will see other implications. I want to take the christological implication of eucharistic theology. Are you with me? The christological implication of eucharistic theology.

You have before you bread and wine. As the divine and the human coinhere, so also God coinheres within his created order, and especially at those points where he so chooses to coinhere to be uniquely present. The Eastern Church in her Christology, which wants to emphasize the union between God and man, expresses in her eucharistic theology a concept of real presence, a union between body and bread. You see the christological implication of eucharistic theology? Do you know what I mean when I am talking about eucharistic theology? The Lord's Supper. What is that bread? Is that bread just bread? Or is that bread more than bread? Is it body? The christological implication is that God may use the creation as a worthy vehicle for divine grace. It is a key statement that I will be discussing again and again. The christological implication is that God may use his creation as a worthy vehicle of divine grace, or a worthy vehicle through which he himself is present. Is God present in the man Jesus Christ? Yes. There should not be any Christian who would reject that. God is present in Jesus Christ. He is a man. Pinch him and he says, "Ouch." Cut him and he bleeds. Hit him over the head and he falls. I think we have to use these dramatic illustrations to emphasize how human Jesus was. He was not an apparition. That is gnostic heresy. He was not some sort of a phenomena that floated around. It is flesh and blood and guts, toenails and fingernails, hair on his head and a mustache and a beard, right? But that flesh and blood was more than flesh and blood. It was God incarnate. Therefore, when he said, "This is my body, this is my blood," it was more than common bread and common drink. It is his body and blood. Not his body and blood in the sense that if you bite it, you would bite Jesus. But what? Coinherence. As God coinhered in his Son Jesus. Not a mere conjunction, but an actual incarnation where he was really present. Not destroying the humanity but uniting with the humanity so that he was there, not as though it is divine flesh, for it was human flesh. But divinity was present in humanity. Therefore, creation may become a vehicle of his divine presence. So the water of baptism is more than water. So bread is more than bread, and wine is more than wine. You see the implication of an Eastern Christology. The Eastern Orthodox Church is relatively unhappy with the Chalcedonian Statement. They have had several other ecumenical councils, particularly the Council of 553, which is known as the Sixth Ecumenical Council. Chalcedon is the fifth, in which they came back and reinterpreted the Chalcedonian Statement more in keeping with the Cyrillian perspective. I was only going to give you one illustration, but I think you understood that illustration so well that I am going to give you another. How many of you have been to an Eastern Orthodox service? The eternal can be present to us in the material. Thus an icon is more than mere paint and wood and whatever else goes into making an icon. It is a window into the eternal. Now I do really quickly want to make a qualification. An icon is not an incarnation. The bread and wine is not an incarnation. There is only one incarnation in Eastern Orthodox thought, not more than one. However, the incarnation is extended in the created order. So that God through his energy—energy is an Eastern concept which I want to talk about sometime—is made present by his energy through his created order. Thus holy water, which sanctifies the creation, because the whole of creation has been assumed in Jesus Christ, and only that which is assumed is saved, thus the whole creation is saved, Romans 8. Creation is under bondage to decay, but now is waiting, eagerly anticipating, the glory of its redemption. So therefore the whole relationship of incarnation in Jesus, where God makes himself present, is extended into the presence of God in the whole created order, so that the whole creation may lift its hands and give glory to God. The created order is not something that is unrelated to God. He brought it into being. He upholds it by the word of his power. He is present in it and through it.

Student: But is not the created order and the confusion and the trouble and sorrow it is going through, isn't that just a consequence of man's sin? It was cursed by God, as we see in Genesis 3.

Webber: Oh, yeah. If it was cursed by God.

Student: The fall was caused by man himself, but is not the creation unfallen?

Webber: No. From an Eastern perspective, the created order is fallen. . . .

Student: Could you explain to me briefly what the Protestant mindset is? You said that the human is never invaded by the divine, and the divine is never invaded by the human? I am not sure I understand.

Webber: Okay, let me use the word *coinherence*, which I used last week and used a couple of times [today]. Coinherence is accepted here in the basic christological formula of the Eastern and the Catholic. Now the Protestant, by and large—I say "by and large" because this is not really going to be everybody—but the Protestant will, by and large, accept coinherence but not its implications. So therefore, by the way in which a Protestant does his or her eucharistic theology, let's go from the eucharistic theology back to Christology. The Protestant seems to be rejecting a coinherence, or the implications of christological coherence, and therefore tends in their interpretation of the Chalcedonian Definition to go the Nestorian way. May I also say that in terms of mindsets, the Protestant mindset is basically rational. This [Nestorian] is a much more rational perspective, whereas this [Cyrillian] is much more mystical. Your Eastern and Catholic are more mystical, although Eastern is more mystical than Catholic, because the Catholic has been somewhat reshaped by the wedding of Aristotelianism with Aquinas, and that has given a different shape to Catholic thought. Nevertheless, they have maintained a more mystical spirit than the Protestants. Protestants are Enlightenment rationalists, by and large. When I say Protestants, I would tend to see both Luther and Calvin themselves as being closer to this [mystical] position than they would be to this [rationalist] position. It is the followers of Luther and Calvin, the seventeenth century onward, that comes closer to this position over here.

Student: In the Eucharist, or the Lord's Supper, or whatever you want to call it, and you compare it with the divine and human in Jesus, you said that when God chose, he could use creation as a worthy vehicle of his presence. I think a lot of the difference would be that a lot of people would say that God chose in Christ to do it, but, for instance, if you accept that Eucharist as being his choosing to do it at that time—I am not saying he would not be present, because he is omnipresent—but if you say he manifests himself in that, he would manifest himself in a lot of other things too, like a rock in the wilderness would have to be something like that, and would have an awful lot of implications for icons and things like that, and you sort of have to interpret how much of that kind of thing God chose to do.

Webber: That is true. They are different levels. You do have to look at that rather closely. In terms of sacramental theology, just to give you a foretaste of what will come at the end of the course, you have to distinguish between the dominical sacraments of baptism and the Lord's Supper, the church sacraments (the other five) and a general sacramental conception of the universe. . . . There are implications in that soteriologically, which I will deal with in Eastern Christianity, but I better finish up this illustration on the Eucharist because it is 5:00 o'clock. Not that I do not want to answer your question, it is just that I will be spending a whole two hours on that.

Okay, the Catholic position is really relatively close to the Eastern position. The Catholic position recognizes the coinherence and therefore also comes out with an understanding of eucharistic theology, where bread is more than bread, and wine is more than wine. The Nestorian position, however, so separates the human from the divine that the human is only human and always human and is not invaded by the divine, and the divine is always divine and does not invade the human. Do you see Protestant eucharistic theology, then, related to that Christology? The bread is bread and nothing more. The wine is wine and nothing more. Or rather, the grape juice is grape juice and nothing more. The point that I wanted to make, and I hope that you followed all the development of it, is that if you are going to understand the differences between the Catholic and the Orthodox and the Protestant points of view, you have got to begin with both Trinity and Christology. Actually, Christology is the most central notion. But I began with Trinity, because Trinity is what we would call the ontological basis for the theology of coinherence, to which Catholic, Eastern, and Protestant all agree, unless you are either a Unitarian or a tritheist or a ditheist. I think that there are many of them running around in the Protestant church, they just do not know it, because they have really never thought about their theology. Our churches are full of tritheists and ditheists. But that does not mean they are heretics, and it does not mean they will go to hell. Just purgatory, the Protestant purgatory. There is a special one for Protestant people. It is not quite as severe. You do not need indulgences. You just need to learn your theology. I will be there teaching. That will be purgatory. You are going through it now. This is it. It gets awfully hot. This whole thing is purgatory right here, isn't it? Okay.

But that is why it is important to start with the Trinity and Christology, because these are basic. After Christmas we are going to see how important this all becomes to soteriology, to ecclesiology, to Scripture, to sacraments, then you will have a fairly good basis, I think, to understand the differences. That would be ridiculous. I could have walked in here today and in ten minutes I could have told you the difference between Eastern, Western, and Protestant. That is not the point. The point is I want you to understand *why* there are these differences, and that is why ecumenical relations between these three groups are just not snappy like this. You see very definite, deep philosophical differences between these three schools of thought. I am not telling you where you should plant your feet, but I think that what you want to do is open yourself up to thinking about all of these perspectives, and not just simply automatically accepting one over the other, regardless of which one. Otherwise, you won't learn them quite as well. But the thing to do is to put yourself into this subjectively and ask yourself, "Where do I fit?" Do not take a Protestant position blasé, or an Orthodox position blasé, or a Catholic position blasé. Work it through. Now we have only begun, and it has taken me four hours to get to this place where we can begin looking at the differences.

Student: I do not see how one could necessarily imply how all these others had to be. I can see how you can accept it from Jesus and not for the Lord's Supper. . . .

Webber: There is a lot of other theological data that needs to be taken into consideration. For example, the relationship between God and creation in what we call, theologically, transcendence and immanence. How do we understand that? What was in fact happening in the Old Testament with all of those instances? What does it mean that God came on the mountain and made himself known? What does it mean that he localized himself in the ark, made himself present in the Holy of Holies, and then finally enfleshed himself in Jesus? What do all of those things that we often overlook, what do they mean? There is a tremendous amount of depth to the ancient way of seeing things, and the Eastern and the Catholic churches are closer to the ancient way of seeing things. But I think the Eastern Church is the closest. That is an academic statement.

The next judgment that you have to decide is whether or not that in fact is biblical, and some people would say, "Well, what you have in the early church is an immediate departure from biblical truth." Which seems hard to assume that the church went wrong that quickly. At any rate, I do not want to throw too much more out at this time because it is 5:10. You need to catch trains and eat food and do all that sort of stuff and go and have a good vacation. So Merry Christmas, Happy New Year. Do nothing but think about all this stuff until I see you again.

9

Orthodoxy, Catholicism, Protestantism

SESSION #5, JANUARY 4, 1979

Webber: Today we are talking about the subject of the Catholic view of salvation. As I was saying to you before I was rudely interrupted by this crazy tape that we have to turn on for these people who do not come to class, who have to listen to this stuff, I was saying that this is the area of the greatest differences. There are tremendous differences in ecclesiology and sacramental thought and all of that as well. But it is the difference in soteriology, or the doctrine of salvation, that lays the groundwork for the differences that we find between Catholics and Orthodox and Protestants. What I would like to begin with today is an opportunity for you to share with me some of your ideas of what you think the Roman Catholic doctrine of salvation is. It does not matter to me whether your view is correct, whether it is a caricature, whether it is totally and completely off the wall, out to lunch, whatever you want to call it. What I want to do is hear from you what you think at this particular point the Roman Catholics teach on the doctrine of salvation. The floor is open.

Student: From my understanding, the salvation is based on. . . . Let me speak right into the mic. This is your roving reporter.

Webber: Yeah. Salvation is based on what, right?

Student: Salvation is based on the accepting of Jesus Christ through the Eucharist and also by means of the works of the baptism, the washing with baptism that Christ has received, and by that receiving of Christ, they enter into a state of salvation from sin.

Webber: Okay. That is a good place to start. Who else has something that they would like to say?

Student: The members themselves and what they experience in their lives is different from the historical Catholic doctrine of salvation. For example, I found many people on the street while witnessing, saying that if I try to follow the Ten Commandments and try to lead a good life and do not hurt anybody, and make sure I go to Catholic church.... If I just try to live the life, I am pretty much assured of heaven, and we will all end up there anyway. And most of them say that even the non-Christian religions have a chance at salvation.

Webber: You are speaking about Catholics that you have talked to on the streets? Well, I think we have to recognize that there is a distinction perhaps between what we might call the official doctrine of the church and the understanding of the people. I think you would probably find that in Protestant churches too, don't you think? If you went to the Wheaton Bible Church or College Church and yakkety-yakked with the bulletin giver-outer, would you find that there is some kind of a failure there to communicate the Protestant theology of salvation to the people, and that there are, in fact, some erroneous conceptions within the minds of Protestant people, as well about the theology of salvation? Would that be true?

Student: I am not sure about this, is there something to do with having to participate in all seven sacraments, also with the doctrine? It is a progressive thing from one to the other?

Webber: Are you asking me or telling me?

Student: If it is right, I am telling you. If it is wrong, I am asking you.

Webber: Well, we will determine at the end of the class whether you told me or asked me. But that there is a conception of the relationship of sacraments to the doctrine of salvation is true. Exactly what that means, we have to take a look at that.

Student: I have the knowledge or the assumption or whatever that what is the basic doctrine of the Catholic Church, is very right on as far as—if you read it and you look at it, it seems very Evangelical and very Protestant. But there are other things like the traditions that go beyond just the basic documents. A group of us looked into basic Catholic doctrine, and the basic things are very Evangelical. If you look at them, they did not look any different than what you might find in the front of a Baptist hymnbook. Maybe that was just something that was wrong, and I did not read it right, but that is the way it appears. I know that there is more to it about which I do not agree. But the basic doctrines about receiving Christ and that type of thing are very, very Evangelical. That's my thinking.

Webber: That is interesting, because I think that is true. Maybe we should say that the Evangelical doctrines are really very Catholic, rather than turning it around, since the Catholic came first, that maybe Evangelicalism is a kind of reduction of Catholic teaching with certain shifts. I think that we will see that that is in fact true when we get to the Reformation to study the Protestant doctrine of salvation, because it comes out of the Roman, and of course it is a response against excesses in the Roman Church in the fourteenth and fifteenth centuries. But there is also some additional insight or information that comes from the Protestant point of view that had not been clearly understood, say in the medieval period or even in the patristic period. But then we have to evaluate that to ask whether or not that is in fact biblical. So what we see then by the discussion is that there are a lot of different ideas perhaps floating about as to precisely what the Catholics teach, and we recognize specifically the distinction between church doctrine and peoples' doctrine, or what you might call popular Catholic Christianity.

First, let me say that what I am going to do today is somewhat preliminary and must be interrelated with what I am going to be doing for three weeks, because for three weeks we are going to discuss the doctrine of salvation, and I think that we will have a better understanding of the whole thing, even a better understanding of the Catholic point of view, two weeks from now than we will today. But I want to begin laying the groundwork for understanding the doctrine of salvation by taking this doctrine of salvation apart, looking at the pieces, and then try to put it together toward the end of the class. Let's think in terms of a puzzle. It is just a three-piece puzzle, except that you could take each one of these pieces and break them up into many other little divisions. We will start with the easiest thing and take our puzzle apart in three sections and then look at each one of those sections. There are three things that belong to this puzzle.

First, when discussing the theology of salvation, we must discuss the nature of man. Second, we must discuss the work of Christ. And third, the application of two to one, the application of the work of Christ to the nature of man. In short, to put this in terms that we are probably more familiar with, what we are talking about in the nature of man is the question of sin and free will. There is a lot more to it than that, which I do not think we have time to take up, but such things as the image of God in man, such things as the question of predestination and election, which I am going to try to look at more closely when we talk about the Protestants than today. Second, with the work of Christ, we are basically talking about a theology of atonement. The death of Christ. How are we to understand that? And then third, when we talk about the business of applying the work of Christ to man, we are really talking about the theology of grace.

So what I plan to do now is to talk about each one of these areas from a Roman point of view, which means that I will be skipping the Orthodox and the Protestant material, and we will have to kind of tuck all of that back in again in the next couple of classes. But I will look at this from the Roman point of view and then toward the end of the class, I will try to put it all together in terms of a Roman Catholic synthesis on the theology of salvation.

Let's begin with this question of the nature of man. First of all, on the nature of man, I want to go back into the New Testament and just refer to a couple of passages of Scripture that would be familiar to us and familiar to a Roman Catholic development of the doctrine of man as well. We are familiar, I think all of us, with Romans 1–3. There we definitely see a doctrine of sin. In Romans 1 it appears that Paul is specifically referring to the Gentiles as sinners. In chapter two, he appears specifically to refer to the Jews as sinners. Sort of an interesting way to get at this whole thing. And then in the third chapter he concludes that therefore all are sinners. So you go from Gentiles, to Jews, to a recognition that everybody is fallen and in need of a savior. You will see more statements by Paul, particularly in Ephesians 2. This is a passage that we are all rather familiar with. "You are dead in trespasses and sins."[1] "You follow the course of this world."[2]

---

1. Ephesians 2:1.
2. Ephesians 2:2.

And then he talks about becoming "alive in Christ."[3] So there is a great deal of material in the New Testament, in addition to those passages, that would talk about the problem.

So in finding a schema or a way of treating this, I would like to suggest that the biblical view of man looks something like this and that this would be bought by Roman Catholics and Orthodox and Protestant alike that in the biblical view of man. There are three models or perspectives on man. First, what we would call original man, and the idea is that original man is perfect or innocent. I am going to put the word *innocent*, because that is a word that is preferred by the Eastern Church and also by the Arminian church as opposed to the word *perfect*. Then the second man is what we would call fallen man, and we all recognize that because of the sin of Adam, the whole human race has been affected by his sin, and therefore we refer to man in the unfolding of culture as fallen man. And I think all of the verses that Paul uses there in Romans 1-2, and three, as well as Ephesians 2 that I quoted would refer to this fallen man.

Now the third man that we have here is redeemed man. It is recognized in the Scripture, and by all the various denominations, except those that would be liberal, it is recognized that it is Jesus Christ who redeems man, who restores man to something that would look like original man, except he is a new man. He is a new man in Christ Jesus. So in the nature of man, you have original man, fallen man, and redeemed man.

The question that comes up in reference to this is, how far fallen is man? Now we are getting into the issue here of free will. I would like to suggest that there are three approaches to this question that developed within history itself. First, man is fallen to the point where he is totally and completely dead. This would be an Augustinian understanding. Then a point of view that would be completely opposite to that of Augustine is the view of Pelagius. Pelagius insists that man, in fact, is not fallen, that the free will remains intact and that it is possible for man to actually be perfect too, to maintain his perfection of the original man. The third one, which I am not going to cite here yet, but I am going to get back to that after I have described Pelagius and Augustine a little bit more closely, is the semi-Pelagian point of view, but we will come back to that in a moment. Let's begin with Pelagius's point of view, and then take a look at Augustine's reaction, and then thirdly, at the semi-Pelagian consensus, which becomes the Roman Catholic consensus on the nature of man.

---

3. Ephesians 2:5.

Pelagius was a fourth-century monk whose basic concern was the Christian life. He was a very pious man, a man from a monastery, somewhat concerned about what he felt to be a failure to strive for perfection in the Christian community. Therefore, Pelagius went out with the message that you can be perfect. You might say that he was a moral preacher. He was concerned about ethics. He was concerned about the character of people, about growth and development and perfection in Jesus Christ. Now in his preaching, he set forth a theology of the nature of man that had its corollary in the doctrine of grace. I cannot help but get into the doctrine of grace, although I shall look more specifically at this later. But the doctrine of man and grace looked something like this—build a couple of steps there on your paper if you are taking notes on this. Original man is perfect. There is the possibility, Pelagius says, that there are some people who would continue to be perfect, that is to say, that Adam's fall affected only Adam. Are you familiar with that kind of thinking? Usually in the West we think of Adam's fall affecting and polluting everybody. But Pelagius's point of view was Adam's fall affected only Adam, so we are all Adams. You are an Adam, and you have to do what Adam did. There is the possibility that you will never do what Adam did, so that you could be perfect, and he cites some illustrations in Scripture of people who were perfect. Enoch, for example, is one that he says was perfect. I believe he refers to Mary as having been perfect, and several others. It is the exception rather than the rule. Now in this class, it is probably the rule rather than the exception. But for most people in this world, like Wheaton students, it is definitely the exception rather than the rule that I probably am the only perfect one up there. So I know that that it is the exception.

When man fell, God's grace went to work. There are two things that really went to work. Let's put it this way: the environment became evil. This is the way evil is passed down to people, and you have a bad environment, and the environment leads you into sinning. It is not that you are born with a sinful nature. But the grace of God is also at work in this, and the grace of God is the means by which you are once again able to attain to your perfection. Now what has been given? Well, first of all, Adam had free will and reason. I should not just say Adam, but mankind has free will and reason. That is to say, it is reasonable to elect to become perfect, and you have the free will to overcome your sin in order that you may become perfect. So reason and free will may be seen as little ladders taking us up to the gift of perfection. And reason and free will, you see, are grace. It is the grace that helps you to become perfect again. However, the world became increasingly sinful and all that stuff because of the environment, and most people did not select to be perfect. So God introduced the law. Keep the law. Do this and you should be perfect. Here is the ten general words or commands. If you can obey them, you will be all right.

So what is the law? The law is an act of God's grace, whereby in this world he gives us the means by which through free will and reason we have another help, another aid. We can read it, we can understand it, we can follow it. Finally, Christ came into the world. The significance of Christ is not so much in his death, as we are generally trained to think in our own background, but the significance of Christ is in the example which he gave. The example of Christ is an example of someone who did keep the law. He used his free will and his reason to keep the law. Therefore, those of us who stand on this side of Christ, can look to Christ, and we too, following the example of Jesus, we too can ultimately arrive at perfection. Right. We look at that and say, "Pelagius, you dirty, low-down heretic. You scum of the earth. Give me my matches. I am going to pile the pews of your church around you and burn you sky high." That is what you are thinking, right? You are not thinking that? Oh, you are such loving persons, you would not even burn a heretic. Well, that is because you are afraid you are going to get burnt.

At any rate, this looks like a doctrine of works, doesn't it? There is not an awful lot of reliance on Jesus. There is not a great deal of stress on faith. It is, "Work it up, baby. You can do it. Hey, I know you can do it. I know that you have committed one sin in the last twenty years, but you can do it." You can overcome, except you know that is not that case with most of you. Nevertheless, it is sort of a pull yourself up by your bootstraps theology. You too can have perfect character. Now Pelagius said, "Yeah, but I give all the glory to God." Oh? How come? Well, because in the nature of man, there are three things that we need to think about: *posse*, *valet*, and *esse*. Possibility or ability. I use that word, it is shorter. Ability. Will. Actualization. Pelagius says, "Look, it is all to the glory of God. It is not to work, because it is God who, in creating you, gives you the ability to do good." The ability is actually basic to the will. He has given you the will. He gives you the will to determine to function or to actualize the possibility.... So all to the glory of God, because God created you and made you in such a way that you can actually do this. As you can see, Pelagius's point of view would create some differences of opinion, which of course it did. And the major person with whom it created significant differences of opinion is our buddy Augustine.

Augustine said, "Oh, you're crazy." Instead, Augustine said, "Look, you are dead in your trespasses and sins." And when he talked about a person being dead, he meant that there is no free will to choose God. That is absolutely an impossibility. No free will. With Pelagius you can choose God. Augustine said, "Rather, grace must be understood in terms of three things: 1) prevenient grace; 2) irresistible grace; and 3) persevering grace." Let's take a look at these. Prevenient grace is the grace that gets you started, that is to say, you are dead, dead, dead. Rhoda is dead. There is not a blooming thing that Rhoda can do. Nothing. So the Holy Spirit must come along and give Rhoda life. The Holy Spirit turns Rhoda toward God, so that that dead person now receives life, and this prevenient grace is the burst of life itself. Irresistible grace means that as God gives Rhoda grace, she cannot resist it because God—now this goes back into election and predestination, which is going to come out more in Calvin and Luther, particularly Calvin—but she cannot resist it because this is the gift of God, and therefore as God turns her toward him, she turns toward him. It happens willingly. As God turns her toward him, she turns toward him. It is not anything that she did to turn toward him, but that because grace is irresistible, she finds herself irresistibly turning toward God, and accepting the provision in Christ. This is followed by persevering grace in the sense that because God created grace, and she turned as a result of that grace, God gives persevering grace for her through [to] the end of her life. As you can see from the context of this fifth-century battle, Augustine reacts to Pelagius's point of view. Many people looked at both of those at that time and determined that what we have got here are two extremes. So a number of people opted for what is called a semi-Augustinian, I suppose you could call, approach, but it has come down in history as the semi-Pelagian point of view. It is known as the semi-Pelagian point of view, used in the pejorative sense from those who would take the Augustinian position. But the trick in the semi-Pelagian point of view is to say that your will is not completely dead, but it has been affected to the point where it is sick, wounded. What God does, then, is when he gives you grace, you respond with cooperating grace. This business of cooperating grace is an extremely important thing to understand, if you are going to understand the Roman Catholic theology of salvation. So cooperating grace is, you might say, the middle ground between what people considered to be these two extremes, the Augustinian and the Pelagian. So you see three possible positions in terms of the nature of man. Just keep that in mind, and then we will come back to that later and put that together. Are there any questions or responses on that before we go on?

Student: Why did you call that cooperating grace?

Webber: Because that is what they call it. But I think what you are really asking me to do is to describe that a little bit more, which I did not do.

Student: Grace is something that God gives, but when you say "cooperating," that sounds like something man is doing. So how is that grace?

Webber: Yeah. That is right. Well, you remember my little description of this with Rhoda. God wakes her up, gives her irresistible grace, and she does turn toward him. Look back for example at your own salvation experience. Did you not make a willful, conscious decision to be a disciple of Christ? To rest and trust in him and follow after him? You were not coerced. God did not beat you over the head. It is not a puppy dog theory, where you were standing there with all fours stretched out, saying, "No, no!" and God is pulling, "Come on! Come on!" And you say, "All right, I give up. You are tougher than I am." Not the case. It was *yes*, I am in need of a savior. I recognize my sin. Yes, whatever way you did it, you know, whether it was raising a hand, dropping by your bedside, whatever. It was real. And it came from you. It came from inside. Cooperating grace is just simply another term for defining this process, except that it recognizes that man's will is only sick and not dead. See, that is the key to it. The key to it is understanding man's will. Rhoda is lying here on the floor. She is not dead. I want you to know she is not dead. Yeah, she is just lying on the floor. But she is sick. I get down on my knees, and I say, "Rhoda," but there is hardly even a whimper. A little eyelash is fluttering. I say, "Rhoda, will you follow after me?" And the eyelashes flutter a little faster, indicating yes, yes, yes. So I pour a little grape wine—uh, grape juice—into her mouth, and I sort of nurse her along. She is getting stronger. "Do you still want to follow me?" Yes, yes. As I nurse her and strengthen her, she gets stronger. But you see, I am doing something, and she is doing something. It is a cooperating kind of thing. Now she is down there, and I say, "Rhoda, do you want to come after me?" And then later, "Rhoda!" Ultimately poor Rhoda is going to die and go to hell, because she refused to accept my grace. I offered her my grace, which was universally offered to everybody, but Rhoda would not take it. So that is Rhoda's tough luck, so to speak. After all, she resisted it. She turned her back on it. She rejected it. I had nothing to do with it. See, in this business over here you can get into this predestination. I predestined that Rhoda should not accept it. Ah, double predestination. You predestined this one to go to heaven and that one to go to hell? At any rate, we will take a look at that a little bit more a couple of weeks from now when we talk about Calvin's point of view. But do you see what I am doing here in terms of focusing on the will and its relationship to grace? So you see, grace is cooperating. Let's see if maybe there is another question or two, and then we will take a break. I do not want to stop in the middle of the discussion about the atonement.

Student: What about Philippians 2:12–13, "So then, my beloved, just as you have always obeyed, not as in my presence only, but now much more in my absence, work out your own salvation with fear and trembling; for it is God who is at work in you, both to desire and to work for his good pleasure"?

Webber: That verse, of course, is misinterpreted if you use it that way. It is not meant to be used that way in Philippians. It is taking it out of context, but the principle of "work out your own salvation with fear and trembling" is definitely a Roman principle, yes. It is rooted first, consciously rooted, in this battle where the Roman Church gradually becomes a semi-Pelagian church with an emphasis on the will as being sick and not dead. Your Reformation church, at least your Calvinistic and Lutheran church, and then your English Reformation, is going to come from this perspective, and thus they are going to have a different view. You Arminians—anybody here Arminian, Wesleyan, Nazarene, Holiness, Charismatic?—you are mostly going to be standing in the same tradition as the Catholics, except you are going to come out with a different theology of salvation, because some of the shifts that occurred in the Reformation have crept into your thinking. But you are not election and predestinarian thinkers, as the Protestant Reformers, who, incidentally, were scholars in Augustine. See, Augustine's view on this matter did not prevail in the Roman Church.

That does not mean to say that there were not some Roman theologians who emphasized this, but the bulk of Roman theology from the medieval period was basically a kind of what is called a synergistic theology. Have you heard that term before? I will give you that word, because you will often run across this with the Reformers, who reject what they call synergism. Synergism simply means the energy of two cooperating elements synthesized. So this would be called synergism. It lies at the basis of the Roman view of salvation.

If there are no other questions, I think we better take a little break. It is kind of warm in here and you need to relax for a moment. Go outside. Run around the block a couple times. Throw some snowballs. Drink some coffee.

* * *

Webber: The second thing that we want to look at today in developing our doctrine of salvation in Roman Catholicism is the question of atonement. Let's begin with the passage in the Scripture, and the passage that I want to begin with is Romans chapter 3. I am going to read it and speak about this for just a few minutes, because it is an important passage for us to keep in mind, not only from a Roman point of view, but also from a Protestant point of view. So let me read [beginning at] Romans 3:23:

> for all have sinned and fall short of the glory of God, being justified as a gift by His grace through the redemption which is in Christ Jesus; whom God displayed publicly as a propitiation in His blood through faith. This was to demonstrate His righteousness, because in the forbearance of God He passed over the sins previously committed; for the demonstration, I say, of His righteousness at the present time, that He might be just and the justifier of the one who has faith in Jesus.[4]

This is a passage of Scripture that is generally cited by both Protestants and Catholics as having to do with the whole substitutionary atonement. I think that is a word that all of us are quite familiar with, the fact that Christ died for me. I would like to go back into the early church for just a moment and talk about this concept of a substitutionary atonement, and how it developed and how it shaped into the Roman Catholic concept of substitutionary atonement and what it means. You may find some shifts from this in the modern Roman point of view. To begin with, I want to assert very clearly, I want you to write this on your mind. Write it on your hand, if you need to. Keep hitting your mind until it gets in there. Write it on the wall of your room, and lie in bed at night and look at it. Learn a dance around it, and dance around the campus through the

---

4. Romans 3:23–26, New American Standard Bible. Hereafter cited as NASB.

door into Peter Deyneka's[5] office, singing this, so that everybody remembers this point of view. Are you not allowed to dance?

Now with that introduction, what I want you to underscore is that there is *no such thing* as a theory of substitution in the early church. Let me say that again in a different way. The word that I want to underscore is "theory." There is definitely a view of substitution, that is to say, Christ died for me. The Isaiah 53 passage is quoted almost in full by Clement, for example, at AD 96. You find the works of Ignatius and the works of other early church fathers who are quite conscious that Christ died for me as a substitute, but there is no *theory* of substitution. By the time you get up to the Cappadocian fathers, this would be up in the late fourth century, say 350 to 400, a theory about substitution begins to emerge. The theory about substitution is basically connected with the ransom idea.

Student: What do you mean by theory in this instance?

Webber: A theory means a systematic view of the doctrine of substitution. It is just that there was not a conscious theoretical understanding of substitution. Remember when I was talking about the doctrine of the Trinity, I said there was a consensus that we have Father, Son, and Holy Spirit. But you do not even have the word *Trinity* until you get up into the third century. So while there was a consciousness of diversity in the Godhead, let's say, there was no theoretical Trinitarian doctrine in the early church. What I am doing here is making the distinction that I have made both in Trinity and Christology between common faith and the formulation of that common faith, in a theoretical, analytic, or systematic expression of it. So what I am saying that the common faith is, yes, Christ died for me. But there is no theory of exactly how that is to be understood.

Student: In other words, it is a vague understanding without the details?

Webber: That would be a good way of putting it. That does not necessarily mean that the detailed understanding of it is particularly better than the vague understanding.

Student: More divisive?

Webber: More divisive. Definitely, yes, without question.

---

5. Peter Deyneka Jr. was a Russian-American evangelist whose father founded the Russian Gospel Association, later renamed Slavic Gospel Association. Their headquarters was in Wheaton, Illinois.

Student: Why [do] you think that is?

Webber: I think it is because we are constantly doing theology through cultural grids, philosophic grids that arise within culture. I will show you how this actually is a theology that is determined through a cultural grid, when I get into the Roman view of it, which you will immediately see is very similar, probably, to your own view of it. And in that way, I will show you how your view of atonement is very close to the Roman view of atonement. But let me give you a little bit more, then we will stop and come back and reflect on this, because I think this is raising some very good questions, and I want to pursue these questions, but perhaps with a little more content first.

Now the Cappadocians in this business of ransom, which is connected with the whole concept of substitution, said, "Aha. A payment was made." To whom was the payment made? Well, put your feet on your desk, lean back, drink a ginger ale, and think about it for a while. What do you come up with? Well, let's see. The devil kind of moved in, took things over, captured man. Hmm. The ransom must have been paid to the devil to release the souls of man. See, that is some of the preliminary thinking along this line, that the ransom was paid to the devil. This is what is further elaborated by Gregory as the fish hook theory, because the devil did not get his ransom. He was fooled. He was tricked. It was like, you put the worm on the fish hook, drop it in the water and the fish comes floating by and—*gulp*. You tricked him. He thought he was going to get the worm, and instead you rip him up out of the water, you cut off his gills, and you cook him and eat him. Poor fish really lost out in the end. Aha, so does Satan. God gives Christ as a ransom to Satan for the release of all the souls in Satan . . . Christ is resurrected, sitting on the right hand of God the Father, and God looks down at Satan and says, "You lost! I tricked you. Ha, ha!" What occurs, then, is as the consciousness of what was really implanted in the bosom of the church develops within the context of history, it is filtered through various cultural grids, and the church reflects on it in different periods in different ways. This is the way the church is reflecting on it, for example, in the fourth century. Now we move from AD 350 to 400, up to the twelfth century, 1110, that is not an exact date, to a fellow by the name of Anselm. I think you will immediately recognize the Anselmic doctrine of the atonement, because he says, "Hmm, let me reflect on this." He does it in a very systematic and analytic fashion in a discussion with Boso. (Not Bozo the Clown[6] who works over at Gary-Wheaton Bank.[7] This is a different Boso. I must make that clear.) Anselm says that in the nature of God, which God is a person, and God is to be understood as a moral person—we will make this one of the attributes of God—and in this moral person he is righteous, he is holy, there is wrath, there is justice, there is mercy, there is love, etc., etc. See what he is doing. He is connecting the whole question of the atonement, the death of Christ, or the work of Christ, with the character of God.

Let me write it out this way for you. God is holy. Sin is an offense against the holiness of God. Thus, sin must be punished. All of that is connected with the characteristics of his being a moral being. God has two ways to punish this sin, two possibilities before him. One, he can punish each individual for his sin. Or he can elect to punish one individual for the sins of all mankind. He chooses the latter. He chooses to punish Christ, who receives this punishment for the sins of the whole world. Thus, back to the Romans passage, he is just and the justifier of the unjust. For God to extend his grace, apart from the punishment of sin, would be pure sentimentality. Let's relate it to life. Suppose somebody goes out and kills somebody in cold blood. He comes to the judge, who says, "That's all right, Joe. I know you have a temper. Just don't do it again. See ya later." You would not call that love, would you? You would say that the judge is a sentimental fool, a sentimental idiot, to do something like that. Now if God said to the whole world, "All right. Forget it. I will be your big buddy. I am your finest friend. Forget it. Forget it. Forget it." You would say, "Hey, pure sentimentality. God is sentimental." No, God *ain't* sentimental, because love is not sentimental. Because love demands punishment. It is just like when you are a kid, and you are bad. If your father overlooks it and says, "Oh, go on, play in the traffic. It doesn't matter." You know that is foolishness. But you go on doing what you are doing, it does not matter, and you know good and well it is something that is going to hurt you. That is sentimentality. Love punishes. Love corrects. Love chastises. By punishing Christ, then, the love of God is shown, and through that punishment, which is—note that it is a payment to God, not a payment to the devil—a payment to God to satisfy God's demands of righteousness, which is connected with his holiness so that he may be just

---

6. Bozo the Clown was a well-known children's entertainer on Chicago television from the 1960s to 1980s.

7. Gary-Wheaton Bank was a local chain of banks in the Wheaton, Illinois, area that merged with a larger Chicago bank, then was acquired by a large national bank.

and the justifier of the unjust. You follow that? That is, in the eleventh, twelfth, thirteenth centuries and since that time, the official Catholic doctrine of atonement. My guess is that you see that that is quite close to your own doctrine of atonement. You will see a completely different doctrine of atonement in the Orthodox church, but let's put it up here.

The Anselmic doctrine of atonement is what we would call a meritorious doctrine, that is to say, Christ merits your salvation, Christ merited your salvation. What we need to look at the third point, and we need to do this quickly so we can start putting all of this together and talk about the application of the work of Christ. How is the work of Christ applied? I wish we had a longer piece of chalk. Let's take a look at this concept of application and see where we go with this.

In Ephesians 2 we read, "For by grace you have been saved through faith; and that not of yourselves, it is the gift of God; not as a result of works, that no one should boast."[8] Grace is a gift, that is to say, that grace is the gift of faith. God gives us the gift of faith, but not apart from our cooperation. You see where in the application the nature of man's free will and cooperating grace, connected with this doctrine, is going to come to focus. Let me try to do this symbolically for you, because I think we will best understand it that way. Christ came on Earth and established a church. This is the church. The church is the body of Christ, so there is a mystical connection between Christ, and here we are thinking of resurrection, the whole concept of atonement. Soteriology is rather complicated. I think maybe through discussion we can pull some of this together a little bit better. But as a result of the death and resurrection, he has created for himself a body, the church. The church is that body of people who have received grace. Right? The question is, what means has God set up in the church through which grace is given to the individual? Well, it is what is called the sacramental means.

Let's stop for just a moment and define the word *sacramental*, because we need to have an understanding of that so we understand where we are going with this. The word comes from two words. *Sacra*, which means holy. The suffix *mentum* means "to make." To make holy. The sacramental system means that means by which God gives you his grace. Let's reflect on that for just a moment. Let me try to connect with what I believe to be the experience of most of us in this class in terms of our Christian faith. My guess is that our experience is that we have received

---

8. Ephesians 2:8–9, NASB.

grace through an encounter with Christ through the preaching of the Word and the hearing of the Word and the conviction of the Holy Spirit, followed by the raising of hand or the walking forward and kneeling at an altar, or kneeling at the front of the church, and being spoken to about how one becomes saved. My guess is that that probably fits the majority of us in this classroom. The thing that I want to stress, as to whether that fits all of us or not, is that there was a method involved in receiving grace. We would say that in that encounter, God was gracious to me, and I became a member of the church of Jesus Christ or of the body of Jesus Christ. Right?

Now in the early church, and then throughout the medieval period, the question was asked, how does one in fact come into the body of Christ? The first way in which one comes into the body of Christ, or the initial means by which is through baptism. Baptism is what is known as the initiation rite. In the early church it was mostly adults who came into the church through baptism. They were converted and baptized and brought into the church.

But later, by the time you get into the medieval period, you are talking mainly about infant baptism. So in infant baptism, the application of the work of Christ has already begun. This is the initial movement of God toward man in bringing man toward himself. Because the child does not really know what is going on, there are godfathers, godparents, mothers and fathers and people of that sort who present the child in and because of their faith. It is a promise that is made to God, that in bringing this child to Christ, we promise to bring this child up in the church, and in the understanding of the faith, so that when this child becomes of age, he will use his or her free will to turn to Christ. Thus grace has begun. But simply because baptism has been the beginning of God's grace, it does not guarantee salvation. The reason it does not guarantee salvation is because baptism must be confirmed by the free will or the free choice of the individual. Therefore, confirmation, which comes at about age twelve or so, is the opportunity for the child to make that personal confession and also to receive the Holy Spirit, because confirmation is a reception of the Holy Spirit, when persons become, as Aquinas called them, little soldiers of Christ. Once a person has made that personal commitment to Christ, the way in which that commitment to Christ is continued is through the Eucharist. Because the Eucharist, you see, is feeding on the body and blood of Christ, that is to say, nourishing on the body and blood of Christ, and therefore being transformed.

Let's note for just a second how this works. Every time one comes to receive the Eucharist, what is one receiving? Christ. What is the Eucharist? The Eucharist is the presentation of the death of Christ on your behalf, so that when you take the bread and drink the wine, you are in fact saying yes again to Christ again, an exercise of free will. You see how free will is working in here right now? However, suppose once a person is in the body of Christ and in the church, and following after Christ, but sins? Well, then we have the doctrine of penance, where one can come and confess and show contrition and do satisfactions and be absolved. In other words, the doctrine of penance is a means through which one continues with Christ. This is because the Eucharist is continuing with Christ too. This is a matter of nourishment. This is a matter of the dialectic of confessing, being forgiven, and continuing with Christ.

Let's stop and think for just a moment. Don't we, as Protestants, do that? We do not call it a sacramental approach to the Christian faith. But don't we confess? Don't we stress confessing your sins, continuing with Christ, growing into Christ, all of those kinds of things are emphasized in a Protestant point of view too?

Of course, marriage and holy orders are sacraments, but we won't put those up there because they are special, and neither one of those are necessary. But unction is another holy order. These keep us going from birth, and unction brings us up to death. It is the final sacrament before death, although originally unction was not a sacrament of death but a sacrament of healing. In the Roman Catholic Church since Vatican II, it has been shifted back again to the sacrament of healing. But I am trying to go back and give you sort of a medieval development.

When you look at this, you look at it in its original inception or conception and you would say, "Oh, it doesn't look too bad. It looks fine." Because in all of this there is also faith. There is no rejection of faith in this. Faith is the beginning of the work. Hope is the continuing of the work. Love is the expression of the work of God's grace in one's life. So faith and hope and love, recognizing that only Christ merits our salvation. Only Christ. No one else. Because we have free will, we must continually choose Christ, and the context in which we continually choose Christ is the sacramental context. I will put another circle up here, and I will show you a circle that is somewhat similar to this in the Evangelical Protestant community. We begin with conversion. Sometimes that is followed by baptism. Sometimes in the Protestant community, it is said that it is not necessary. Bible reading. Prayer. Witnessing. Church attendance, twice on Sunday, once on Wednesday. And if you go to a Christian college, five chapel days a week. Why knock that when we have this?

We have created a context. The Catholics have a context. Actually, this context here is a little bit more biblical than this. However, I am not saying that this is not biblical in the sense that I think that the Scriptures certainly teach the necessity of continuing in Christ, but this circle over here is also a circle for continuing in Christ. We have a very mixed up theology here in terms of we are not really sure whether man is fallen, or whether he has a free will. As a matter of fact, we say, who cares? What difference does it make? Except those of us who are Reformed Baptists, or something of that sort, who have a very strong Calvinistic bent. I am not saying that you should not have that, but what I am saying is that the normal crop of Evangelicals are a rather sloppy group theologically. There is no precise theology among Evangelicals. The Reformed Baptists or Presbyterians or people who are really interested in doctrine have a much clearer concept of what their theology is. What I want to point out, however, about this Roman view is what it becomes, what it may become. I am not saying that it necessarily has to become this, but what I want to point out is in history, what it became.

By the time you get into the fourteenth and fifteenth centuries, this became what we call sacramentalism. You know what I mean by sacramentalism? It is different than sacramental theology. This is sacramental theology over here. That is to say, the application of the work of Christ continues to us in faith and hope and love as we seek to follow after Christ within the context of the church, using the sacraments of the church as means for nurture and growth and continual encounter with Jesus Christ. Now, sacramentalism is the perversion of this, which did happen in the fourteenth and fifteenth centuries. It is a point of view that argues for what we call an *ex opere operato*, the Latin meaning "it works the work." That means it works the work without faith. In other words, it does not really matter whether you believe or not. It does not really matter what you do. Just get your body over there to church. Get baptized and run through the confirmation and make sure that you receive the Eucharist at least two times a year. More often, if you can. The church will see you through. That is bad, lousy, rotten, smelly Roman theology. That is not good Roman theology at all. It is not even Roman theology. It is a perversion of Roman theology in the fourteenth and fifteenth centuries. Added to that, then, was the whole meritorious system of works for man. That is to say, the work of Christ was not sufficient merit so that to the merit of

Christ, we must add our own good works which establish merits. Thus, the sale of indulgences, good works for the establishment of merit, and various things of that sort, so that ultimately we can be saved. It is this perversion, the creation of sacramentalism, that the sixteenth century reacted against. Luther reacted against that, Calvin reacted against that, and the Roman Catholic Councils of Trent reacted against that.

In order for you to get a view of the Council of Trent, I am going to take a moment here to read some of them, and let you get a feeling for what they had to say. These are the documents on justification that I am going to read from, the decree concerning justification. I am going to skip through this rather quickly, but I want to try to let you pick up as much of this as you can. "Chapter 1. The impotency of nature and of the law to justify man." So this would be a rejection, for example, of a Pelagian point of view.

> The holy council declares first, that for a correct and clear understanding of the doctrine of justification, it is necessary that each one recognize and confess that since all men had lost innocence in the prevarication of Adam, having become unclean, and, as the Apostle says, by nature children of wrath, as has been set forth in the decree on original sin, they were so far the servants of sin and under the power of the devil and of death.[9]

So man is a sinner. Roman Catholic doctrine officially states that. "Chapter 2. The dispensation and mystery of the advent of Christ." I will just read the concluding sentence.

> Him has God proposed as a propitiator through faith in his blood for our sins, and not for our sins only, but also for those of the whole world.[10]

So there is only one way, from an official Roman Catholic doctrine, to get to God, and that is through Jesus Christ, his death and his blood, which was shed for our sin. "Chapter 3. Those who are justified through Christ." Again I will read one sentence.

> But though He died for all, yet all do not receive the benefit of His death, but those only to whom the merit of his passion is communicated.[11]

---

9. Council of Trent.
10. Council of Trent.
11. Council of Trent.

So far, my guess is you are following, saying, "Hm. Sounds good." "Chapter 4. A brief description of the justification of the sinner and its mode in the state of grace."

> In which words is given a brief description of the justification of the sinner, as being a translation from that state in which man is born a child of the first Adam, to the state of grace and of the adoption of the sons of God through the second Adam, Jesus Christ, our Savior.
>
> This translation however cannot, since promulgation of the Gospel, be effected except through the laver of regeneration or its desire, as it is written:
>
> Unless a man be born again of water and the Holy Ghost, he cannot enter into the kingdom of God.[12]

While the Protestant would stress personal faith, the Catholic is stressing the baptismal waters. But not without personal faith, as you will see later. There is a stress on the physical side of doing things. "Chapter 5. The necessity of preparation for justification in adults, and whence it proceeds."

> It is furthermore declared that in adults the beginning of that justification must proceed from the predisposing grace of God through Jesus Christ, that is, from His vocation, whereby, without any merits on their part, they are called; that they who by sin had been cut off from God, may be disposed through His quickening and helping grace to convert themselves to their own justification.[13]

Did you note that phrase? ". . . may be disposed through his quickening and helping grace to convert themselves to their own justification by freely assenting to and cooperating with that grace . . ." Cooperating grace is a very important aspect of the of Roman theology.

> . . . so that, while God touches the heart of man through the illumination of the Holy Ghost, man himself neither does absolutely nothing while receiving that inspiration, since he can also reject it, nor yet is he able by his own free will and without the grace of God to move himself to justice in His sight.
>
> Hence, when it is said in the sacred writings: Turn ye to me, and I will turn to you, we are reminded of our liberty; and when

---

12. Council of Trent.
13. Council of Trent.

> we reply: Convert us, O Lord, to thee, and we shall be converted, we confess that we need the grace of God.[14]

See how central to that whole statement is the concept of cooperating grace. "Chapter 6. The manner of preparation." I will skip through most of this and just read one sentence.

> ... that is, by that repentance that must be performed before baptism; finally, when they resolve to receive baptism, to begin a new life and to keep the commandments of God.[15]

Now "Chapter 7. In what the justification of the sinner consists, and what are its causes."

> This disposition or preparation is followed by justification itself, which is not only a remission of sins but also the sanctification and renewal of the inward man through the voluntary reception of the grace and gifts whereby an unjust man becomes just and from being an enemy becomes a friend, that he may be an heir according to hope of life everlasting.
>
> The causes of this justification are: the final cause is the glory of God and of Christ and life everlasting; the efficient cause is the merciful God who washes and sanctifies gratuitously, signing and anointing with the holy Spirit of promise, who is the pledge of our inheritance, the meritorious cause is His most beloved only begotten, our Lord Jesus Christ, who, when we were enemies, for the exceeding charity wherewith he loved us, merited for us justification by His most holy passion on the wood of the cross and made satisfaction for us to God the Father, the instrumental cause is the sacrament of baptism, which is the sacrament of faith, without which no man was ever justified finally, the single formal cause is the justice of God, not that by which He Himself is just, but that by which He makes us just, that, namely, with which we being endowed by Him, are renewed in the spirit of our mind, and not only are we reputed but we are truly called and are just, receiving justice within us, each one according to his own measure, which the Holy Ghost distributes to everyone as He wills, and according to each one's disposition and cooperation.
>
> For though no one can be just except he to whom the merits of the passion of our Lord Jesus Christ are communicated, yet this takes place in that justification of the sinner, when by the

---

14. Council of Trent.
15. Council of Trent.

merit of the most holy passion, the charity of God is poured forth by the Holy Ghost in the hearts of those who are justified and inheres in them.[16]

That word *inheres* is very, very important, and I will come back to that again in my own explanation of this.

... whence man through Jesus Christ, in whom he is ingrafted, receives in that justification, together with the remission of sins, all those infused at the same time, namely faith, hope and charity.[17]

Now "Chapter 8. How the gratuitous justification of the center by faith is to be understood."

... that we are therefore said to be justified by faith, because faith is the beginning of human salvation, the foundation and root of all justification, without which it is impossible to please God.[18]

So we see a rejection of *ex opere operato* and in the counter-Reformation movement, and in official Roman Catholic theology. "Chapter 10. The increase of justification received."

Having, therefore, been thus justified and made the friends and domestics of God, advancing from virtue to virtue, they are renewed, as the Apostle says, day by day, that is, mortifying the members of their flesh, and presenting them as instruments of justice unto sanctification, they, through the observance of the commandments of God and of the Church, faith cooperating with good works, increase in that justice received through the grace of Christ and are further justified.[19]

Now "Chapter 11. The observance of the commandments and the necessity and possibility thereof."

For God does not forsake those who have been once justified by His grace, unless He be first forsaken by them.[20]

See, no doctrine of eternal security here at all.

---

16. Council of Trent.
17. Council of Trent.
18. Council of Trent.
19. Council of Trent.
20. Council of Trent.

> ... no one ought to flatter himself with faith alone, thinking that by faith alone he is made an heir and will obtain the inheritance.[21]

Okay, there is more, but let's see. . . . Yeah, maybe I should read this section right here.

> ... it must be maintained that the grace of justification once received is lost not only by infidelity, whereby also faith itself is lost, but also by every other mortal sin, though in this case faith is not lost; thus, defending the teaching of the divine law, which excludes from the kingdom of God, unbelievers and those who are unfaithful.[22]

Well, there is more, but I want to stop and just explain it, because I am not sure that we can always communicate best through reading a lot of material like that. Basically, what I would like to do is to give you again a picture of this and see where we go with it. God first gives his grace to man in baptism, which is continued through the sacraments of the church, as I have defined here, which is continued and expressed in faith, hope, and love. Faith, hope, and love, from the Roman point of view, are the expression of your good works. Justification, then, occurs at the end of life and not at the beginning. Justification occurs at the end of life and not the beginning. If in the process of life itself, you have not followed after Christ sufficiently, there is, then, a view of purgatory in which you really might say this is a second chance theology, that in purgatory itself you have the opportunity to be purged of your sins. Now, why is that? It is because grace is looked upon as an infusion. Grace as infusion. In that grace is an infusion, where grace is properly infused, through this earthly means, through this earthly system, there is created, then, a habit of life. The habit of life is that growth in Christ, that development, that becoming more Christlike, because becoming more Christlike is to receive more significantly the infused grace. The infusion of grace, then, is the gradual changing of the individual into the image of Christ. And you never, in that process, ought to be so presumptuous as to say, "I'm justified," because until the end of life or beyond, you do not know. You may turn your back because you have free will.

While it is only Christ who saves, because of free will, synergism, the semi-Pelagian point of view, it is only man who can grasp hold of that

---

21. Council of Trent.
22. Council of Trent.

salvation by his choice and by the energy of his own will, and continue with it, who in the end accomplishes that salvation.

Just one point here for you to see where the difference lies with the Protestant view of salvation. The Protestant view regards the gift of God's grace as imputed rather than infused. It is something that is put upon, rather than put within. Because it is put upon, then the life of good works is an expression of what has been put upon. Whereas in the Catholic theology of salvation, the life of good works is the infused habit of Christian living, which is the means by which one accomplishes that justification, which in fact is rooted in Jesus Christ. And the church is that visible institution in life itself which nourishes one and ultimately is the context through which one comes to Christ. I need to stop. I have been gibbering here for a while. I want to find out whether or not you got those distinctions.

Student: Doesn't the Catholic church emphasize that faith without works is dead?

Webber: The Catholic church definitely emphasizes faith without works is dead. The Catholic church really pushes the statement of James there, that if you cannot show me the habit of love, see they bring faith, hope, and love together, if you cannot show me the habit of love, then you do not have faith.

Student: As seen in public good works?

Webber: Yeah, it would be expressed in the general Catholic community by the doing of good works and various things of that nature. The problem here is the problem that, as Protestants, we all see very clearly, standing outside of the Catholic church, and I think if you went inside of the Catholic church, you would be shocked to discover how many genuinely Christian people there are, just as they would be shocked to come here and discover that there are genuine Christian people in the Protestant world.

We develop these caricatures. We build these walls. Wheaton is the apple of God's eye in the world. If you are a graduate of Wheaton, there is no question that you are secure. All those nonsensical ideas, and we carry that stuff around, whether we articulate it or not. "Oh, you are a graduate of Wheaton! Oh, you went to the Institute for Slavic Studies! Oh, you came in contact with His Holiness Bob Webber himself!"

Student: I do not know if I lost something along the way. Does it mean that through that process of the infusion of grace that you are not fully sure about your salvation? It's still up in the air?

Webber: Right. We got that. It's still something that you are working toward. God has already done his part. Now you must do your part.

Student: So if you are going along and you still think you are doing your part and you really believe it, but you know you are going to die the next day, wondering about eternal security, you are still not sure?

Webber: That's right. Because you can always, because you have free will, you can always choose to turn your back on the work of Christ. And life seems to suggest that there is a degree of truth to that. By that I am not saying that I am Catholic in my theology of salvation, but what I want to do is to try to present a fair picture of the theology of salvation in Catholicism, so that we rid ourselves of these caricatures, where we almost feel like they dismissed the work of Christ.

Strict Catholic doctrine, whether or not in popular Catholicism this has been forgotten, is Christ and Christ alone saves—however, you must do your part. The Catholics stress that you must do your part, whereas the Protestants stress that Christ and Christ alone saves. What you find in the Protestant community is a community of people who sort of trust and rest in Christ, almost an antinomianism. "Nooo, he did it all!" they insist.

10

Orthodoxy, Catholicism, Protestantism

SESSION #6, JANUARY 11, 1979

Webber: Today we are going to talk about the Orthodox view of salvation. Right? Is that what you are prepared to talk about? Let's take a look at where we began last week. I am trying to remember whether or not I went into the book of Romans, chapters 3 and 5. We have two different approaches to the subject of the atonement. In Romans 3, perhaps we should look at this passage of Scripture, unless I looked at it with you last week and I cannot recall. I did not think that I did, but I was not absolutely certain about that. I want to begin at this point because I think it is very important for us to see a couple of different points of view in regard to the doctrine of the atonement. Begin with Romans 3:24:

> being justified as a gift by His grace through the redemption which is in Christ Jesus; whom God displayed publicly as a propitiation in His blood through faith. This was to demonstrate His righteousness, because in the forbearance of God He passed over the sins previously committed; for the demonstration, I say, of His righteousness at the present time, that He might be just and the justifier of the one who has faith in Jesus.[1]

I think you are probably more familiar with the King James translation of that last statement, which says, "in order that he might be just, and the justifier of the unjust." Note the triple use of the word "justice" there. What is going on in Romans 3 is what I would like to call a legal view of

---

1. Romans 3:24–26, NASB.

the atonement. Let me try to clarify that just a little bit. Basically, another way of saying that is what we have here has been interpreted in history as being the substitutional view of the atonement. I think that is a view that all of us would be highly acquainted with, because most of us come from Evangelical traditions which emphasized that Christ died for me.

Student: Before you go on, are you explaining the mechanics of the Evangelical position, or are you explaining the Orthodox view?

Webber: I am going to explain the Orthodox. I am revving up for it, so to speak. I am trying to show that in the Scripture there are two different approaches to the atonement, and the Western approach is one, which I am discussing now very briefly. Then I will jump into the Eastern approach, which comes out of Romans 5, and show you how both of these approaches are somewhat biblically grounded.

So the legal transaction works something like this. God's holiness has been offended. Therefore, his righteousness demands that a punishment to be made. God can either choose to punish every individual sinner who has offended his holiness, or he could choose to punish one for all. He chose to punish one for all. It is a kind of transaction that occurs in the Godhead, so that he is just and the justifier of the unjust through penalizing Christ, who is the substitute for all people. Thus Christ satisfies the righteousness of God. God, then, is free to save or to forgive and be loving towards sinners without demanding any penalty or sacrifice of themselves.

See, there is a difference between pure sentimentality and justice. Sentimentality would say, "So you all sinned. That's all right. Everybody does that sort of thing. Forget it." That is sentimentality. True love says, "There has been a wrong, and there must be a punishment." When the punishment or chastisement has been meted out, then love, which is based on justice—true love is always based on justice—is capable of freeing that person who has committed the offense. So this is what you might call a legal transaction. You see that that would be reflected through a Roman view, a judicial point of view.

In Romans 5 you have another approach to the interpretation of the atonement. I am not saying that this would be an interpretation in contradiction to what you have in Romans 3. It is just another way of seeing it, another way of talking about it, another way of emphasizing it. I want you to notice what we have in Romans 5. We will begin with verse 12 and then I will jump down to verse 18. "Therefore, just as through one man sin entered into the world, and death through sin, and so death spread to all mankind, because all sinned."[2] Here is the connection we all have with Adam. As Adam sinned, we are all sinners. Next read verses 18–19,

> So then, as through one transgression there resulted condemnation to all men, even so through one act of righteousness there resulted justification of life to all mankind. For as through the one man's disobedience the many were made sinners, even so through the obedience of the One the many will be made righteous.[3]

What you have going on here is not so much a legal transaction, as you see in Romans chapter 3, but you have a kind of poetic, imagistic, allegorical expression. You have a comparison between the first Adam and the second Adam. The first Adam did something to us. He brought us into sin, death, condemnation. The second Adam did something for us. Instead of sin, he brings righteousness. Instead of death, he brings life. Instead of condemnation, he brings justification. So the second Adam is responsible for reversing what the first Adam did. This kind of poetic expression is not really oriented around a legal view at all but is really oriented around what we may call a physical view, which is expressed somewhat poetically. And this [other view] is expressed really almost rationally. Do you see the contrast between those two views? It is very important for us to see that if we are to understand the difference between Eastern and Western approaches to trusting your salvation. Let me stop there for a minute and get a little bit of feedback, making certain you have caught the nuances.

Student: Yeah. I understand what you're getting at. I am just curious if you have dealt much with why Paul dealt with it this way? In other words, he kept the legal aspects of it first in chapter 3, and then in chapter 4 he discusses some of the historical, Israelite background. Is there some significance?

Webber: I guess I would have to say that I do not [know] for sure whether there is or not.

---

2. Romans 5:12, NASB.
3. Romans 5:18–19, NASB.

Student: For example, does the legal view clear the way for the physical view? Is that being too analytical?

Webber: Yeah, I think so. I do not know that I would want to see it that way. I would rather think that what we are dealing with here are just simply different ways of talking about the atonement. One of the things that we need to recognize is that there are different ways of talking about salvation, as we saw last week. I think the main thing that I am trying to do today is not so much deal with which of these would be correct, that is to say, if they are opposed to each other. I do not think they are opposed to each other. But rather, what I am trying to deal with here is the fact that you do have two different viewpoints coming out of the Scripture, which shaped the perspective of the Eastern and Western church. For example, when the Western church looks at the Scripture, the Western church is more oriented around law and reason. It is more judicial, more pragmatic. Therefore, the Western church tends to see the atonement as a legal transaction. So the strong emphasis that you get in the Western church—this is both Catholic and Protestant—the very strong emphasis is on substitution. That does not mean to say that there is not a substitution motif here. But this is a kind of legal substitution, a transaction occurring in the mind of God, in the character of God. The physical view, which really fits more the Eastern mindset, which is more aesthetic, more poetic. When we think, for example, of the contribution of the Greek world, the Eastern world, it is in the area of poetry. But the Roman world is in the area of law. The poetic, the imagistic, the allegorical, all of this is an Eastern way of thinking. What we are doing in theology is we are translating biblical motifs through philosophic and cultural grids. When the biblical motif is translated through a Roman or Western philosophical and cultural grid, that comes out emphasizing the legal transaction. When it is filtered through the Greek Eastern perspective, it comes out emphasizing the poetic and imagistic, so that the motif in the Western world is almost always going to be justice. The motif in the Eastern world is almost always going to be a comparison between the first Adam and the second Adam. The allegory. The poetry.

Student: Is there a difference, then, in the legal view . . . when we say substitution, is this salvation for all, but all cannot receive it? In the other view, is it symbolic of Adam? When Adam sinned, we all became sinful. Is that automatic, then, because Christ is the symbol of Adam? When he died, we all became righteous, so that it isn't a matter of accepting Christ, or is it just that from now on, whoever is born is righteous before him?

Webber: Strictly speaking, according to, say, Russian theology, the answer to that question is no. I will show you at the end of class today, because I will read from the Russian catechism to show you how this is interpreted. But if you want to talk in terms of leanings, this view leans toward universalism. The other view leans toward only a few people getting saved and the bulk of humanity going to hell. That is just the way it is from the mindset.

Of course, the physical idea is that as Adam was a physical human being and sent in time-space in history, he therefore affected the whole of the created order. Christ came as a physical being, was the righteous one, was obedient and therefore affected the whole created order. So you do have a redemption of creation motif in the in the Eastern worldview, which you do not really find in the atonement theology of the West. It is there, but it is kind of hidden under all of the legal transaction. This lends itself more to individualism, whereas this lends itself more to a solidaric understanding of humanity. I do not know why I did not start at this point last week, but we are going to do the Eastern point of view today.

There are several people, several sort of spots here, by which we can take a look at all of this. I want to look, first of all, at Irenaeus, an Eastern theologian at about AD 180. Then I want to look at Athanasius. Again, an Eastern theologian, at 325. By then—actually, I could go into the Cappadocians, but the Cappadocians do not have that much more to add to it. By then you have got a pretty solidly worked out view of salvation in the Eastern Church. Then I will carry it all the way up to a contemporary Russian catechism and try to show you how that catechism is related to the theology of these two people back here.

So let's begin, then, with the theology of Irenaeus. What I am going to do is to read from Irenaeus's work and then comment—or I will let you do the commenting. There is quite a bit of material on this, but I am going to read the section where Irenaeus gives us an explanation of what is called Recapitulation Theology. Have I given you that term before? That is a special Eastern term. It is also a biblical term, a biblical concept. Let me read Irenaeus's Recapitulation Theology, and then we will discuss what that is and how it affects our understanding of Eastern theology. I am going to read about two pages, so listen closely:

> So the Lord now manifestly came to his own. Born by his own created order that he himself bears, he by his obedience on the tree renewed and reversed what was done by disobedience in connection with a tree. The power of that seduction by which the virgin Eve, already betrothed to a man, had been wickedly seduced was broken when the angel in truth brought good tidings to the Virgin Mary, who already by her betrothal belonged to a man. For as Eve was seduced by the word of an angel to flee from God, having rebelled against his Word, so Mary by the word of an angel received the glad tidings that she would bear God by obeying his Word. The former was seduced to disobey God and so fell, but the latter was persuaded to obey God, so that the Virgin Mary might become the advocate of Eve. As the human race was subjected to death through the act of a virgin, so was it saved by a virgin was precisely balanced by the obedience of another. Then indeed the sin of the first formed man was amended by the chastisement of the First Begotten, the wisdom of the serpent was conquered by the simplicity of the dove, and the chains were broken by which we were in bondage to death. Therefore he renews these things in himself, uniting man to the Spirit; and placing the Spirit in man, he himself is made the head of the Spirit, and gives the Spirit to be the head of man, for by him we see and hear and speak. . . . The enemy would not have been justly conquered unless it had been a man [made] of woman who conquered him. For it was by a woman that he had power over man from the beginning, setting himself up in opposition to man. Because of this the Lord also declares himself to be the Son of Man, so renewing in himself that primal man from whom the formation [of man] by woman began, that as our race went down to death by a man who was conquered we might ascend again to life by a man who overcame; and as death won the palm of victory over us by a man, so we might by a man receive the palm of victory over death.

I am interested in knowing what you heard when I read that, and then we will go back and put it all together. What did you hear? What is the Theology of Recapitulation?

Student: There is beauty.

Webber: A poetic kind of beauty. What else?

Student: To put it very crudely, Christ is undoing what Adam did, in the sense of Philippians 4, where Paul speaks of Christ taking on himself the form of a servant and emptying himself, that he was laying down his divine prerogative, in opposition to what Adam did, where Adam sought to grasp divine prerogatives, by the suggestion of Satan, having no right to those prerogatives, Christ having already possessed them, willingly surrendered them so man could be redeemed.

Webber: That is a good way of explaining it. Anybody else? How about the Reformed Baptist over there in the corner? . . . It is interesting. You are all describing this in symbols. Nobody is using "rational empirical language." You are all using poetry to describe symbolic language. What do you think of the references to the Blessed Virgin Mary?

Student: It's interesting, too, that she is just as significant, perhaps more so, than Eve in her humanity.

Webber: I would like to hear some more women respond to this comparison of Eve with Mary.

Student: Her virginity does not seem to be the issue, as far as I am concerned. . . . The issue is the disobedience of the woman led the man to disobey. And the obedience of Mary to the words of the angel to her, "Behold, I am the servant of the Lord; may it be done to me according to your word," is the means by which the salvation of mankind is realized. . . ."[4]

Webber: That is the real issue, the obedience of Mary. . . . But I suppose the real reason I am interested in having some of you women respond to this is because it does seem to be in Protestant theology that the woman in the whole salvific process is really sadly neglected. Mary is not the co-redeemer, as our caricature of Roman Catholicism sometimes suggests, but rather it tends to give Mary her rightful place, as Luke records in the Magnificat. We are to call her blessed, and we bypass Mary for John the Baptist and everybody else. But there is not very much talk about the significance of Mary in the Protestant community.

Student: I think that is just a reaction to Catholicism more than any actual feeling of disregard or disrespect.

Webber: I guess my feeling is that in the Protestant church, the neglect of Mary is as much an error as is the overemphasis of her in the Orthodox church. We need not pride ourselves in our neglect of Mary. If anything,

---

4. See Luke 1:38.

we need to be brought under conviction that we have, in fact, overlooked one of the most important servants of God. We elevate Abraham, Moses, David, Isaiah, and we totally bypass Mary. Is it because she is a woman? Is it because of Roman Catholicism? What is it? I really think that there is a need to recover the place of Mary. I am not calling for worship of Mary or anything of that sort, but just simply the place of Mary.

Student: I do not think the Roman Catholic Church is calling for that either.

Webber: No. Well, in some branches and movements within the Catholic church, but generally I do not think there is worship of Mary.

Student: I see what you are saying, that Scripture does say that we should call her blessed and things like that, but when people start getting that close to comparing Jesus's salvation of us to Mary in that same context, I start to get scared. I have heard some great sermons on Mary at the cross, when she visited Elizabeth, and things like that. But when people start putting it into such a close context as Jesus was to Adam in this matter of saving us, and then they compare Mary to Eve, I start getting scared. It's as if she were saving us.... Irenaeus did say that it was through her obedience that we are saved.... What does it mean that Mary is the Mother of God? When I hear that phrase, to me that says that Mary was before God, or that she has something that makes her different from humans. Like what you just read, it seems like Mary's obedience is something that saved us. But God could have saved us regardless of Mary. He could have asked another girl.

Webber: I think not. I would challenge that notion. It is a very hypothetical thing, that God might have chosen another. Let's go back and recreate that scene. Do you think Mary was sort of "La-dee-da," sweeping the floor and doing the dishes, when all of the sudden an angel of light appears to Mary. "Oh! What's going on?" And the angel says, "*You*, baby, have been chosen!" And Mary is distraught. "What's going on? I've never even heard of this stuff before. Explain. Play this again. What did you say about Genesis 3:15? Me? That sounds pretty good. Let's do it." Or was Mary like Simeon, deeply pious, deeply religious, and carrying within her the whole hope of Israel? I think I would come at it from the second point of view, that Mary was a child of God, that she, like John the Baptist and Simeon and like other unusual people in the process of redemption, were filled with that hope of God, longing for, wishing for, hoping for the coming of the Messiah. So when she was selected, so to speak, she did not have to ask any questions. "Me? The bearer of God." Theotokos means that, bearer of God. Immanuel, God with us.

Student: But I would blame her being that way on God, and I would say that God could have developed a girl to be like that, who is not necessarily named Mary, nor necessarily lived in her land. It was just that God chose it to be that way.

Webber: Yeah, if you are coming at it from that point of view, except that I would personally be a little bit careful about the strong predestination notion who is coming through that in the causal sense, that God is kind of sitting up there with a checkerboard. He moves this piece, that piece. See, the whole causation notion of predestination is related to Newtonian physics and the Enlightenment view that arose later. I have no question about the sovereignty of God over all things. I just do not know how it works. To say that God elects and selects somebody and builds that up within them, denies also the operation of the person's will by which there is in fact a genuine and true seeking after God.

Student: But do not you think that somebody else really could have sought God?

Webber: Oh, yes. Somebody else could have, and somebody else probably did. I am not saying that that could not happen. But what I am trying to say here is let's get a vision of Mary as a woman of prayer, as a deeply spiritual woman who was hoping for the coming of the Messiah. And when I use the word *hope*, I do not mean to use it in the sense, "I hope it doesn't snow," but hope in the biblical sense, in which that which was being longed for was actually being formed as a result of the longing. We need to see Mary from that point of view. If we see Mary from that point of view, then truly without Mary the Christ would not have been born, and sin would not have been conquered. Just as John the Baptist was the forerunner. "Prepare ye the way of the Lord."[5] Just as David was the king after whose kingdom Christ's would be modeled, etc.

Student: How could she be called the mother of God? I always thought it to mean, "Well, Jesus Christ is God and Mary was his mother and

---

5. Luke 3:4, King James Version.

therefore she is the mother of God. And I keep telling myself that they have got to have a better line of reasoning than that.

Webber: Remember we talked about Theotokos a couple weeks ago? It was defined in the Chalcedonian Definition that Mary is the Theotokos— I forget the exact phrase—as pertaining to his manhood. Jesus is fully God and fully human, and Mary is not the Mother of God in the sense that somehow she generated God. I admit that this can be a misleading statement. Any statement can be misleading. My guess is that there has been, particularly in medieval Roman Catholicism, a tremendous amount of piety that has been attached to that Theotokos, and wrong notions have been attributed to Mary as the mother of God, and therefore raising her to a level higher than what she should have been raised. No question about that. But that does not give us the right, as most Protestants have done, to simply "dump" Mary. Mary is almost seen in a lot of Protestant churches as some sort of lifeless channel. What is she, a womb? She is a little bit more than a womb. She is a woman. She has a mind and a heart and a will. She has a reputation to be concerned about. We must see Mary. Somehow we have over-divinized Jesus and we have under-humanized Mary.

Student: I want to try to clarify a statement. What you say about Mary, wouldn't that be the same as if David had not existed? It's the same basic principle. Abraham, David, they were all chosen of God, and if they had not preceded Christ, Christ would not have come.

Webber: Yeah. It is putting everything in the redemptive process, and I am saying that as Protestants we do honor many of the others, but we simply deny any place to Mary at all. We even talk about John the Baptist as having a unique position, because he's the last of the Old Testament prophets and the first of the New. So we call John the Baptist the forerunner of Christ and give him a special place. So there is a very special place that should be given to Mary. We give Paul an incredibly special place. We seem to give him a greater place than we do for James, for example. There is nothing wrong with having levels of importance or levels of significance, but there is only one through whom we are saved, and that is Jesus Christ, not the Virgin Mary, not David, not Abraham, not Moses, not Paul. Only Christ saves. Okay. We will take a break, then we will look at Athanasius, who comes right out of Irenaeus's position on soteriology. Grab a cup of coffee and wake up.

Webber: The second person we are going to look at in the development of soteriology is Athanasius.

Student: I would like to ask a question about this Theory of Recapitulation before we move on. In the type of relationship that Adam had with God at that particular point in time was a real fellowship of walking with God in the garden, and there was no separation, when Christ came . . . okay, in between, we had the law and all the traditions of the Jewish church, being the means of mankind of getting to God. When Christ comes, does the Theory of Recapitulation say that it goes back to the original type of relationship, or do you still have the traditions and the law of the Jewish faith?

Webber: Well, the Theory of Recapitulation, as developed in the Eastern church, would recognize that the ceremonial laws of the Old Testament are done away with, and that they are not necessary. It would maintain the moral law, and the continuity between the Old and New Testament in the moral law. However, as things developed in the Byzantine culture, the principle of the ceremonial law came back into the Byzantine church. Therefore, you have elaborate systems of worship and means by which a person's growth in Christ continues to occur. So the principle of Old Testament ceremony is found again in the structure of salvation. With Athanasius, I would like to give you a picture, because I am going to have to discuss Athanasius' point of view in symbolic manner. . . . Athanasius stands in the tradition of Recapitulation with our friend Irenaeus. This is the specific way in which he develops the Theology of Recapitulation.

First, we are going to refer here to original man. In Eastern theology in general—I am not going to make all of this to be just strictly Athanasius—I am going to talk about Eastern theology in general, which is rooted in Athanasius's point of view . . . but in Eastern theology, you do not have such a thing as original sin. You have instead man being referred to as innocent. The original motif here is that man is created innocent not perfect, but that perfection is the goal of man. Again, this is poetic kind of language, so do not try to read it in a purely rational way.

Student: When you say that man is created innocent, does that mean every man is created innocent?

Webber: Yeah. It is going to mean that, that all men like Adam are created innocent. Adam is created innocent, and this little sign right here indicates the fact that man's responsibility is to grow into union with God. This is called the process of maturation. We mature into union with God, and thereby we become perfect. Adam and Eve at this particular [point] have the choice to either move upward toward God or to move away from God by being disobedient to God. Adam and Eve both choose to move away from God. So rather than moving into union with God, Adam and Eve begin a movement, not only for themselves, but also for all mankind and also for all creation. What occurs here in the entrance of sin is of course the fall of man. The fall of man brings about death, mortality, corruptibility. You will find these terms in Eastern theology. This occurs not only for man, but it also occurs for his culture. So man and culture, and you could say creation. Creation is affected by the fall of man. For example, in the early chapters of Genesis, after God talks with Adam and Eve, he discovers their sin and curses the ground. What does that mean that he cursed the ground? From an Eastern point of view, it means that the whole of creation has been affected by sin. Sin is not an individual thing. It affects individuals, yes, but it affects and infects—*infects* is one of the significant words of the Eastern Christian point of view—the entire created order. You see some poetic language about this in Romans 8 in terms of the terms of the recapitulation. For example, see Romans 8:

> For I consider that the sufferings of this present time are not worthy to be compared with the glory that is to be revealed to us. For the anxious longing of the creation waits for the revealing of the sons of God. For the creation was subjected to futility, not of its own will, but because of Him who subjected it, in hope that the creation itself also will be set free from its slavery to corruption into the freedom of the glory of the children of God.[6]

You are beginning to see here the whole recapitulation notion that you find in Irenaeus and Paul and Romans 5, and now again in Romans 8. The recapitulation notion touches not only man being recapitulated, but it touches the entire created order, so that the redemption sets the creation free from its bondage of decay and obtains the glorious liberty for the children of God.

> For we know that the whole creation groans and suffers the pains of childbirth until now. And not only this, even we ourselves

---

6. Romans 8:18–21, NASB.

groan within ourselves, waiting eagerly for our adoption as sons, the redemption of our bodies.[7]

The whole business of sin and redemption is connected with creation, in that creation is affected by sin, and creation is now going to be affected by the redemption. I want you to notice how all of this fits into the concept of Christology that we talked about several weeks ago. Christ enters into history and takes upon himself full humanity. The emphasis we see in Romans 5, in Irenaeus and now in Athanasius, which permeates your Eastern tradition, is the emphasis on Christ assuming the tangible, visible, physical world. It is kind of a mystical point of view. You would never find an Easterner who would deny the historicity of Jesus Christ. It is only in the West that that is really happening. A Western person can come along and say, "Well, it doesn't really matter whether Jesus was a historical person or not. The important thing is the idea." But that would pull the rug right out from under an Eastern soteriology, because in the Eastern point of view, Jesus had to be human, he had to be physical, he had to be visible and tangible. He had to be part of materiality. Why do you suppose that is true?

Student: Put very crudely, I'd say he had to become one of us so he could redeem us.

Webber: Okay. But if you were to stop at that point, you can still get into a kind of mere individualistic salvation. He became a man, therefore all men are redeemed. But let's look at this from a larger, broader scope. The Orthodox Church emphasizes the union between the human and the divine in Jesus Christ. Not a conjunction. Not a side-by-side relationship, but a union of the human and the divine in the person of Christ. This fits into their whole soteriological perspective, which is a recapitulation theology of salvation. . . . Jesus must be human in order for humans to be saved. This is the Second Axiom, for example, of the early church fathers. Only that which is assumed is healed. Remember that axiom? It is hard to remember these things from one week to another.

Look at this for a moment. Only that which is assumed is healed. Let's go back here for just a minute. What was affected by sin? Everything. The whole created order was affected by sin. Recapitulation argues for the salvation of the whole created order. Therefore Christ, coming into the created order, assumes the entire created order. . . . The entire created

---

7. Romans 8:22, NASB.

order mystically participates in Jesus Christ. He takes the whole created order into himself. There really is not any rational language to describe that. It has to be received in an allegorical or poetical or imagistic way. It is beyond the possibility of language. Actually, it is a Christology, or a christological soteriology, that is going on here. The human and the divine are so united, and the created order is so brought into the Christ, that the created order is pulled up into him, allegorically, imagistically, poetically, so that in his death and resurrection the whole created order is renewed and restored and begins again. It is the idea that the creator, Christ, enters the creation in order that he may recreate creation. It is a second creation that we have happening in Jesus.

Student: I follow that line of reasoning. But it seems that it does not necessarily have to be as mystical as they are making it, because when Jesus Christ died, his body was broken as well. It is said in the book of Isaiah that God made his soul an offering for sin,[8] but his body was broken also. And according to the book of Genesis, our body is made from dust and returns to dust. This type of thing. So why isn't it that creation is seen as being redeemed simply by the fact that his body was broken as well as his spirit, and his soul being made an offering for sin?

Webber: Well, there is another side to this, another way of reflecting on it from classical point of view, as well as an Eastern point of view of the atonement. That is the next thing that I want to talk about, which I think will fill out what I have been trying to describe to you in terms of creation being pulled up into Christ. Let me give you a bit of that, and then we will come back to discuss this more.

In the beginning of my lecture today, I talked about the atonement from the Western point of view, drawing from Romans 3 as being a legal transaction. The atonement from the Eastern point of view, drawing from Romans 5 and Colossians 2 and passages of that nature, is understood not so much in terms of a legal transaction, but in terms of a cosmic victory. Let me try to describe that for you. There is a kind of dualism that runs through the Scriptures, which I think all of us would recognize. It is not a metaphysical dualism, but a dualism that pertains to light and darkness, good and evil. The dualism in the Scripture is described by Paul, for example, in Ephesians 6, when he says, "We wrestle not against flesh

---

8. See Isaiah 53:10, King James Version.

and blood, but against principalities, against powers, against the rulers of darkness, against spiritual wickedness in high places."[9]

We are all familiar with that kind of motif in Scripture. From an Eastern point of view, and from Athanasius's point of view as well, the creation is made and declared by God to be good. There is an evil influence on the created order. I do not want to draw that as though that was some kind of metaphysical entity, in and of itself, but I am speaking of evil as a power. The power of evil affects the creation, so that as a result of that the entire creation is stained and affected by sin. When Christ died on the cross, his death is to be understood as the victory over the permeating power of evil in the created order. For example, let's take a look at Colossians 2:14–15.

> . . . having canceled out the certificate of debt consisting of decrees against us and which was hostile to us; and He has taken it out of the way, having nailed it to the cross. When He had disarmed the rulers and authorities, He made a public display of them, having triumphed over them through Him.[10]

The Eastern Church interprets Colossians 2:15 as that the cross of Christ enters into that evil, and as a result it is sort of an all-permeating destruction of that evil. It is a victory of Christ over evil. So for example, when you read 1 Corinthians 15, "O death, where is your victory? O death, where is your sting?"[11] Christ is the victory.

If you attend an Eastern Orthodox church, you usually find in front of the ambo[12] an icon of Christ in Hades with his hand stretched out as though to say to Satan, "Give me the keys," and he has a foot on the fallen door. The image that comes to us from that icon is that in Christ at the cross in his death disarms the powers and principalities of the air. He is victor over them, and therefore he can go down into hell. He can knock down the door of hell, he can shout, so to speak, into the channels of hell, "You are free." You get the whole idea of the souls that have been imprisoned in hell or hades pouring out and the graves opening up and releasing their dead. It is an Eastern motif. You do not find that kind of thinking in the West. It is there, but you do not find a strong emphasis

---

9. Ephesians 6:12, King James Version.
10. Colossians 2:14–15, NASB.
11. 1 Corinthians 15:55, NASB.
12. An ambo or ambon is a large pulpit or reading desk in Eastern churches from which the Gospel is read.

on it because the Eastern Church emphasizes the victory of Christ over sin and death. This victory of Christ, then, begins something new in the created order. Maybe we could say that within the created order there is a gradual erasing of the effects of evil, so that ultimately by the time you get to the new heavens and a new earth in the second coming of Christ, the whole created order has been released from its bondage to sin and decay.[13] The created order still has, at this particular point, still has the taint of sin, but nevertheless, as Romans 8 says, it is longing for, it is waiting for, with eager anticipation, its release from bondage and decay, and the whole created order lives in that hope. And we, who have been redeemed, live in that hope. And it is that hope, which is being born within us, which is carrying us forth in history and in life, by which we are saved.

The work of Christ is completed in the consummation. That view, which is the classical view of the atonement, has a lot of ramifications for the whole theology of the church and everything else that we can look at in terms of soteriology. But I will stop at that point and get some feedback from you before I go on.

Student: According to this conception, if the earth is stained by evil, needing redemption by Christ, why does the Bible speak of the necessity for the new heavens and the new earth? It has been redeemed, but it is not totally clean. It must be restored by fire the second time.

Webber: The problem is with your interpretation from an Eastern point of view is that you interpret that literally and symbolically, not allegorically, not poetically. The poetic interpretation of that is that the new heavens and the new earth is this earth, released from its bondage. All of the imagery of the second coming of Christ and the destruction of the heavens and the Earth and the new Earth simply means that sin fizzles out. It is like the last gasp of sin.

Student: What about when Peter says that the earth shall melt with fervent heat?[14]

Webber: That's all figurative language, not to be taken in a literal sense at all. It's as though God says, "Okay, Earth," and then zaps it like one of these movies where they disintegrate things with guns. That's not the

---

13. See Romans 8:21–22.
14. See 2 Peter 3:10.

point of view that an Easterner would take. It's a release, a movement of sin out of the created order.

Student: Do you think that conception of the reality of the universe was limited to that, because until the Einsteins or physics came along and it could be realized that matter could indeed be converted to energy, and things could be melted with fervent heat to the point where they no longer existed as matter but existed as energy?

Webber: Um, I do not know about that . . .

Student: For example, I can see why they would understand that purely figuratively prior to the twentieth-century physics, but now that twentieth-century physics are a more literal private interpretation, particularly of Peter, it seems perfectly plausible to me, whereas previously it required a significant stretch of the imagination.

Webber: Well, I guess I disagree with that. Contemporary physics in its conception fits the reality of the universe closer to the Greek theologians of the third and fourth centuries than it does to, say, the Newtonian world view.

Student: I think the Einsteinian type of thing differs significantly to Newtonian. It is a progression so far beyond anything that we are no longer dealing with a Newtonian physical worldview.

Webber: That's right. And what I am saying is that in the conception of the universe by the Greek Fathers it was, in fact, a dynamic conception that fits much more closely to the twentieth-century quantum physics and relativity.

Student: So in other words, the reason that they did not accept this particular dispensational, millenarian type of interpretation of Peter wasn't because of their restricted view of the physical world, it was just their particular theological orientation, right?

Webber: Right. It is their aesthetic, poetic, imagistic orientation, probably. I do not know that for certain, but I would say that it is probably that grid.

Student: Inclusion in Christ is a prerequisite for sanctification. Therefore, if you abide in him, he abides in you. Just as the cross is not applicable to him who would legally refuse God's offer of salvation, so salvation becomes non-applicable to people who refuse him.

Webber: This is the next point. What occurs here in Christ coming into the world, being victorious over the permeation of sin over the created order, is that a new creation begins. So we finish out the schema with this other line. This new creation that begins—as a matter of fact, it is here now—is moving toward union with God, even as Adam was originally called to grow into union with God. What would be the new creation? Where do you find it? Where do you see it? The church. There are just numerous implications of this in Eastern Christianity. Let me give you a few examples.

If the church is in fact the new community, the new creation, then the responsibility of the church as at the center of the world is to continue expanding in the world, eradicating [sin], or sanctifying man and nature. Let me give you an example of this business of sanctifying nature. If in fact God has redeemed the whole created order, and it will be totally and completely accomplished at his second coming, and the church now is the heart of that redemption in the world, called to permeate the world with it, then you can begin to understand the significance of holy water in the sanctification of nature. If all things have been redeemed, then by the name of Jesus Christ, and in the power of his victory over sin and death, water can be named and sanctified and set apart, even as a man and woman can be named and sanctified and set apart. Water, of course, has the imagery of creative power in the Old Testament and the New Testament. We often think of water as cleansing. The underlying motif to water as cleansing, however, is creativity. The earth is made out of water. God separated the water from the land. Look in Genesis and see the creative use of water. Man's first birth is in water. Jesus said, "Except ye be born of water and the spirit, ye cannot enter the Kingdom of Heaven,"[15] putting together both the spiritual and the physical. The physical and the spiritual are always put together in Eastern Orthodoxy. The physical is always the outward sign of an inward reality. Water is set aside as an outward sign of the reality of that permeating redemption or sanctification of the whole created order. So that water can become a symbol, then, of our being born anew into the kingdom, and it can become a symbol of the power of Christ over the evil in the universe. For example, the sprinkling of holy water on people. Sprinkling of holy water on buildings. Sprinkling of holy

---

15. See John 3:5.

water in the home. Sprinkling of holy water on the ground. These are all symbolic ways of expressing the ultimate victory of Christ over the evil that permeates the created order.

We are not talking about magic or pagan rites. What we are talking about is a theology, or the application of a theology, that is rooted in an atonement reality, a conception of salvation where not only man but the whole created order is recapitulating. This does not mean that there still is not sin in the world. We wrestle against principalities and powers to the end of the world, to the new heavens and a new earth. But it means that the sanctification of water and the sprinkling of water not only looks back to the redemption, but also conveys an eschatological symbol, in that it looks to the second coming at which time the whole created order would be released, and thus fully and completely sanctified.

Student: So the church in this particular schema is referring to the organizational structure, as opposed to the Protestant conception of all believers?

Webber: We will be looking more closely at this when we get to the subject of ecclesiology in Eastern Orthodoxy. The answer to that question is basically no. Eastern Orthodoxy has a much more organic conception of the church, and it is not just a pure hierarchy, or the organization that we sometimes think. Another thing, too. The process of sanctification is really what is known as the process of deification. It is drawn from 2 Peter: "... in order that we may become partakers of the divine."[16] How do we become partakers of the divine? There is a strong emphasis in the Eastern Church that Christ's life is in the church.

When I draw this connection between the church and Christ, I mean to show what is often referred to in Eastern Christianity as the incarnational dimension of the church. Where is Christ now? Christ is in the church. There is an indissoluble union between Christ and the church brought about by the gift of the Holy Spirit. The whole church, then, is growing up into its union with God through Jesus Christ, and individuals within the church are growing up into union with God through Jesus Christ. Not all individuals are on the same level of growth and development. But the whole church will ultimately be corporately united with God through the work of Jesus Christ. So the doctrine of salvation in the Eastern faith is not so much an individualistic doctrine, but it is rooted in

16. See 2 Peter 1:4.

the Theology of Recapitulation. What I would do in the closing minutes of the class is read from R. W. Blackmore's *The Doctrine of the Russian Church*. When we get into the subject of the church and the sacraments and all of that, it is going to be closely related to what I have given you here today.

> Q: How came it to pass that Jesus Christ was crucified when His doctrine of works should have moved all to reverence Him?
>
> A: The elders of the Jews and the scribes hated Him, because He rebuked their false doctrine and evil lives, and envied Him, because the people, which heard Him speak and saw His miracles, esteemed Him more than them, and hence they falsely accused Him, and condemned Him to death.[17]
>
> Q: Why is it not only said in the Creed that Jesus Christ was crucified, but also added that He suffered?
>
> A: To show that His crucifixion was not only a semblance of suffering and death, as some heretics said, but a real suffering and death.
>
> Q: Why is it also mentioned that he was buried?
>
> A: This likewise is to assure us that he really died, and rose again; for His enemies even set a watch at His sepulcher, and sealed it.
>
> Q: How could Jesus Christ suffer and die, when He was God?
>
> A: He suffered and died, not in His Godhead, but in His manhood; and this not because He could not avoid it, but because it pleased Him to suffer.[18]
>
> Q: In what sense is it said, that Jesus Christ was crucified for us?
>
> A: In this sense, that He, by His death on the cross, delivered us from sin, the curse, and death. . . .
>
> Q: How does the death of Jesus Christ upon the cross deliver us from sin, the curse, and death?
>
> A: That we may the more readily believe his mystery, the word of God teaches us of it, so much as we may be able to receive, by the comparison of Jesus Christ with Adam. Adam is by nature the head of all mankind, which is one with him by natural descent from him. Jesus Christ, in whom the Godhead is united with

---

17. Blackmore, *Doctrine of the Russian Church*, 65.
18. Blackmore, *Doctrine of the Russian Church*, 66.

manhood, graciously made Himself the new almighty Head of men, whom He united to Himself through faith. Therefore as in Adam we had fallen under sin, the curse, and death, so we are delivered from sin, the curse, and death in Jesus Christ. His voluntary suffering and death on the cross for us, being of infinite value and merit, as the death of one sinless, God and man in one person, is both a perfect satisfaction to the justice of God, which had condemned us for sin to death, and a fund of infinite merit, which has obtained him the right without prejudice to justice, to give us sinners pardon for our sins, and grace to have victory over sin and death.[19]

In that statement you see how the Eastern position actually brings together Romans 3 and 5.

Q: How can we have Fellowship in the sufferings and death of Jesus Christ?

A: We have fellowship in the sufferings and death of Jesus Christ through a lively and hearty faith, through the sacraments, in which is contained and sealed the virtue of His saving sufferings and death, and lastly, through the crucifixion of our flesh with its affections and lusts.[20]

You get right down to the nitty-gritty of how a man is saved. The Eastern Church says three things are involved in salvation: 1) faith; 2) sacraments; 3) holy living. The Protestant tends to emphasize faith and holy living without the sacrament. Let me just briefly describe the role of the sacrament and see how this fits together.

In an Eastern point of view, there is always a strong emphasis on the visible and the tangible. The tangible is always the means through which God works to accomplish his salvation. The point at which that is most clearly seen is in Jesus Christ. Jesus Christ is visible, tangible materiality, physical. The physical man is a worthy vehicle through which divine grace is made known to us, for the divine unites with man, so that in our Christology we have brought the human and the divine together in man, in the physical.

Therefore, the way in which God's grace continues to work in the life of his church, which is visible, tangible, material, is through the visible, tangible, material, the sacraments. So baptism, the washing with water. It does not deny the interior renewal by faith, but rather it is the external

19. Blackmore, *Doctrine of the Russian Church*, 66–67.
20. Blackmore, *Doctrine of the Russian Church*, 68.

expression of the internal occurrence. The sacrament, for example, the bread and the wine is more than bread and wine. It is body and blood. To receive the bread and wine in faith is to receive Jesus Christ, and to become, as Saint Cyril of Jerusalem says in his *Catechetical Lectures*, Christ bearers. That does not mean that if you bite the bread, you have bitten the body of Christ. It just means that the bread and wine is a worthy vehicle through which the saving reality of God in Jesus Christ is communicated to his people. So we do not neglect the external, nor do we simply function in the external as just a pure rote action, but it is always accomplished through faith.

Student: So they would say that faith and holy living is not enough to be saved? I must partake of the sacrament?

Webber: Yes. Another thing which I should add to this is that the emphasis in the Eastern Orthodox point of view is really on free will. I would say that Calvinism would be closer to the Western position, but Arminianism is closer to the Eastern Orthodox position. Just because you have been baptized and brought into the church does not mean that you will be saved in the end. That is true of strict Calvinism too. As I said last week, the matter of eternal security is really not a Calvinistic notion, because Calvinism stresses the necessity of the perseverance of the saints. This is the way in which the Eastern Orthodox Church deals with the whole question of the perseverance the saints. You do not talk about Christ is "in" and the church is "out," because the church is Christ. The church is the presence of Christ in the world. So you cannot neglect the church and neglect the sacrament and assume that you are saved, because you are neglecting Christ. You are turning your back on Christ by neglecting the church. This does have the danger, of course, of observing the sacraments of the church and involvement in the church just for the sake of observing it without faith. But I think we have that same problem in Evangelicalism. We stress Bible reading, prayer, attending church, twice on Sunday, once on Wednesday. We would say that if you neglect the church, if you are not here, the Christian life is not solo. There is no such thing as freelance Christianity. We would emphasize the necessity of being involved in the church. But that also has the danger of being legalistically involved in the church, the same danger as in the Orthodox Church. So what do you think about Eastern Orthodox salvation?

Student: You've given me so much material, I'm trying to figure out what in the world *I* believe about salvation.

Webber: Do you think if somebody believed this way, they would go to hell?

Student: I wonder if they really have faith in the Lord Christ. We run into a lot of people who are in the Catholic Church. They are faithful Catholics, observing sacraments and such, and are far better Christians than a lot of people in our own fellowship. Far better. Their doctrine is more concise, they follow the Scripture even closer than some of our own people. Yet they are still Catholics. What do you do with something like that?

Webber: You are asking me? I would *never* ask an Orthodox Christian or a Roman Catholic Christian to become a Protestant Christian. Never.

Student: Would you ask a Protestant Christian to convert to Orthodoxy or Catholicism?

Webber: No. If that person's understanding moved that way . . . Let's put it this way. I think in some cases some Orthodox are going to have to become Protestant, because there is a certain amount of rebel in everybody—maybe not everybody, but a lot of people. There is a desire to find reality for ourselves. So I am never concerned about any crisscrossing, whether an Orthodox becomes a Protestant, or a Protestant becomes an Orthodox, or Anglican, or whatever, if in that context there is a greater sense of the presence of Christ. Strictly speaking, that is a rather liberal point of view from an Orthodox perspective as well as a Catholic perspective, for this reason: that the person who becomes a Protestant is putting himself or herself pretty much outside of the realm of the sacraments. . . . Of course, a lot of my concern for Protestantism is that they recover the meaning and the sense and the use and the practice of the sacraments. Well, I think it is time for me to stop.

11

Orthodoxy, Protestantism, Catholicism

SESSION #7, JANUARY 18, 1979

Webber: Today is Saint Peter's Day. How often do we think about what day it is, and what that means to us? Right now is Epiphany. How often do we think about our life and its relationship with the church year? These days come along, Mother's Day, Father's Day, Boy Scout Day, Girl Scout Day... oh yeah, Christmas and then Pentecost. What's that? When does that come, anyway? Yeah, we kind of lost track of the whole Christian perception of time, history, space, and all of that in the Western world, where we think we are so religious, where we think we have really got it all together. Yet in the Eastern and Catholic world we tend to think, "Oh, they have no habit of Christian life at all." Yet this has permeated their very culture. That does not mean that every person takes full advantage of it, nor does it mean that every person in the Western culture does not have a consciousness of God. I do not mean to say that. But I just mean to make that comparison between cultures that has been spawned by the Byzantine Eastern Christianity, by a Catholic Western Christianity, and by the industrial, technological secular society that has been formed as a result of the Protestant and Renaissance movement. There is a huge difference. You must think about that in terms of this business between imputed grace and infused grace.

Student: How would you answer someone who says that when you read printed prayers, you routinely follow vain repetitions?

Webber: I would say that you must, when reading prayers, approach the prayer with the doctrine of intention. It is true that you can really be sloppy about reading. "Most merciful God, blah blah blah . . ." Of course, you can pray the same rote prayers. A Baptist minister I knew years ago, nearly twenty years ago, as a matter of fact—isn't that incredible?—did that. I found myself in that church, during the morning prayers, simply falling into an incredible pattern, and I had to really work to get myself out of it. I remember hearing one preacher I admired, who, when he preached about the government, said, "O, Lord, bless the ship of state as it sails turbulent waters. . . ." And when I found myself repeating that every Sunday, I thought, "Wait a minute, wait a minute . . ." But look at the prayers that have developed and grown in the soil of the church over the centuries, tested by time, carefully integrated with Scripture and biblical notions, just as the Old Testament has written prayers. When we approach them with intention to pray what they pray, they are more inclusive, more expansive, and they open us up to things we might not have even thought about praying before, and become a guide, a discipline to us. It is like saying that it gets boring when the sun comes up every day or goes down. Life is made up of routine, and routine has been sanctified and redeemed by Jesus Christ. Through creation and incarnation the routine becomes sacred, a sacramental perception of the routine. So I cannot see that kind of argument against routine and prayers as having any significance, because the routine itself is sanctified.

Student: Another point is that in periods of dryness it is better to read something that is creative, or at least where the phrasing is different, rather than the routine patterns that we have fallen into in our own terminology. We say some things every day . . . The likelihood that some of that will catch fire is greater than if some of our more familiar readings will catch fire.

Webber: Right. Because the content is there. The gospel is there. Even when the church goes astray, so to speak, it still has her liturgy and the whole gospel, and the church is committed to the perpetuation of it. It is always there. It is true that the greatest renewals, as far as the context of liturgy, John Wesley's renewal, the whole Great Awakening, are all rooted in the Anglican liturgy. The phenomenal renewal that is occurring today in the Roman Church is connected with her liturgy. I really think that worship is the road to renewal. The problem in Evangelical circles is that we have such a reduced worship. It is such a reductionistic form. There is hardly any content left. If you want to see a completely contentless worship, go to a Unitarian church. It is just one step away, really, from our Protestant reductionism. There is just nothing left. We read one Scripture, maybe one responsive reading, say a couple of little off-the-cuff prayers, smile at everybody and act enthusiastic. The whole thing is geared around the media. We are so affected by the media in today's world. We really evidence the secularization in Protestantism, a movement away from that content orientation of liturgy. Yet the danger of liturgy is not to intend what is being done. So they are always dangers on both sides. We need some balance.

Student: Could you briefly comment on what you think of Harvey Cox's book *The Secular City*?

Webber: Very briefly, I think Cox is really off the wall in *The Secular City*, because of the way in which he has redefined the church, the gospel, everything . . . To say that the gospel is anything, any word of promise that releases you from bondage, really just simply posits the principle of the gospel without its content. To flatten everything out, as he has done, and he has just flattened out sacraments, church ministers, everything, and incorporated that totally into the light of the world, so that anybody who does a good deed is in fact being the church. I do not really think that that is true, because biblical theology seems to suggest that a new thing is happening in the world, a new creation, and that the church is the presence of that new creation, that it must be done in the name of Christ. Sometimes it is not consciously done in the name of Christ, and that is the church acting. But it seems to me that Cox just simply secularizes the gospel to such an extent that it goes away like our snow goes away, hopefully in a few months, when there won't be anything out there, no content left. . . . Do you feel that you see the differences between the Catholic, Orthodox and Protestant points of view?

Student: I personally had some questions in my mind. . . . If you are talking about soteriology, as I have been reading in some of the Orthodox literature, and what I know of Catholic belief about salvation, and what Luther had to say is that salvation is by faith alone. From the Catholic and the Orthodox position, there is no salvation at all outside the sacraments. If you do not participate in them, there is no salvation for you. But Luther comes along and says, yes, there is salvation in faith alone, and sure, we have to continue the works. . . . But as I look at it from the position of my Protestant upbringing, that is the way I see it. If that is the case, then how do we get away from this aspect of trying to deal with Catholics and Orthodox that salvation is not in the sacraments?

Webber: Let me comment on it this way. It is a matter of emphasis, whether you are Catholic or Orthodox or Protestant. The problem that we are talking about is the relationship between form and spirit. The Catholic and Orthodox tend to emphasize the form, whereas the Protestant tends to emphasize the spirit. Faith fits under the spirit. The actual washing of water and baptism fits under form. And the actual taking of the bread and wine, the Eucharist, fits under form. In the literature, Catholic and Orthodox, as well [as] most Protestants, especially Reformation Protestants, the form and spirit are in reality brought together. They really are. When Luther says faith alone, if you read his *On the Babylonian Captivity of the Church*, he does not at all, in no way, deny the significance of baptism as that external expression of the inward reality of faith. Nor does he deny the significance of bread and wine as the means by which he encountered Christ, and which becomes real to us. However, he always says that baptism and Eucharist hold out promises. There is an implicit promise, the promise of God, which must be grasped by faith. Now late medieval theology is *ex opera operato*. We talked about that a couple weeks ago. It "works the work without," it simply works the work without faith. It would say, "The form is all that's important. Come and be baptized. Come and take the Eucharist on holy days," and various things of that sort, and in the end you'll get there. That is as much a perversion of Roman Catholic and Orthodox theology as it is to insist that Luther says, "Don't worry about baptism or the Eucharist," or that Calvin says, "Don't worry about baptism and Eucharist," because they do not say that. It is a matter of emphasis. It appears that the Catholic and Orthodox overemphasize the external rites and underemphasize the necessity of faith. And it appears that Lutherans, Calvinists, and Protestants overemphasize faith and underemphasize the external, as somewhat reaction against, really, fourteenth- and fifteenth-century Catholicism, not Catholicism earlier than that. And I can take you into the sources of the Fathers and show you again and again how they bring form and spirit together. What we are working against in this class, to a certain extent, is the caricatures that we carry around of the Catholic and Orthodox, and in some cases even Protestant Christianity, and we need to look at them from the sources.

Nevertheless, that would be my answer to your question. Well, it's 4:30. Let's take a break.

***

Webber: We are going to talk about the subject of the Protestant perspective on soteriology, and therefore draw to a conclusion the soteriological lectures in which we have tried to make a comparison between the Catholic, the Orthodox, and the Protestant points of view. To begin with, let me go back and remind you a little bit of what we have done over the last couple of weeks. We began by looking at Romans, recognizing that in Romans we have two different approaches to the whole subject of salvation.

First of all, in Romans 3 you see a rather legal point of view, that he might be just and the justifier of the unjust. We recognize that this is the basic Western position. And then in Romans 5 we had what we called the physical idea of salvation, the imagistic, the poetic, the allegorical, the whole contrast between the first Adam and the second Adam. We recognize that this is basically the approach that is taken in the Eastern church. I do want to make one somewhat corrective statement in regard to this, and that is that we need to recognize the fact that it is not as though the Eastern church is only Romans 5, or that the Western church is only Romans 3. But that they do bring together both of these passages, both the Eastern and Western churches—but that if you are talking about which way do they lean, that is what we are talking about. How do they lean? We recognize the fact that there is a degree of ambivalence in the Scripture. There are different ways of seeing the same truth, and it depends in terms of our cultural, geographical, philosophical interest, and perhaps in some cases even our individual sort of personality, how we ourselves are going to interpret various biblical concerns. So there are some people, as the Eastern, which lean more toward the physical interpretation, and there are some people, as in the West, which lean more toward the legal transaction.

It is interesting to note that in the Western Church, when you get up into the medieval period, the Roman viewpoint does stand in this tradition of the legal. The interesting thing to notice is that almost all of the theologians of the medieval church were lawyers. Your bishops were almost all lawyers. In many ways they were very tied into the political situation too, as you well know. They were in a sense tenders of the land,

and therefore it was necessary for them to have law degrees. Well, the juridical interest that law requires, the detailed way of seeing matters, pretty soon that obviously filters through one's theological preconceptions.

We noticed that the law orientation of salvation in the Roman Church becomes stronger and more articulate by the time you get into the medieval church than it is, say, in the early church. We must recognize that the Protestant point of view also comes out of the same Western milieu, so that the Protestant point of view is going to be more closely oriented to a Western legal transaction than it will be oriented towards an Eastern physical conception.

Student: Doesn't the Orthodox Church more or less accuse the Protestant church of saying that this is nothing more than a logical conclusion of Catholicism?

Webber: The accusation that Protestantism is that? Oh, yes.

Student: In their hyper-rationality?

Webber: That you can find Protestantism implicit within Catholicism simply because Catholicism went the way of rationalism, and that rationalism leads in fragmentation rather than unity, because the mystical seeks to hold ambivalence together, whereas rationalism always seems to separate. That is what we have done in the West, fragmented over soteriology. We have insisted that it must be this way and this way alone. One of the things that we have got to keep in mind is that Orthodox, Catholic, and Protestant theology in its soteriology is all the same in the sense that all three groups would insist that the only way in which one gets to God is through Jesus Christ. It is the death of Jesus Christ that saves us. The Orthodox say that. The Catholics say that. The Protestants say that. However, the difference comes in describing it, and in detailing how that salvation is applied, how we receive it, how we get it, how it is obtained. We will see some of that today as we deal with the Protestant point of view.

So my first point is that we must recognize that Protestantism stands in the legal Western tradition and tends to be rather rationalistic. I would say that there are exceptions to that. It does not mean that all are rationalistic. I think Luther himself was not so much a rationalist. He was a kind of existentialist. We will take a look at Luther, and then see where we go.

Now, in discussing the soteriology of Luther, there are a couple of things that I want to begin with here.

Let's take a look at the medieval background from which Luther emerged and what kind of ideas he may have had as he came into an understanding of justification. First of all, in reference to Luther's background, we need to pick up on the fourteenth- and fifteenth-century notion of the righteousness of God. This is an important thing for us to understand. How did Luther in his early days before his conversion understand the righteousness of God? Anybody want to venture on that? Nobody has read enough of Luther to comment.

Student: Luther's motive was an attempt to placate God by works?

Webber: I am going to read selections from Luther in a moment. But let's pick up on this comment and develop it a little bit more. The reason why Luther tried to placate God was because he thought that is what he had to do. In the fourteenth- and fifteenth-[century] Catholic notion, the righteousness of God was something that was demanding.... Luther saw God as the perfect and holy one who said, "Be like me. You have to be like me to attain salvation." Stop and think about that for just a moment. Maybe at some point in your own Christian experience, you have had some legalism put on you, because this is legalism of the nth degree. God is good and holy and just and righteous. You are not acceptable in the sight of God, unless *you* are good and righteous and holy and just. From that perspective, the righteousness of God becomes a very demanding kind of thing. Now in connection with the righteousness of God, there is another concept here that needs to be taken into consideration, and that is the concept of penance, which is really the concept of repentance. Repentance, or penance (that is how it was understood at this particular time), was something that you do. This is a really important thing for you to understand, if you are going to understand Protestant theology. It is something that you *do*. You do penance. Doing penance is doing the good works by which you receive the perfection of God. So it is a works system. Let me relate this just a little bit in terms of Luther's background, and I will read to you from Gordon Rupp's book *Luther's Progress to the Diet of Worms*. By the way, the Diet of Worms is a city. If you do not know that, it does sound funny, doesn't it? Luther's progress to the diet of worms? Crazy. Luther progresses until he gets on this diet of eating worms. When Luther at an early age gave up his profession, he too was going to become a lawyer. But he gave up that profession and entered the monastery. The statement that was posed to him when he entered into the Augustinian monastery was this, "Keep this rule, and I promise you, eternal life." See how that fits into the whole concept of righteousness? God in his righteousness gives us rules by which we can obtain the righteousness. Doing penance is doing the good deeds and contains that righteousness. Luther later wrote, reflecting on these early days of his in the monastery,

> I tried with all diligence to live according to the Rule, and I used to be contrite, to confess and number off my sins, and often repeated my confession, and sedulously performed my allotted penance. And yet my conscience could never give me certainty, but I always doubted and said, "You did not perform that correctly. You were not contrite enough. You left that out of your confession." The more I tried to remedy an uncertain, weak and afflicted conscience with the traditions of men, the more each day found it more uncertain, weaker, and more troubled.[1]

Luther, later in developing his whole understanding of what was occurring in his life, said that the more he tried to do these good works to satisfy the righteousness of God, the more he felt the wrath of God. Now that is interesting. There is a lot of theology in Lutheranism that grows out of this. Let me run that one through once again. If you have a standard of perfection that is set before you, and you really try to keep it, that standard of perfection is going to become a thing of wrath, because it becomes a measurement of judgment. Maybe you have never experienced this, but have you ever lived with someone who was sort of on the verge of perfection? The more you are around this person, the more you feel judged. Think about that for a moment. You compare yourself with this top-flight perfection. To really live with somebody who's got it together and seems to be doing everything right all the time. . . . Luther kept measuring himself against the perfection of God, against the righteousness that he saw in the law of God. The more he measured himself, the more he discovered that it was absolutely impossible for him to measure up. Yet the demand that was laid upon him was, "Measure up, and you will be saved." Now, in our world today, most people would say, "Ah, the heck with it." But Luther was not that kind of person. He was a man of piety, a man who really wanted existentially to experience reconciliation and

---

1. Rupp, *Luther's Progress to the Diet of Worms*, 27.

oneness to God but found that he could not do it that way. So let's follow his route a little bit more and see what happens.

> In the monastery I did not think about women, or gold, or goods, but my heart trembled, and I doubted how God could be gracious to me. Then I fell away from faith, and let myself think nothing less than that I had come under the Wrath of God, whom I must now reconcile with my good works.[2]

He goes on to say,

> Then God appears horrifyingly angry. . . . There can be no flights, no consolation, neither within or without, but all is accusation. . . . I am cast away from thy face: Lord, accuse me not in thy Wrath. In this moment, the marvelous to relate, the soul cannot believe it can ever be redeemed, but that it is suffering a punishment not yet complete . . . and left only with the naked longing for help, and terrifying trembling, but it knows not whence help can come. This is the soul stretched out with Christ so that all his bones can be numbered, nor is there any corner not filled with the most bitter bitterness, horror, fear . . . but all these things seem eternal.[3]

Then he talks about being under this sort of wrath of God, seeking to be good, and Luther was a good man. When he says he was not thinking about women and gold and all that kind of stuff, he wasn't. Testimonies of Luther's early life was that he was a man who spent a considerable amount of time in his cell praying, and sometimes beating himself. As a matter of fact—I do not know if we could call him a cellmate or not, but well call him a cellmate for lack of better term, right?—discovered that Luther had not shown himself for about three days and went to his room, and found him there in his cell, bleeding and nearly at the point of death, because he had been beating himself in order to attain goodness. He had been trying to beat evil out of himself. He was that much existentially concerned about finding peace with God.

This is no superficial jaunt that Luther is on. He is really searching for the strength of God. The better he became, in terms of his own person, the worse he believed himself to be, because the closer he got to God, the more clearly he could see himself. . . .

---

2. Rupp, *Luther's Progress*, 29.
3. Rupp, *Luther's Progress*, 30.

There is not an awful lot known about Luther prior to his monastery experience. What we do know about Luther is that he was always a very sensitive boy to religion. He was nearly struck by lightning one time during a tremendous thunderstorm. He fell to the ground and cried out to the Holy Mother that he would be saved and give his life to the church. Then he drifted away from that and went into law, but that terrifying experience stuck. It was that, in part at least, that led him to quit law and enter the monastery. But yes, he was a man of very sensitive conscience, even from what little we know from his boyhood days. It was the thing in those days to be a lawyer or a businessman. With a rising, changing economy, that is what everybody hoped for. . . .

So we see the righteousness of God, which produces in the person who seeks to attain the righteousness of God, a sense of the wrath of God, and one's unworthiness and unholiness. Luther writes this, which I think is very interesting:

> I remember, dear Father, that once, among those most pleasant, wholesome talks of thine, with which the Lord Jesus often gives me wondrous consolation, this word "penitence" [*poenitentia*] was mentioned. We were moved with pity for many consciences, and for those tormentors who teach with rules innumerable and unbearable, what they call a "method of confession." Then we heard you say, as with a voice from heaven, that there is no true penitence which does not begin with the love of righteousness and of God, and that this love which others think to be the completion of penitence is rather its beginning. This word of yours stuck in me like a "sharp arrow of the mighty" (Psalm 120:4) and I began from that time onward to compare it with the steps of Scripture with speech penitence. And then began a most joyful game. The words played up to me smiling agreement and jostling one another on all sides. So that whereas before there was no word more bitter to me than "penitence" which I feigned sedulously in the presence of God, and sought to express in a forced and fictitious love, now none has to me a more sweet and pleasant sound. For thus the precepts of God grow sweet when we seek not so much to understand them in books, but in wounds of the most sweet savior.[4]

Rupp continues,

---

4. Rupp, *Luther's Progress*, 31–32.

> Luther goes on to tell that when he came to study Greek, he found that the authentic meaning of "penitence" as "repent" rather than, "do penance," confirmed what Staupitz,[5] had told him.[6]

See, there is a tremendous difference there between repenting and doing works of penance. The whole system that Luther was reared in was a legalistic system of doing penance. I am going to read this paragraph about his conversion experience, because it is so excellent.

> Meanwhile, in that year [1519] I turned once more to interpret the Psalms, relying on the fact that I was the more expert after I had handled in the schools, the letters of St. Paul to the Romans and Galatians, and that which is to the Hebrews. I had indeed been seized with a great eagerness to understand Paul in the Epistle to the Romans and, as Virgil says, "It was not in coldness of blood" which held me up, but this one word, that is, in his Chap. 1. The Justice [*Justitia*] of God is revealed in [the gospel]. For I hated this word "Justice of God," which by the use and custom of all doctors I had been taught to understand philosophically as they say, as that formal and active justice whereby God is just and punishes unjust sinners.[7]

See how this is going to fit into Romans 3. If you connect this with the righteousness of God, it is an active righteousness, that is to say, God is righteous and he demands that you be righteous, act out righteousness in order to be saved.

> For, however irreproachable my life as a monk, I felt myself in the presence of God, to be a sinner with the most unquiet conscience, nor would I believe him to be pleased with my satisfaction. I did not love, indeed, I hated this just God who punished sinners, and if not was silent, blasphemy, at least with huge murmuring I was indignant against God, as if it were really not enough that miserable sinners totally ruined my original sin should be crushed with every kind of calamity by the law of the Ten Commandments, but God through the Gospel must add sorrow and sorrow, and through the Gospel bring his wrath and justice to bear on us. I raged with a fierce and disturbed conscience in this way, and yet I knocked with importunity at

---

5. Johann von Staupitz was a German Catholic priest and theologian who mentored Martin Luther.

6. Rupp, *Luther's Progress*, 32.

7. Rupp, *Luther's Progress*, 33.

Paul in this place, with a burning desire to know what St. Paul could intend.[8]

God is an ogre to him, just demanding, demanding, demanding.

> At last, God being merciful, as I meditated day and night, pondering the connection of the words, namely, "The Justice of God is revealed, as it is written, the Just shall live by faith", there I began to understand that Justice of God in which the just man lives by the gift of God, i.e., by the gift of faith."[9]

See the whole different swing that is coming. Formerly, the righteousness or the justice of God demands that you be just, so you work, work, work. But you feel wrath. You shake your fist at God, asking, "Why do you demand so much, when you know I can't make it?" Then all of a sudden Luther, while contemplating this, says,

> There I began to understand that Justice of God in which the just man lives by the gift of God by faith, and this sentence, "the Justice of God is revealed in the gospel" to be understood passively as that whereby the merciful God justifies us by faith, as it is written, "The just shall live by faith." At this I felt myself to be born anew, and to enter through open gates into paradise itself. From here, the whole face of the scriptures was altered. I ran through the scriptures as memory served, and collected the same analogy in other words, as *opus dei*, that which God works in us; *virtus dei*, that in which God makes us strong; *sapienta dei*, that in which he makes us wise; *fortitude dei, salus dei, gloria dei*.[10]

Blah, blah, blah, on and on. You can feel with Luther the conversion he went through, when all of a sudden, he realized that God was not saying, "You have to be righteous." Luther expands on this a little bit more. He now understood that God gave his Son Jesus Christ, who is our righteousness. The justice of God, the righteousness of God, has been met, not by you or me, but by Jesus Christ, so that the gospel is a gift. The gospel is proclaimed, it is done. The righteousness of God has been satisfied in Jesus Christ. Rest and trust in Jesus. Therefore, Luther says, *sola fide*, faith alone. This is likely the background from which most of us come. Most of us see salvation from this particular perspective, and

---

8. Rupp, *Luther's Progress*, 33.
9. Rupp, *Luther's Progress*, 33.
10. Rupp, *Luther's Progress*, 33.

it is a very clear, Christ-centered perception of salvation that Luther arrives upon. It is not without its problems, however. The greatest glory of the Protestant concept of justification also has within it its greatest problem. The greatest glory of it is that everything that ever needs to be done to make you acceptable to God has been done in Jesus Christ. That is explored. The problem is, unless balanced by other aspects of Scripture, it can lead into antinomianism. So it is this thing that the Orthodox and the Catholic church have already struggled with, as we have seen. That is to say, that works is also part of the saving reality. The difference between a Lutheran Protestant point of view, and the Catholic and the Orthodox view as well, is that Luther is teaching imputed grace. You know what I mean when I talk about imputed grace, or put upon grace? The righteousness of God, which is given to you, put upon you. He talks a lot about sinners being saved.

The sinner-saint is the fact that before God, in the eye of God, we are 100 percent saved, because justification is complete. It is all over, it is done. We wear the righteousness of God as a cloak. We are covered by the blood of Christ, and therefore we are saints in heavenly places. But on the earth, in the world of history, time, space, where we are now, we are sinners. So there is the struggle between the sinner and the saint going on as we in life are working out what it means to be a saint. The danger in this position, however right it may be, is resting in the heavenly statehood and assuming, "Oh well, everything is okay. God's grace and Jesus Christ is imputed to me. My name is written in the Lamb's Book of Life. I can lean back and rest on that."

There is [here] no sense [of] what you see in the book of Hebrews. Keep on keeping on. Do not slide. Do not turn your back. The greatest perversion of this notion, I suppose, is the eternal security doctrine, which, as I have said before, is neither biblical nor historic. It is a modern, radical, innovative, unchristian, unbiblical concept. That leaves you a lot of room for discussion, doesn't it? I express [it] that way because I want to make a point. Now, on the other hand, both the Orthodox and the Catholic teach what is called infused grace. Those schools of thought come at it a little differently in terms of sacrament. How do you understand the word *infused*? Infused grace means to form a habit of life within. If you have had occasion to read some of the saints, particularly the Russian saints, and become acquainted with the Jesus Prayer where the whole approach of spirituality in the Eastern church, the whole quest is that of becoming infused by the grace of God, the whole desire to come divinized, to become deified, to become like God, to grow in union, to mature. The idea of having the life of Christ infused in us. There are a lot of biblical motifs for this. The vine and the branches. The mystical relationship between Christ and the church. The concept of the church as the extension of Christ. The church, built by the presence of Christ. The church living out the life of Christ. The church having Christ present in her through the sacrament of body and blood, the bread and wine. Eating, nourishing, growing as a result, a continual feeding upon Christ through the sacrament, through the Scriptures, and through prayer, where our life is united with him. The danger of your Catholic and Orthodox view is just the opposite of the danger of the Protestant, because the danger is not being aware that in fact everything that ever needed to be done to save has been done in Jesus Christ. The danger of Catholicism and Orthodoxy is legalism, the attempt to work out our own salvation, the assumption that somehow what we do is going to gain us merit for salvation. Whereas the danger of the Protestant point of view is antinomianism, so rested in the grace of Christ that we consider the doing of good works or the development of the habit of life, the habit of Christian life, as being relatively unnecessary. You see those two extremes. Let's talk about this.

Student: If you observe the lifestyles of Orthodox and Protestant and Catholic people, you will probably find the Protestant disregarding good works, or the merit of good works. But he will probably live a more good working life in terms of Bible reading, church attendance, piety, than a lot of Catholics and Orthodox. How do you explain that?

Webber: Well, my response is that I am not really positive that is true.

Student: I think a definition of good works is in order, because good works to Protestants and Catholics are different. Good works to Catholics or Orthodox often mean attendance at church on holy days, receiving the sacraments at certain times, fulfilling other obligations imposed upon them by the church. Beyond that, it often doesn't mean living [a] Christian lifestyle as we understand it. Do you see what I mean?

Webber: Yeah, I do. And I think that your question arises out of popular Catholicism and Orthodoxy and popular Evangelicalism. I think that you are probably right in turning that around within the popular masses to a certain extent, except that would be a hard thing to prove statistically. I know myself in trafficking more with Anglicans and Catholic and Orthodox over the last five years, I have been just overwhelmed by the depth of spirituality in the most unsuspecting person. On the other hand, I have been absolutely shocked at the superficiality of the most unsuspecting people in Evangelicalism, our leaders. So I do not really know how to answer that question, because it does seem to me that that is a caricature that we have of the Orthodox and the Catholics and the Anglicans, and that we hold a caricature of great depth and spirituality among the Evangelicals. And I have been shocked at both levels and find that neither one is necessarily true.

Yet at the same time I know that there are deeply spiritual Evangelicals as there are very worldly Catholics and Anglicans. We all have the same problem. But if you were to take this, for example, into the lives of the saints, the Catholic, the Orthodox, and the Protestant church, we too have our saints, our Spurgeons and Billy Grahams and so forth. . . . If you take this into the lives of the saints, you may find that the analysis I have given you is more correct. But that is an opinion. To really prove that, you would have to generate a statistical analysis. Let me give you a couple of examples of this business of forming a habit of life. I remember a couple of years ago that Don Mitchell, the vice president of academic studies [at Wheaton College], had been in South America. He was comparing the lifestyles of South American people with the lifestyles of the Americans. He said he was there assuming that everybody was Catholic. He was talking to a person who was Roman Catholic. Don said, "Another person who knew us better rushed up to us and said, 'So and so,' whom we both knew, 'has just died.' My response was to say, 'Oh, I'm so sorry. Is there anything I can do?' He said, 'My Catholic brother dropped on his knees, did the sign of the cross and prayed. Whose response was more Christian? Mine was a very secular response. His response arose from a habit of life.'"

Last night we were interviewing a person for St. Barnabas Church.[11] We are in the process of finding a new pastor. This man was formerly a Lutheran but became an Episcopal priest. I asked him, "Why did you shift from the Lutheran church to the Episcopal?" And he said, "Because the Lutheran Church does not have the fullness of catholicity in it." I said, "Could you explain that a little bit more?" He said, "I was always frustrated in the major events of the personal life, and not having the tools of the church to deal with them. For example, when a couple came to me

---

11. St. Barnabas Episcopal Church in Glen Ellyn, Illinois.

to talk about marriage, I could never talk to them. I was limited, because I could not talk to them in terms of marriage as a sacrament. Here is another example. When I went to the hospital to visit a sick lady, I felt within myself the burning desire to anoint that person with oil and pray, but because of my church canons, I cannot do that." He went on, giving five or six examples. All of this arises from what? A habit of life.

Let's make a comparison very briefly with what you may regard as a pagan sort of habit. You walk into an Orthodox home, and what is there in the corner? An icon. Before you even greet that Orthodox person, you look at the icon and do the sign of the cross. Then you turn back and say hello. Okay, maybe that has been corrupted to a certain extent. I have no question that it has been for a lot of people.

Let's take the business of the prayer life. This man last night gave another example. He said, "One Sunday I was preparing to preach, and all of a sudden it dawned on me that I hadn't prayed once this entire week." That has happened to every one of us in this room, no question. It's probably happened to every Protestant minister in the world. He said, "I went over to my Episcopal friend and said, 'What do you have as a discipline of prayer?'" Then the priest introduced him to the Book of Common Prayer, the Morning and Evening Prayer, which is a habit of life. Every Episcopal priest is under oath to develop this habit for his life. It is something that those of us involved in freelance Christianity do not have. Not only that, but there is the discipline even in the written prayer of praying for things we would not even think of. We tend to be too casual, saying, "Oh, Lord, I'm really wiped out tonight. I've been doing your work all day. It's getting late. I'll see you in the morning. You know my prayers anyway." We smile, because we have all done it.

In other words, if you look at the liturgy, look at the Byzantine culture for a moment and see how integrated a Christian view of reality is with it. . . . It struck me so much when I was in Russia a year and a half ago. The most pleasant trip I ever took. As I was standing on top of one of the churches looking out over Moscow, what do you see everywhere? Domes. The architecture speaks so loudly about the faith and existence of the church, because they are so suppressed in Russia, but cannot be destroyed. It is built right into the very fabric of the architecture of that country, the music of that country, the literature of that country. Talk about bringing the habit of life into the warp and woof of society itself, so that the very landscape of nature shouts forth the existence and glory of God.

12

Orthodoxy, Catholicism, Protestantism

SESSION #8, JANUARY 25, 1979

Webber: Today we are going to discuss the subject of ecclesiology, the doctrine of the church. This is the first day that we are not going to be concentrating on one particular church point of view, but rather attempting, as far as possible, to reflect on the Orthodox, the Catholic, and the Protestant points of view regarding the church. There are two things with regard to the church that we need to talk about. We need to talk about the nature of the church and the organization of the church. Either one of these subjects could consume a considerable amount of time for us. I think that what I am going to do is just speak briefly to the question of the nature of the church, because to tell you the truth, this can get so complicated that I am not certain that it would be profitable for us to get into that subject on too much of a level.

But I would begin by saying that the nature of the church from the New Testament perspective is that the church is to be regarded as incarnational. The incarnational dimension of the church. When we talk about the incarnation, we always talk in terms of "God with us," is what the incarnation means. So when we talk about the incarnational dimension of the church, we talk about that way in which God is in fact with us now. Let me try to illustrate this. I heard a preacher preach last year at Wheaton College, who said something like this, "When Jesus Christ ascended into the heavens, he cut the apron string from the church." Really dramatic. But that is a complete repudiation of the whole notion of the incarnational dimension of the church. The incarnational recognition of the church is that God in Christ is still uniquely present with us in the church. Paul talks about this in his mystical union of the church, the body with the head. The way in which I like to symbolize this is in terms of Christ continuing to be present with us in the world through the church, so that the church, you might say, is an extension of Christ until the second coming, the rapture, whatever you want to call it. So there are a lot of interesting ramifications of that.

The thing that I want to examine in terms of the incarnational dimension of the church is that the church is a presence of Christ in the world. The comment that I would like to make is this. This becomes very personal and very practical from a spiritual point of view. We say to ourselves, "How can I relate to Christ?" We talk about the personal relationship to Jesus Christ, which is really kind of nebulous. Sometimes we are not exactly sure what that means, how that looks, and what that feels like, what the experience of a personal relationship for Christ is all about. It is a very nebulous concept. When you talk about Christ being present in the church, then you concretize your personal relationship with Christ by your relationships in the church. I see a furrowed brow. You are not exactly sure what I mean by that? You want me to go over that again? If Christ is present to the world in the church, then the way in which we concretize a personal relationship to Christ is in and through the church.

Student: What do you mean by concretize?

Webber: To make visible. To make manifest. Make it real. For example, we all know that the body of Christ is people. That is the most primary designation of the church. The people of God. Christ is in us. We mystically participate in him as the head of the church, the community of the people of God, mystically belong to Christ, and we are visible and tangible. If I pinch Jan, she says ouch. If I kick Tom, he kicks me back. There is a tangible, physical, material reality. We are talking about a very material, not a nebulous, kind of thing that the church is not something that goes *whirrrr* in the dark. The church is something that you can see and feel and touch, because the church is people. My relationship to Christ, then, is expressed and concretized and fulfilled in my relationship to people. Jesus said anyone who gives a cup of cold water in my name is giving it to Christ. There is more to it than that because the church, which is that fellowship of faith, speaks of the fabric of human relationships in the church. The church is also organized—I do not want us to see this organization in terms of temporal organization, because it is a divine institution. It is the only institution in the world which is divine, created by Christ. It *is* Christ.

Student: What about the family?

Webber: Okay, I see what you mean. The family is an order that belongs to creation, so the family is in that sense a divine institution, but not on the same level in which the church is a divine institution. That is to say, the church exists as the new creation, that therefore the creational activity of God in the church is incarnational rather than creational. The family arises from creation. The church arises from incarnation, death and resurrection, Pentecost, Holy Spirit, all these others. So it is the unique institution which is divine. That is to say, we speak of the presence of Christ in the family, but in a different way than we speak of the presence of Christ in the church, because the church is the unique body of Christ. So there is a uniqueness in that divine institution. My point is that we concretize our relationship to Jesus Christ in the life of the church, which is the life of Jesus Christ in the world. Jesus is not only sitting at the right hand of the Father. See, we tend to put him up there and forget him. We pray upwards. Our visual imagination of Jesus is always that he is seated at the right hand. He is there, no question about that. That is true, but he is also very manifest in the world in the church, so that we can never say, "Christ is in, the church is out." Because the church is Christ, thus the worship of the church, the prayer of the church, the Scriptures of the church, the ministries of the church, the gifts of the church, the workings of the church as described in the New Testament are all a very vital part of our life in Christ. In our mechanized age we tend to separate our relationship to Christ from our relationship to the church. You do not think so?

Student: No, I wouldn't disagree. You are blowing my mind, that's all.

Webber: Okay, you are not sure. I am blowing your mind? Good! I did not think I would be able to do that!

Student: But this does not fit into *The Four Spiritual Laws*.

Webber: Oh, I am sorry. Ha!

Student: No, it's great.

Webber: Well, what would you expect me to say about the church? It fits right into everything I have been talking about this whole quarter. What do you think I am, a radical? This whole business of belonging to the church, fellowshipping with the church, is in fact our fellowship for Jesus Christ. That speaks of the incarnational dimension. I want to give you a couple of things here that hopefully won't throw you, because they are somewhat complicated and I do not want to spend an awful lot of time on it, not more than three weeks. And then we will stop and discuss it. What I want you to notice is that there are other dimensions of the church as well. There is the Trinitarian dimension. The christological. The soteriological. The pneumatological. The sacramental. And then the eschatological. I could come up with more, but I think these would give you the basic idea. What I am trying to illustrate in terms of discussing the nature of the church, talking about the essence of the church, is that within the church you find the fullness of all theological considerations. Let me try to describe each one of these. Let's being with the Trinitarian. The key to Trinity is unity and diversity. Thus you find in the church the fullness of the Trinitarian Godhead is to express in the midst of all of the diversity of the church, the unity that belongs [to] the church. Just as you have the diversity of this distinctions of Father, Son, and Holy Spirit in the church in the Godhead, so you nevertheless have the single essence of Godhead in Father, Son, and Holy Spirit, thus describing the unity. This breaks down, or ought to break down, all the walls that we seem to build toward each other in the body of Christ. Because there is only one body of Christ, and that body is not the Evangelical body. It is not the Catholic body. It is not the Protestant body. It is not the Orthodox body. The body of Christ is expressed in all the wisdom of those diverse cultural expressions of the church of Jesus Christ. So that when we think in terms of Trinitarian fullness, we want to recognize that in these cultural differences, which express themselves in the Byzantine soil as Orthodox, in the Western soil as Catholic and then Protestant, and in the more modern world, Evangelical. These cultural shapes of the church, while quite distinct, find their unity in Jesus Christ, and that therefore the Trinitarian fullness helps us to become inclusive in our understanding of the church, rather than exclusive. The exclusive attitude is *I am right*.

The Orthodox often say that this is the body of Christ. The poor Catholics, the poor Protestants, the poor Evangelicals, they are outside in the cold. So it is not only the Evangelicals who think they alone are the body. It [includes] the Catholics too. We all have this problem. But I think what we need to do is to see that Trinitarian fullness calls us to an inclusive, not at exclusive, understanding.

The key to Christology is that Jesus Christ is both fully human and fully divine. The christological dimension of the church, which is an extremely important thing for us to understand, is that the church is both fully human and fully divine. If the church has the life of Jesus Christ in it, then the church is divine. Those tangible ways in which we see the light of Jesus Christ in the church would consist of such things as Scripture, the sacraments, and the ordained minister. I want to include with that not only the ordained ministry but all the ministries and the gifts and the workings of the Spirit as they are alive in the church. All of these represent the divine activity.

The human side of the church is our inability, you might say, to keep things together. Our cultural, geographical, and personal differences that find expressions in the church. Thus we have Catholic, Orthodox, Protestant, Evangelical, and whatnot. Because that is the human side of the church. But the divine side is found in Scripture, sacraments, etc. Are you following?

Now the soteriological dimension of church. The church is our means of salvation. Let me qualify that. First of all, Christ and Christ alone saves. Nothing else. Not works, not water, not communion. Nothing else. Only Christ saves. But the church, which is the extension of Jesus Christ, is therefore the continuing, redeeming activity of Christ in the world. Thus St. Cyprian, a good old Church Father in AD 250, said, "He who hath not the church for his mother, hath not God for his Father." How can you have God for your Father if you do not have the church? If, in fact, the church is the extension of Jesus Christ in the world? You cannot be outside of the church and be a Christian. So the soteriological dimension of the church is that the saving work of Jesus Christ is communicated to us within the context of the body of Christ, the church. There is no such thing as freelance Christianity, American rugged individualism. I am going to do it on my own. I will show God I can get there without his church. No. Not possible. Because the church is the corporate body of Christ to which we must belong if we are to be saved.

Now the next one, the pneumatological dimension of the church. The Holy Spirit is what pneumatology is about. The Holy Spirit stands in inseparable union with the church. We speak of ourselves as having the Holy Spirit, which we do, we are the temple of the Holy Spirit. The church is an inseparable union with the Holy Spirit, so that through the activity of the Holy Spirit, Jesus Christ is really and savingly brought to us. Do that one again? Okay. We speak in terms of the Holy Spirit being inside of us, right? We become temples of the Holy Spirit. If you look at Ephesians and study Paul's development of the concept of the church in Ephesians, you will see that the whole church is growing up into a temple of the Holy Spirit,[1] not just individuals. The whole church corporate, and that is the thing that I am trying to get after here. The Holy Spirit has his activity within the church, the maturing of the church corporately into Christ. Therefore, there must be some tools that the Holy Spirit has within the church by which this is accomplished, and this is where we come into the sacramental dimension of the church.

The sacramental dimension is the visible, tangible means through which the Holy Spirit works in order to bring us the saving experience or encounter of Jesus Christ. We get ourselves into a lot of the problems here unless we are careful. One thing that we need to keep in mind is that *form and spirit must be kept in balance*. For example, baptism is the form, faith is the spirit. You really should not have one without the other. In some cases, you have baptism without faith; sometimes you have faith without baptism. But the best thing to do is to bring the two together, because baptism is the external sign by water of the internal conversion renewal, cleansing that has taken place, which is our passageway into the church. Once we are in the church by the work of the Holy Spirit through baptism as the external sign of faith of the internal sign, then we are in the body of Christ. Now in the body of Christ we are fed and nourished by his body and his blood. What is it that makes the body of Christ alive? His body and blood. We are speaking poetically, imaginatively rather than literally. But it has a literal meaning that stands behind it. You do not keep a body alive without food and drink. The body of Christ feeds by faith on the body and blood of Christ, which proclaims to the body of Christ that the body of Christ has been redeemed by the death and resurrection of Jesus. So that by feeding on him by faith, we are continually reminded of the redemptive motif, out of which the church is created, from which the church derives its meaning, toward which the church is moving in terms of the goal and consummation of history. Her redemption is connected to consummation. There are other elements, such as confession and various things [like] that, which we will look at more closely when we get to the subject of the sacraments.

---

1. See Ephesians 2:21–22.

But finally, the eschatological goal or dimension of the church is that the church not only looks to the future—the Eucharist proclaims the future, because the Eucharist proclaims the ultimate banquet in the new heavens and new earth—but the church is also the future. The church is the presence of the future in the world now. I have thrown something at you that I prefer to have spent two or three hours talking and going through rather slowly. What I would like to do is give you a chance to react. Maybe I have gone through too many things too quickly, so you are not exactly sure what I said.

Student: I experienced that this weekend when I went alone on a retreat.... I really missed Christ.... It really hurt.

Webber: There is an activity in the Holy Spirit of bringing us to Jesus Christ in the body that we do not experience at the same level when alone. That is something that Protestantism does not tend to understand because of its secularization, so informed by the individualistic spirit of rugged, Western individualism. Sometimes we tend to think we can go it alone, and we forget the corporate nature of the church, and that God works in the church by the Holy Spirit through the whole body. I put it like this: the Christian faith is not individual, but it is a person ... to get away from the rugged individualism, but also to retain the necessarily personal characteristics.... I saw your hand up. I saw your brain working.

Student: Well, it's always doing that, though it's not always producing. Would you go over the last one again, the eschatological?

Webber: Okay. The church points [to] the future. See it? If the church, as we have suggested, is the new creation, then it points to the future. It points to the new heavens and the new earth. It has a sort of prophetic ministry, pointing to the future. But more than that, it is also supposed to be ideally the experience of the future in the present world. That is to say, we are in a sense caught up in the heavenlies in the church, and we experience the heavenlies. Paul speaks of this in Ephesians. St. John speaks of this in the Apocalypse. There is an awful lot of material in the New Testament that we sometimes overlook, recognizing that even though we live here, there is another realm in which our presence finds its meaning. The church, therefore, gives meaning to the structures of normality, and the meaning that it gives is rooted in the ultimate goal of the church, which is the new heavens and the new world as a final reference point....

I would like to talk about this for a while, because I think these are rather complicated notions, and I gave them very quickly, and I am not going to be satisfied to walk out of here having just dumped them on you. I want you to do something about them. I can sense best what you are thinking when you interact with me. . . .

Student: I think the Orthodox Church looks at the Protestant Church as being a by-product of the Catholic Church falling short and succumbing to rationalism. . . . Protestantism is simply a reaction to the errors latent in Catholicism.

Webber: So how to respond to that? Okay, I think basically what you are asking is how does this fit into our comparison between Orthodox, Catholic, and Protestant? First, I would say that in terms of theoretical understanding, the Orthodox Church understands this better than either the Catholic or the Protestant. I first stumbled across these ideas myself [when I] was reading the Eastern Fathers. These ideas were developed by ninth- and tenth-century Eastern theologians. You will find them in Eastern theologians today, like [Vladimir] Lossky and [Nikolai Fyodorovich] Fyodorov and [Alexander] Schmemann. But I have not seen any Eastern theologian develop these motifs to any great extent. I have only seen it as being a sort of a reflective method of doing theology in the Eastern Fathers. So I am in a sense pulling this out, doing my own thinking. Second, in regard to the Catholic Church, I think that the Catholic Church, like the Orthodox Church, has a fairly good understanding of this. But I am not exactly sure how to comment, except to say that you won't find it in all the Catholic theologians. If you pin them down in their ecclesiology, they would talk about it in terms of their ecclesiology, but there is not as clear a spelling out of this in Catholic theologians that you find in the Orthodox. And you do not find it at all among the Protestants. Why would that be the case? Let me reflect on this for just a moment. The methodology of doing theology in the East is poetic. . . . The method of doing theology in the West with the Catholics, particularly after Aquinas, became rational. And thus church is defined more institutionally than it is defined poetically. . . . The Orthodox church is defined poetically. For Catholics, the church is defined institutionally. . . . And with the Protestants the church is basically defined humanly. When I say the Protestant church seems to define itself humanly, that is to say, that there is not a great deal of ecclesiology in Protestant thought. There is a lot of confusion, I think, as to what the church is. What is it? "Well, we come together every Sunday." More recently in Evangelical circles there have been some books written attempting to get at the nature of the church. Possibly one of the most popular books that you would all know about would be Ray Stedman's *Body Life*.[2] I think what Stedman is trying to do in that book is see the poetry of being the body of Christ. The word *body* is a poetic word, perceived intuitively rather than rationally. What he is striving for is a way to express the church for Protestants, who are so humanly oriented. "Well, it's a bunch of us people and we go into this building on Sundays, and we sit there, and we listen to our sermon." What is the purpose of being there? To learn! Or is it? Should we walk away and say, "I'm not getting anything from the church. I did not learn anything." Ever say that? All right, now immediately it seems to me that there is a misunderstanding of what is the meaning of the church, if you think you are going to a Calvinistic lecture hall. Or as some people would say, "Oh, I took all my problems to church with me today. Alas, it was no help." What do you think church is, a psychiatric couch? "I took my unconverted neighbor with me today. Good grief, nothing happened." What do you think the church is, an evangelistic tent? The church is primarily a worshipping commune. This does not mean that is all the church is. The church is more than that. But primarily the most basic calling and function of the church is to be a community that worships and adores God in Jesus Christ. Let me give you a first-hand illustration that will get at some ideas of the church. I've mentioned that at St. Barnabas Episcopal Church we are looking for a new priest, and for the last three months I've been involved with this process on the search committee. Late October, when the search committee made the mistake of making me the chairperson, I said, "Well, before we can even determine the kind of man we are looking for, we must decide what the church is." And we spent two months deciding what the church is, wearing off our edges. And then we made a profile of the church from the people in the church. We came up with five things which are all biblical: 1) The church is a worshipping community. 2) The church is a teaching community. 3) The church is a fellowshipping community. 4) The church is a healing community. 5) The church is a serving community. Let me go through each one of those and define them a bit, to help you see where our pastor or priest or whatever fits into that. . . .

---

2. See Stedman, *Body Life*.

If the church is not worshipping, nothing else is really going to fit into place with what happens in the church. For example, if you look at Isaiah 6 and Revelation 4-5, you get a glimpse into the heavens. Both Isaiah and St. John are lifted up into the heavens and see what is going on. It is worship. We see all this imagery in ever increasing concentric circles to the throne of God. . . . There are angels and seraphim and beasts and apostles and martyrs and saints. What are they doing? They sing, "Holy, holy, holy," the eternal chant, the eternal adoration of God. The church on earth is connected with the church in heaven; it just so happens that we are in different spheres. There ain't no dead people in Christ. All the dead are very alive in Jesus, and they are there worshipping. That is their calling. Their God created the world to be for his glory, and our rightful place is to be at worship. The whole creation in the end will worship God. We Earthlings find our true meaning in life by worshipping. That is basic. Because the moment you begin to worship God for who he is, it is like Isaiah, who said, "Good grief! Woe is me, for I am a man of unclean lips." What happened? He saw himself for what he was. He saw God for who he was in all of his holiness and beauty. . . .

Student: In Isaiah's particular situation, he had a personal revelation of God, and on the basis of that personal revelation he had the Law and the prophets and the book of Leviticus. He had these things which he could have worshipped in the same way, but he did not. In the same sense, when we go to worship, can we worship only on the basis of what we read in the Scriptures, or can we expect God to give us the revelation of himself in this?

Webber: Well, in that Isaiah and John saw the same thing, I think we already have a revelation and vision of what worship is all about. And I would personally hesitate to ask for anything more than that. I do not believe in continuing revelation of the same magnitude as the revelation of Holy Scripture, which is our final, ultimate authority. But I do believe that God, the Holy Spirit, makes himself very real, and is experientially present in our lives, particularly in the experience of worship. The norm of our worship, the norm of our whole life in Christ, must be determined by the biblical basis at the moment we begin. Someone could say, "Well, I got myself a super-duper revelation here," and moving outside of the context of Scripture itself, we begin creating something other than what the true church is, I think. So I would say that the norm needs to be rooted in the Scripture, but that we too can have an experience like Isaiah and St. John. Not the exact experience, but that our experience of worship can lift us up into the heavenlies so that we can see God and experience the meaning of standing before God, crying holy, holy, holy. When the church is worshipping, these other functions take place too. There is a teaching function, but that is not the primary goal of the church. There is a fellowship fabric of human relationships that exists and belongs to the church, as brothers and sisters in Christ. There is healing that occurs. I would be very open to physical healing, emotional healing, any kind of the work of the Holy Spirit in ridding us of evil and the effects of evil, because the victory of Christ over sin and death and evil is extended to us in the life of the church, by the work of the Holy Spirit. Therefore, I would be open to such things as the sacrament of unction, the sacrament of confession, the means by which we are continually healed in the life of the church. And then, of course, the church has a serving function, in the sense that the church is called to serve the world, to be light in the world, to be salt in the world. These functions ought to be happening in a strong, committed Christian church. But it seems to me that sometimes there is imbalance, where you know the church is great on fellowship, lousy on worship and teaching and everything else. Time for break.

***

Webber: For the second hour I would like to discuss some brief snapshots of the of the church from the New Testament and then jump from that into a discussion of the differences between Protestant, the Catholic, and the Orthodox concepts of the church. Let's begin with the New Testament. What I'm suggesting here is that in the New Testament there are what I call snapshots. The way in which I am using this word is that a snapshot is not a full picture. It seems to me as we work through the New Testament that you find a number of different snapshots, and I want to look at some of these snapshots and then go from that into Orthodox, Catholic, and Protestant points of view, although there are so many even within that that it is going to be hard to deal with.

But nevertheless, let's begin with Acts 2. In Acts 2:43–46, you find an expression of the church. Remember the new Christians after Pentecost were meeting both in the temple and in houses. It says that they were attending to the apostles' teaching, to fellowship, to prayer, and the breaking of the bread. Those four things seem to characterize the church.

As far as the organization of the church is concerned from Acts 2, you do not see much organization, do you? What do you really see?

I want to accent that the apostles stand at the center. There is a great deal of concern in the early church for the apostle. Let's go check with the apostle and see what he says. Did the apostle see that? Did you get that from an apostle? The apostle is the closest one to Christ, and therefore an eyewitness. And there is always a desire, always an interest, in talking to the apostle and getting it firsthand. Looking at the organization of the church at Acts 2, there is not a great deal of organization, but the apostles stand at the center.

When you go to Acts 6, you begin to see not only apostles but also deacons. We are a little uncertain as to precisely what the function of the deacon is. We have all sorts of functions for deacons today, but in the early church it was very fuzzy—at least it is fuzzy from our point of view—in terms of discovering what a deacon is. We know that a deacon here in Acts 6 was called on to share some of the apostles' ministry. The deacon was called on to preach. Steven preached.

And in Acts 21 we seem to get insight into other functions of the deacon which seem to be similar to the functions of the elders, which were appointed later. But at any rate, you have a growing organization by the time you get into Acts 6, and you see both apostles and deacons. There do seem to be some differences in function, but nevertheless there also seem to be areas in which the function is the same.

Now the next snapshot that we have is in Acts 15. I think most of you are familiar with Acts 15, are you not, and what is called the Jerusalem Council? There is an interesting thing apparent here. As you know, the Judaizers were spoiling the Christian message of Paul, particularly in Jerusalem and Antioch, and there was a considerable amount of dissension from the Christian. So Acts 15 says that they appointed the apostles and the elders. This is the first time you see mention of elders. They appointed the apostles and the elders to go to Jerusalem and to discuss the whole matter. Now the picture in Jerusalem appears to look something like this. These guys come from all over, and they are sitting around a table, slugging it out. "I think this, I think that. Blah blah blah. Should we impose these legal restrictions on the Gentile Christians? Yes. No. Maybe. I don't know." On and on. Everybody says his piece. Finally, good old James stands up. James is the elder in Jerusalem, and he says, "Okay guys. I've heard all this discussion. It seems to me that we ought to . . ."—blah, blah, blah. He talks about sending the letter out, and what should be in the letter and what restrictions should be placed on the Gentiles.[3] What I want to talk about in respect to that is the way in which this occurred. It appears to me what you have is the apostle in the center, the elder a little out, and if there were deacons there, we will put them out a little farther. It seems to me that the approach was circular and dynamic, as opposed to hierarchical. The hierarchical approach would look something like this. It would be James at the top, and then the apostles, and then the deacons, and then the people. And it would just be sort of top heavy. The order has come from the top for what we are supposed to do. So everybody falls into place like dominos. It brings up the question of the meaning of authority in the church and the way in which the church is to be structured.

Ray Stedman[4] wrote an excellent article which appeared in *Moody Monthly*[5] titled, "Is Your Pastor the Pope?" It is a catchy title. The thing that he was trying to get at there was that authority in the church, in many cases, is run along the lines of domination. It is kind of a Standard Oil authority, you might say. "Hey, I'm the pastor in this joint. I want you to recognize that. And as pastor, as God's spokesman, I call for all you people to . . ." What Stedman is calling for—and I think this is correct—is getting back to the New Testament, saying, "Wait a minute. Where does authority lie?" Authority lies in Christ. Christ says, "I came not to be ministered unto, but to minister, and to give my life a ransom for many." That is the key to authority. Authority is found not in worldly domination, but true authority is found in service.

There is a comment that the Pope occasionally makes, and not all popes have really lived this one out, but the Pope will say, "I am the servant of all of the servants of Jesus Christ." True authority is being a servant. And that is what we are each called to be in life, servants of each other. Servants of Christ, and therefore servants of each other in the church, which is the extension of Christ in the world. It appears to me that in Acts 15 the church is in fact coming to a decision, a consensus, on that basis, rather than on a model of authority that is designed after Standard Oil.

Student: Wouldn't this domineering sort of pastor justify, perhaps even legitimately to some extent, from the New Testament concept that a pastor, and indeed anybody with spiritual authority, does have a responsibility to

---

3. See Acts 15:19–21.

4. Ray Stedman (1917–1992) was an Evangelical pastor and author.

5. *Moody Monthly* was a monthly magazine published by Moody Bible Institute from 1920 to 2003.

God to review and to correct and so forth, and that this might translate into what appears to the sheep, the congregation, as what might appear to be domineering? For example, Paul, in treatment of the Corinthian church, might be accused of being a pope-pastor by some, but that really wasn't his intention. It would just appear to look that way. Do you think that that is legitimate at all?

Webber: I think you are right. But sometimes the service that the pastor renders to the church may appear to be domination at a certain point. I am sure that the service that I rendered to my children occasionally appeared to be domination. And yet, at bottom, I think that I am more motivated by love. I am concerned for them when I tell them when they must go to bed, or that they cannot play in the snow with a 110 fever. Yeah, I think that needs to be taken into consideration. But in general, we are striking at this authority without love, or authority in love. And authority in love is always a matter of service, a matter of servanthood, rather than of . . . well, the strokes that some people get from being the authority. I am the big cheese in this joint, and do not ever forget it. We know the people who have that attitude. It is not an attitude of service, and it does not rise out of love. It is a power that is based on self-need in many cases, and not on a calling of service. But I agree with what you are saying, yes.

Student: Regardless of those who abuse or misuse their position, is it not true that their authority remains? As servants of Christ, are they still not called?

Webber: It seems to me that this did in fact work in more dynamic ways in the New Testament than it does in many contemporary churches, or in the Catholic or the Orthodox, where domination and authority from the top down is prevalent. It seems to me that it is more of a pulsating dynamic activity of the Holy Spirit—ideally.

Student: I would think that their authority from God remains, whether we like it or not . . . ?

Webber: Well, that is what we are going to try to get at through these snapshots. I think once we get at that, then we have to ask how it has been interpreted. It has been interpreted differently, and that's the way in which I will get into the differences between the Catholic, Orthodox, and Protestant positions. When I get to the conclusion of this snapshot, I believe that we can make those practical inquiries a little bit more closely related to the content given to us in the New Testament. So we will come back to that, if that is okay.

After Acts 15 you jump into a snapshot in 1 Corinthians 12–14, and I think all I want to say about this is that it is a local manifestation of this particular principle. There is a lot of detailed material in there, but I do not think we have time to get into it. But basically, it is a local church manifesting that dynamic principle that we see at work in the more universal church in the Acts 15 situation. What Paul talks about there is the variety of gifts and workings that we have in the single body of Christ, and we must remember the 1 Corinthians 13 should not be taken out of context. First Corinthians 13 appears in the middle of chapters 12 and 14, and . . . it ought always to be read in relationship to 12 and 14. The highest gift of the church is love. What is Paul talking about? We may have different prophecies or helps or administration or preaching or whatever, but the highest gift, the gift that everybody ought to seek to have, is the gift of love. And it is the gift of love that kind of binds or brings together all of the other gifts and ministries in the church. So it is a gift of service expressed in love. However, it becomes a little more technical we get into the pastoral epistles.

This is the next snapshot in 1 and 2 Timothy and Titus, in particular, because what we find here is really that upon which much of what came later is modeled. First, you find the Greek word *presbuteros*, which is translated in the New Testament in two ways. It is translated by the word "bishop," and it is translated by the word "elder." It seems to be indicating two functions. The function of the bishop is a function of oversight, whereas the function of the elder is that of teaching. In addition, you have the deacon mentioned in the pastoral epistles, and his function seems to be that of service, but that is not absolutely clear. It is very fuzzy exactly what the deacon is in the New Testament. It does seem to share some responsibilities with the elders.

The thing that I want to point out specifically here is that you have a threefold function of ministry in the New Testament. Let's take a look at some dates. We are dealing with AD 30 in Acts 2. We are dealing with probably 31 in Acts 6. We are dealing with 49 in Acts 15. We are dealing with 57 in 1 Corinthians 12. And somewhere between 64 and 68 in the pastoral epistles. So through the snapshots that are given us in the New Testament, a progression, a development, because here we had only apostles, here apostles and deacons, here, apostles, elders, and deacons, and finally, by the time you get up to 64 and 68, you have, in addition to the apostles, the bishops, the [elders], and the deacons. The question that we must deal with, from which our differences arise in the Catholic and the Orthodox and the Protestant church, is how you are going to interpret this and organize your church accordingly.

Okay, there are three general approaches to this. There are more, but in general I think we can capture it in three. First, there is the episcopal approach. Episcopal simply means rule by bishop. . . . I am not talking about the Episcopal Church. I am talking about episcopal rule. You will find this in the Catholic, the Orthodox, and the Anglican churches, with some differences. The second is rule by presbytery. Again, we must look at the exact meaning of that word. And then the third, rule by congregation.

All right, let's begin with a general episcopal approach. Let's say that this circle is Chicago. This is St. Louis. And this is Philadelphia. Each one of these areas is going to represent a diocese or district or whatever. From an episcopal form of government, you would have over this particular area a bishop, and the bishop has under his jurisdiction, let's say fifty churches. In each one of those churches, there is a priest. Now the bishop is the pastor of all those churches. He is the pastor, and the priest is there to carry out the responsibilities and the duties of the bishop for that church. And you would also have, not necessarily so, but you would also have deacons. The difference between a deacon and a priest is that the deacon is the first order of the ministry, and while a deacon can preach, counsel, and do a variety of things in the life of the church, he cannot administer the sacraments. Only the priest can do that. In addition, of course, you would have the people. The question is, since the bishop is the priest's pastor, who is the bishop's pastor? Is he the top dog on the totem pole? Or is there someone to whom he is responsible? All right, these other areas are organized in the same way, and there is a unity between these bishops. So these bishops form a unity that transcends their locality, and their locale is ruled by the unity of the bishops. I will get back to that because there are some nuances that I want to discuss, but we will come back to that in just a little bit. What we see is the way in which these three ministries are carried forth in the life of the church. The ministry of oversight is by the bishop. The ministry of teaching and practicing the sacrament, etc. is by the priest. And the ministry of service is practiced by the deacon. But you have the threefold order and the threefold function of the ministry in both your Orthodox and your Catholic Church. So I am going to come back a little bit and distinguish between the Orthodox and the Catholic. Let's go on for just a moment to the Protestant, because I think it is important for us to see the Protestant point of view, and then we will make comparisons.

Let's look first at the Presbyterian. I am going to draw three circles again, and we will say that it is Chicago and Philadelphia and St. Louis again. Let's look inside of that circle for just a moment and see how the Presbyterians are organized. The Presbyterian will have a teaching elder, ruling elders, and a deacon. That is in each one of the individual churches. Let's say there are a number of individual churches in here, represented by all of these little scratch marks. So you have the teaching elder responsible for teaching. The ruling elder is responsible for oversight. And the deacons are responsible for service. Again, the threefold function of the ministry is expressed in the Presbyterian church. Who rules these churches? The churches in the Chicago area are organized into what is called the presbytery. The presbytery has the same function over these churches that the bishop has over [episcopal] churches, because the presbytery is a ruling body. How is the presbytery made up? Well, the presbytery is made up of all the teaching elders, some of the ruling elders from all of the churches, and they constitute, you might say, a sort of a large web of people around here who constitute the ruling body over the many churches, although you have ruling, teaching, and serving in each one of the single churches. So who runs the presbytery, just like who runs the bishops? Well, every one of these areas has a presbytery, and these presbyteries are united together in what is called a synod. The synod is the general ruling body over all the presbytery.

Let's leave it there for just a moment and examine the congregational, and we will choose the Baptists at this point. Again, we are going to draw three circles. But this time we won't put those circles in Philadelphia, St. Louis, and wherever. We will put them all in Wheaton. You have your First Baptist Church of Wheaton, the Second Baptist Church of Wheaton, and your Third Baptist Church of Wheaton. I do not know if there are three in Wheaton or not. In each one of these churches, you have a pastor. Secondly, a board of deacons. And thirdly, trustees. Trustees is not a biblical term, but that is okay, let's say they are entrusted. So in that sense, it is a biblical connotation. The pastor is the teaching elder. The deacons have the ruling responsibility, so they have the responsibility of oversight, and the trustees have the responsibility of service. They are the buildings and grounds [people], you might say. The question is, who rules this church? The church. The church rules the church. There is no such thing as a united web higher than the church itself that rules the church, because every church is the body of Christ, and every church therefore is self-ruled and self-governed. Please note that every single church that I have cited, whether Orthodox, Catholic, Presbyterian, or congregational Baptist, functions according to the three functions. They have oversight. They have teachers. They have service. They do not call them bishops in certain of these churches.

An illustration. Let's say that the First Church of Corinth is having problems. Who is going to solve the problem? There is a split in this church, as in the Philippian church between Euodias and Syntyche, two women who are leaders with problems. Let's see what happens in the episcopal form. They go to the bishop and say, "Hey, bishop, we have a problem at St. Thomas." The bishop says, "What's the problem?" They explain, and finally the bishop visits the church and says, "Hey, listen, as I understand things, this is the way it ought to be. Therefore, I am instructing you to do such-and-such." Ideally, they are supposed to do it, because that is the way it works. The bishop is the final authority of that church, the pastor of all the churches of the diocese. Now in the Presbyterian church there is a problem. What are we going to do? Well, we take it to the presbytery. The presbytery has about sixty, seventy, eighty people. The presbytery discusses it and decides, "Well, we ought to do such-and-such," or they will appoint a committee to do such-and-such. Or they will decide and say, "Okay, the moderator of the presbytery ought to go to the first church on the corner and tell them to do such-and-such." So the moderator says, "Do this," or the committee investigates and says, "Do this, do that." Now go to the Baptist church where a split has occurred. What do you do? Who decides? The pastor, right? The deacons might, but if the people say, "Nah, that's not the way I see it." That could happen in a Presbyterian or a Catholic church too, but less likely, because there is not anything over and above them to keep them in check.

Student: Just wondering, wasn't Jonathan Edwards a Congregationalist? And when his congregation got upset with him, it seems to me like they got a number of the Congregational churches in the area together and hosted a big conference like all these other groups are doing.

Webber: That's interesting, because that does sometimes happen. Technically, it should not happen from their theology, but it does often happen on a more pragmatic basis.

Student: Aren't a lot of Baptist churches affiliated with a denomination?

Webber: The group with which they have affiliated, let's say the Conservative Baptist denomination or the General Association of Regular Baptists or whatever, has no authority whatsoever over the local congregation. They cannot pass canons, creeds, or confessions or rulings that would affect anyone in that assembly, because each church is independent in and of itself, and is not under the jurisdiction of any of the other churches. A church might so choose to seek the advice of a group of other churches, which is often done. The benefit, I suppose, would be awareness of what is happening in the Baptist churches in that area or across the country, and the benefit would also accrue in terms of the united mission boards. It becomes a very practical kind of thing, such as the missionary activities of the General Association of Regular Baptists, who sends the missionaries out. But it is not an authoritarian structure at all. Basically, what you have between the episcopal, presbyterian, and the congregational is, I think, in many ways very similar until you get right down to the congregational point of view, which insists that the whole body of Christ is present in heaven in the local body of Christ. Let me add to that by saying that other churches also recognize that the whole body of Christ, in terms of gifts administered, are present in every local body, but that in terms of authority and organization, the local body must be in relationship with the universal body. How do we prevent a Jim Jones from coming along and instigating mass suicide? Well, I guess I would have to say in the in the congregational motif, there really is not a way to prevent that. With either the presbyterian or the episcopal approach, it can be prevented because they are always responsible to someone above, a council, a bishop, a presbytery, a synod, whatever. Their authority is the means by which you express your submission to Jesus Christ. Of course, what happens when the whole church is apostate? This is the question asked by the Reformers. They broke with the Catholic Church, claiming it as apostate. Rightly or wrongly, in the tragic necessity for the Reformation, they did break from the Catholic Church. Out of that, of course, emerged different governing views.

But it is an interesting thing for us to realize that until the time of the Reformation, with the exception of some relatively small movements within the church, the whole church was organized on the episcopal basis. The first evidence of this episcopal basis is really found in Ignatius. Actually, you find an allusion to it in Clement at AD 96, but by the time you get to Ignatius in 110, which if you are looking at this general development, it is not that many years after 68 or so. Thirty to fifty years at the most, and the church is definitely organized according to a threefold order of ministry. Somewhere it was the consensus of the church that the apostolic ministry, as the apostles died, that the bishop continued the apostolic ministry, so that you do not have apostles, bishops, elders, deacons. You have only a threefold order of the ministry, and the office of the apostle is fulfilled in the office of the bishop. To some extent, you see the difference in organization between Protestant and Catholic. Let's take some questions, and then I want to show you some specific differences between Catholic and Orthodox, which I have not yet shared.

Student: I don't understand how the Catholic Church could be presbyterian rather than episcopal. It seems that with this structure, how can you have bishops and then cardinals above them? Why wouldn't that be a presbyterian type of structure?

Webber: Because in the Catholic system, authority is really placed on the level of a single person, not a group. But it is true that the higher you go, the more complex you become in terms of the spread of the church. The more it appears to be a synodical thing, and yet the authority of the pope would belie any kind of synodical or presbyterial arrangement, because it would appear to be more hierarchical than consensus. The Presbyterian tries to maintain a more consensus approach to the authority, whereas the Catholic church is more dominational. But it should not [be], because the organization of the church became somewhat of a practical thing as it emerged, and any one of these expressions here could be domination, and any one could be service.

Student: So the bishop is over so many pastors, right? But does he go to church somewhere?

Webber: Yeah. The bishop is the chief pastor of the cathedral. The word cathedral means "seat."

Student: Is that the biggest church in town?

Webber: Yes, I suppose so, if you want to look at it from a medieval point of view. Let's say Rome is a small city. It is a big city, so I should probably pick up something else. Okay, let's pick on Rome. So the cathedral in Rome is the seat of the bishop.

Student: He just stays in one place? He doesn't travel around?

Webber: No, he travels around from church to church. But see, the cathedral is usually pastored by the dean. There are lots of different names that have come up here throughout history, like the metropolitan and the archbishop and cardinal, etc., etc., all of which show the increasing complexity of the organization of the church, which in its initial thrust is fine. There's no problem. It is like a college with its president and six vice presidents, academic, finance, dean of students, whatever. And then under them you keep having more people, and more people under them, and more people.... That is the way most administrations seem to function.... You can get a feeling from your college experience—obviously that's not true here—but you can get a feeling for the whole church experience from your college experience. The president says, "Chapel is now going to meet six days a week, four hours a day." So the students say, "What do you mean? I do not have time to study! I do not have time for this or that...!" And the president says, "Shaddup. I run this place. I am the president." Everybody must do what the president says, because authority comes from the top down. But if the president were the servant of the people, he would say, "What are your needs?" Just as a college administration becomes corrupt, so does the church. It is not organized that differently. It also can become corrupt. The central issue in the whole thing is, what is the meaning of authority? If it is understood as service and not domination, it is a totally different type of thing, and the administration that is there to serve the students and faculty in order that they can get the job done. It is unique. It is hard to find.

Student: Why is it okay for the bishop to run around to the churches, but it is not okay for the people?

Webber: Because the bishop is the pastor of all these churches. That's his function.

Student: But who watches the flow of his life? He might be one person in one church, but somebody else in another church.

Webber: Well, that is the function of the other bishops, and the function of his priests and deacons. It is all very ideal, when you get down to it. But the point is that there is the divine and human.

Student: That isn't too far removed from reality, for crying out loud, because living in a goldfish bowl, basically running from one church to the next.... I am somewhat more familiar with the structure of the Methodist Church and the district superintendent. It's the same type of thing. He is literally living in a goldfish bowl. And to say who is going to watch over his life is the main question, because he's being watched twenty-four hours per day. As a ministerial student, I was as close to him as I was to my pastor.

Webber: That's speaking really well for the bishop, because that is his job. You are an extension of the bishop. The bishop is an extension of Christ. And when it is understood that way, and when it functions that way, it works. I suppose I have more confidence with the difference between the Catholic and the Orthodox, because there is a significant difference which you ought to see. Let's draw circles. You like circles? Okay, the Catholic point of view. Let's take a look at the early church in Rome, Constantinople, Antioch, Jerusalem, Alexandria, and Carthage.

Now in the Catholic Church there is going to be a bishop in each one of these churches. Obviously, as I have said, it becomes increasingly complex as you talk about the development of metropolitans and archbishops and all of those people. But they are all basically bishops, even the pope is a bishop. All the bishops are united together, but the Roman bishop is the chief bishop. See, even as you have, say in Alexandria here, all the priests, the chief pastor of all the churches in Alexandria is the bishop. But the chief pastor of the bishop is the pope, or the bishop of Rome. Therefore, the bishop of Rome is the chief pastor of all the churches of the world, because the bishop of Rome is the successor to Peter. Jesus said to Peter, "Upon this rock, I will build my church." This is interpreted institutionally. The Protestants interpret that confessionally. From this rock, meaning Peter's faith. The Roman Church will stress the institution *upon this rock*, that is to say, the church which is established through Peter from Rome. I will build my church.

Let's take a look at how the Orthodox differs from the Catholic, and I will use the same schema again. The Orthodox recognize these areas, and that each one of them is ruled by a bishop. The Orthodox say the unity of the church throughout the world is expressed through the unity of the bishops, but every country, every area, is self-governed. In these circles, therefore, instead of putting Rome and Constantinople and Antioch and etc., what we are going to put is Greece with the Greek Church, the Russian Church, the American Orthodox Church, the Serbian Orthodox Church, the Romanian Orthodox Church. . . .

12

Orthodoxy, Catholicism, Protestantism

SESSION #9, FEBRUARY 1, 1979

Webber: Scripture, tradition, and authority. Let's begin where probably most of us have somewhat of a caricature of this whole question. From our backgrounds, probably very few of us would put these three words together: Scripture, tradition, and authority. We would probably drop the second word "tradition," and just simply talk in terms of Scripture and the authority of Scripture in the life of the church, and say that it is for those good-for-nothing Catholics and those good-for-nothing Orthodox who insert the word *tradition*. That, I think, is a caricature, and I want to try to undermine that caricature and help us realize that Scripture, tradition, and authority really do in fact hang together, not only from the Catholic and Orthodox perspective, but from a Protestant perspective too. So we will try to take a good, close look at that today.

The first thing that I want to do in discussing Scripture, tradition, and authority is to go back and take a look in terms of an introduction about how we think about this question from a biblical point of view. So let's begin with that. How do you think about the question of Scripture, tradition, and authority from a biblical point of view? Let me begin by asking a question. I think that is where I want to put it out in your mind, what is the tradition of the church?

Student: Define "church."

Webber: We did that last week. The body. Using it in the imagistic sense, it is the people of God who constitute the new creation, who constitute the fellowship in Christ, who can be named the body of Christ. That's the church. So I am not thinking specifically of Orthodox, Catholic or Protestant, but the church.... We are trying to go back at the point when the church began, and we have to ask ourselves the question, what is the tradition of the church? Anybody want to venture a guess?

Student: Okay, I think it would have to involve the history of the church, which recognizes the movements of God ... the positions and hammering out of things. The history of it, and interpretation and so forth.

Webber: The history of tradition. Okay.

Student: The history of the church.

Webber: The history of the church within the context of the church. I still have to go back and ask that one question. What is *the* tradition of the church?

Student: Well, that's what I mean. It would need to be built on that institutional structure. It depends on which institutional structure we are talking about, i.e., Roman Catholicism or a particularly nationalistic form of Orthodoxy. Of course, each one of those is going to have their own tradition, their own historical interpretation and accumulation of historical facts and their theological interpretation of the facts, and these are what is going to constitute the tradition.

Webber: Okay, you are standing in the twentieth century and looking back down through the corridors of history at this whole tree, and what I am asking you to do is to come on this side of the tree, this side of the development of Catholicism and Orthodoxy and Protestantism, and standing here, looking forward on the path when the church began at what was the tradition of the church.

Student: Wouldn't worshipping God be the tradition, the practice of Christ?

Webber: The worship of God, the practice of Christ. Okay, that is a start, but it is not quite what I am getting at at this particular point. So let's get a few more things thrown out here, huh?

Student: The sayings of Jesus as tradition?

Webber: Okay. What else?

Student: The apostolic, whatever, practice of the apostles . . . ?

Webber: The apostolic whatever?

Student: At that point there was a lot of Jewish tradition.

Webber: You mean continuity between the people of God and between the Old Testament and the New? Let me draw something up here I love to draw, since I am such an artist, as you all know. Start with something you've never seen before. This is what we were talking about last week. Do you remember what this means? It means the church. This signifies Christ. And we can go like this and say that there are Old Testament traditions that we meet in the New Testament, which find their fulfillment in Jesus Christ. Now let's go to AD 30 at Pentecost. What did [the] church have? The Holy Spirit. The teachings of Jesus. The Old Testament Scriptures. It is so simple that it is difficult to catch. What the church had was Jesus Christ. What I am trying to do is to take you back to focus on the meaning of tradition in order to have a biblical understanding of tradition. Now the church has Jesus Christ. Remember last week we were talking about the theology of the church. Jesus Christ hands himself over to the apostles, and the apostles hand Jesus over to the church. So that you can think of something that looks like this. The apostles hand over the offices of bishop, priest, deacon, which grew—I do not intend to say that they were all here at AD 30, as I am looking at this in the broader New Testament scope. Those are not the offices of that person, but they are the offices of Jesus Christ. And in Protestantism we believe that too, because we say that the one who stands before you to preach the Word is standing in the place of Jesus, declaring the Word of God to us. So we recognize that the offices are the handing over of Jesus Christ.

Now the sacraments. I know that we do not generally use the word *sacraments*, so maybe I should use *ordinances* here, a more Protestant word, but the dominical sacraments of baptism and the Lord's Supper are means by which Jesus Christ is handed down in the church, because baptism is the passageway, the entryway, into Jesus Christ, and the Eucharist is the presentation of the proclamation of the presence of Jesus Christ in the midst of the worshipping community.

We also saw last week that there would be included in this the gifts and workings and ministry and all sorts of things, so that the whole church is always handing over the whole church. Apart from that, let's go back and take a look at something else for just a moment. What was the first thing that the apostles did? They prayed. They met together. They preached. They proclaimed Christ. Let's put the word *proclaim* up there. It is true that they did all of that. The thing that I am looking for here is oral preaching. If we are going to understand this thing from the very beginning, we have got to recognize that at this time, there is no such thing as Scripture. Let me back up for a moment. There is Old Testament Scripture, but I mean there is no such thing as New Testament Scripture. On the day of Pentecost after Peter's sermon, he did not stand there handing out *Living Bible*s.

Student: He handed them King James Bibles, right?

Webber: Yeah, that's right!

Student: I always thought of tradition as something man-made, which contains an element of truth and an element of error. So what is your definition of tradition?

Webber: Your definition is okay, but that is going to come later. The original concept of tradition is the handing down of Jesus Christ. . . . Tradition in the early sense simply means that which the church hands over. Maybe I should put this up on the board, because I think there is a general misunderstanding of the word. The word is *paradosis* in the Greek, but we will just simply put the word *tradition*. The word *paradosis* means to hand over. Obviously, when you talk about handing over something, there is content, whether it is a book or a person. What is it that the church is handing over? What the church is handing over is Jesus. Jesus is handed down in the life of the church. That is tradition. How is Jesus handed down in the life of the church? Well, the office is the sacrament and the preaching. Now the oral preaching, which of course you meet immediately in Acts chapter 2 when you get to the Pentecost, that is an oral preaching of Jesus, which brings the Old Testament to focus, the life, the death, the resurrection of Jesus. And in Acts 2:36 Peter declares this same Jesus we declare for you to be Christ and Lord. So there is an interpretation that the church is immediately handing over about Jesus. It is a true interpretation, but they are handing over Jesus in all his fullness and all of his reality to the church, because Jesus is the life of the church.

We know that oral preaching really went on for a considerable amount of time, because we happen to know by the dating of the New Testament books that the earliest possible New Testament Gospel would be about AD 55, and that is really pretty early. We are talking really 55, 70, 85, possibly 95 for as late as John. Notice that there is a considerable amount of gap between here. You have got at least thirty-year gap between Mark, which is possibly at 55, and Pentecost. So you have twenty-two years at least of oral preaching and more, because your oral preaching continues to be the strongest means of handing over Jesus. In the book of Acts, Paul goes on his missionary journeys. He enters into the synagogue, and he preaches and persuades them of Jesus Christ. So he is handing Christ over by oral preaching. Gradually this oral preaching becomes the written record. By the time you get to about AD 100, you have the whole written record of the Gospels and the whole written record of the epistles, which are interpretations of the Gospels as directed to the ongoing life of the church. But the thing that I want you to notice here, in particular, is that from this chronological point of view, you cannot separate Scripture, nor Christ, from tradition. Christ is the original tradition of the church, passed down in the total life of the church, specifically passed down in preaching. But also in the offices, the sacraments, the gifts, the ministry, etc.

One more thing that I want you to notice about this is, at what point in the life of the church is all of this tradition handed down? If you were to see a highway, so to speak, from AD 30 zipping all the way up into 1979, what would be that highway? Where is the locus of tradition in the life of the church?

Student: The General Association of Regular Baptist Churches?

Webber: Amen! I am going to say that this is right. Okay, now, but we still have not answered the question. Where does it happen? Where today in 1979, where can you go and find the whole tradition of the church present? Bob Jones, right?

Student: In any church in this city where believers are gathered together, where the leaders are presenting Christ and you have a full tradition of Christ being passed down.

Webber: In what activity of the church?

Student: In all of its offices, its working, its gifts, its sacraments, its preaching.

Webber: Uh huh. Where do you find all of those at work at once? The worship is the locus through which the whole tradition of the church was always present and passed down in the life of the church. To have worship, you have got to have people, and there is a procession of people since Pentecost, people who handed over their faith to people. You have got to have offices of ministry and gifts. You have got to have Scripture, which is the product of the oral preaching of the early church, which they did not have, but we have. It is the closest that we can get to the apostles. That is why Scripture is so important. There must be sacrament. All of this takes place in the life of worship. So if you want to talk about Scripture, tradition, and authority, the means by which Christ has been handed down to us authoritatively through history is in worship, which passes down the tradition. Because in worship you also have preaching. By saying that, I have at this particular point tried to portray a common basis, to equalize Protestants and Catholics and Orthodox, because we all have that. Now, you may say, well, there is additional tradition, data that has accumulated since then, and that is true.... Nevertheless at the bottom, we all have Jesus Christ, who has been handed down to us as the tradition in the life of the worship of the church. What do you think about that?

Student: The whole concept all of that is handed down in worship, as if to say nothing else is handed down in any other way but through worship...?

Webber: No, I am not excluding other methods at hand, but what I am doing is asking at what point in the life of the church do you find all of this coming together?

Student: Yeah, but that is like saying that worship is the only way that is handed down, not through things outside of the church like serving other people. No, it is not handed down. That is what it sounds like to me. See what I'm saying?

Webber: Worship is that activity of the church which reenacts those events in history which give her meaning. From that reenactment, it goes forth into the world to serve the Lord. So that service would be included in that, because the primary calling of the church is to be a worshipping community. That's at the bottom of everything. And I think we sense that ourselves as Protestants, because we say, "If you don't have your devotions," and we individualize this more, I think, than the Catholic or Orthodox tradition would. The life of devotion, the life of worship, must be at the bottom of everything that we do. Why evangelize if we don't pray? Why teach if it doesn't arise out of a worshipful attitude or approach toward God? Worship is absolutely primary. If you look into the imagery of the Old and New Testament, the insights of Isaiah and John, for example, when they appear into the heavens, what do they see happening there? Worship. The whole of the created order is gathered around the throne of God, ascribing worth to him, holy, holy, holy, Lord God of hosts. Therefore, our calling in life is also to describe worth and glory and honor to God. Worship includes the re-presentation of the life of God in history by which we are redeemed, which is principally centered around the Word.

Now it is the Word read and spoken, and the Word reenacted. The Eucharist, or the Lord's Supper, is a reenacting of the Word, because the Word isn't complete, as Saint John says in his Gospel, until the Word has been incarnated. So the Lord's Supper symbolically represents the incarnation of the Word, whereas preaching and the reading of the Scripture prior to that symbolically represents the revelation of God to us. But the revelation of God in the Word is not complete until the Word becomes incarnate and dwells among us, crucified and raised again for our salvation. The worship then presents the totality of the history of revelation, salvation history, Old and New Testament, in order that through that reenactment we might ascribe worth and praise and honor and glory to God. Worship is the means through which the Christ of history is communicated to us. So in our worship, all the way down here in 1979, the same Christ who was communicated to the apostles in the early church is communicated to us today, so that we become contemporaneous with that Christ and are brought into communication with the events in history that shape our lives and lend meaning and significance to the world in which we find ourselves.

Of course, we should do a whole course on the significance of worship, because the Protestant community has a very definite sense of the loss of meaning in worship. For us the church is a lecture hall, where doctor so-and-so, one of the great teachers of the Word, stands and intones, "Hello, brethren! Turn with me to Romans 11." Even that exaggerated voice gives a certain degree of credence. And off he goes for an hour, teaching. That is not worship. It is teaching. Or you go to another church that orients itself around giving you an emotional high. "Ladies and gentlemen, today Miss Bobby-wobby is going to sing for us." And Miss Bobby-wobby grabs the microphone, crooning, "*I come to the garden alone . . . .*" And we are sitting there eating it up. It is the television that has crept into the church. Rather than people sitting at home in front of their secular eucharistic tube, we shall bring them to the church and let them see the same kind of gyrating occurrence on Sunday. That is not worship. Or you might see the psychiatrist, musing all week about what's wrong with the brethren, declaring, "Dearly beloved, I know that you have come here today with many troubles on your mind and on your heart, and I am here today to say that Jesus, your friend, can take care of all of your problems. What you must do is have a great deal of faith in yourself. After all, God created you in his image. And if he is successful, you can be successful." My caricature may not be as accurate as I would like, because I had not thought of doing this.

Nevertheless, we have turned the church into a lecture hall, a psychiatric couch, an entertainment center, or an evangelistic tent. You basically hear the same sermon every Sunday. What I am trying to say is worship is something really different than that. I do not mean to say that in worship there cannot be something that teaches, nor that there should not be something that would heal us. I certainly hope that there is. Or that there is not something that reaches our being that speaks to us in the gospel of Jesus Christ and its saving reality. But worship is something different than entertainment or education or psychiatry. Worship is standing before the Creator of the universe, who has entered into the world he created for us, recreating the universe, and ascribing worth, glory, honor and praise to him. Not much of that happens in our Protestant circles. But I am not here to lecture about worship today. I am here to lecture about Scripture, tradition, and authority. But it is related. It is related because we do not see the connection between worship and Scripture, tradition, and authority, because we do not even know what worship is.

So there's the need for an orientation. If there is any branch of Christianity that needs to be revived today, it is the Protestant. It really is in bad shape. I do not mean to say that Catholicism and Orthodoxy are not in bad shape either. The whole kit and caboodle is in bad shape. But I do think that the Lord of the church is doing something unique today in all those branches of the church, and that things are beginning to happen, that the Holy Spirit is very much alive in the twentieth century, bringing renewal to all the churches. But I am poking in this particular way because I think that we emerge from a perspective that we are Bob Jones graduates, Wheaton College graduates, Johnson City Bible College graduates, Gordon Seminary graduates, Moody Bible Institute graduates. As though when we slip between the pearly gates, Peter is going to say, "What school did you graduate from?" . . . I am trying to break down this attitude of superiority that is just nothing more than pure, unadulterated, ungodly pride, and help us to recognize that by God's grace we belong to him, if we belong to him at all. It is by his grace, and not because we merited it through our Evangelical credentials.

And the same thing would apply to the Catholics and the Orthodox too, because you find the same kind of atmosphere there. So I am saying that that must go all the way across the board for the whole church of Jesus Christ. And by understanding that, it shapes and reshapes our attitude and our perspective so that we can be open to God, which is a very dangerous thing. The system closes this up, does not allow us to be open to God.

We must break down the system, all the systems, in order that we can be open to God, because God is a maverick. He does not allow himself to be closed into a system. And the moment we think that we have got him all locked in, he breaks down the doors and he is gone. And he pops up in the most unexpected places, like the Catholic Church . . . or like, on occasion, the Evangelical church . . . or even the Orthodox Church. So what I am trying to do is sort of level things out a bit.

Anyway, back to Scripture, tradition, and authority. Now that I have said that, I would like to say one more thing before we try to get into a comparison of Orthodox, Catholic, and Protestant, and that is to show you that indeed what I am talking about does have some biblical precedent. I want to take you to 2 Thessalonians 2:15. I want us to put what I am going to comment on in context. Second Thessalonians 2:15 was probably written about AD 51. . . . Then I want to take you to 1 Corinthians 15, which was probably written around AD 57. And then I want to take you to the pastoral epistles, in particular to 2 Timothy, which was written at the end of Paul's life, and there is some debate as to whether Paul was put to death around the AD 64 or 68. So let's simply put 64 or 68 or somewhere in between, but in general we are seeing a chronological development. Let's begin with 2 Thessalonians 2:15 and try to interpret this in terms of tradition. Paul writes, "So then, brethren, stand firm and hold to the traditions which you were taught, whether by word of mouth or by letter from us."[1] Note that he speaks of traditions as oral and written.

Let's try to pinpoint this. What is he talking about when he talks about oral and written traditions that he wants these people to hang on to? See, a tradition is not only something that you pass down, but it is something that you hang on to. These two things are going on at the same time. First, if you look at the epistles, you will find that there is a stark contrast between the epistles and the Gospels. That contrast is that the epistles offer no information about Jesus in his earthly life. Where do you find in the epistles stories about Jesus? You do not. They are all contained in Matthew, Mark, Luke, and John, which incidentally, were written mostly after the epistles were written. The epistles were written before the Gospels. How do you understand that? Well, the general consensus of New Testament scholarship is the reason why the epistles do not contain stories about the life of Jesus is because the life of Jesus was communicated already by oral tradition, namely by oral preaching.

Let's go back and take a look at this business with Paul. He goes up into Thessalonica on his second missionary journey and preaches. What did he preach? He probably preached the same kind of stuff that he was preaching in the synagogue, which would be an interpretation of Christ in reference to Old Testament passages of Scripture. A description of his life, a description of his death and resurrection, and an interpretation of that for salvation. Paul says, "Hang on to the oral tradition." That is to say, hang on to the oral original preaching that I gave you, as well as the written tradition. What would be the written tradition? Well, we know that when he wrote 2 Thessalonians, which may very well have been—1 Thessalonians was probably the first letter that he wrote, unless you would put Galatians at the end of the first missionary journey, and there is some debate on that—but in general I think Christian scholarship would say that 1 Thessalonians is at best his second letter, and many people would say that it is his first letter. And it could have been the first epistle written, depending on where you put James, which possibly preceded that. At any rate, here we have a very early epistle, 1 Thessalonians, which was written to the Thessalonian Christians from Corinth, when Paul arrived at Corinth, instructing them about certain things. It appears that they misunderstood the instruction of Paul in the letter. The instruction had something to do with the second coming of Christ, therefore he writes 2

---

1. 2 Thessalonians 2:15, NASB.

Thessalonians to straighten out the misunderstanding that was provoked by 1 Thessalonians, and he says hang on to the oral and written tradition. Apparently, what he is speaking about is that oral tradition would represent the preaching about Christ, which would include the stories, the events, the interpretation of his life and death. And the written tradition would simply be 1 Thessalonians, which he is probably looking at as already part of the tradition of the church. That is the first, earliest use of the word *tradition*.

Student: Do you think he was also including, in terms of written tradition, the entire Old Testament?

Webber: That is possible, yeah. . . . That would be correct, because the Old Testament was regarded as the tradition of the church, since they were interpreting the Old Testament in their preaching and understanding of Christ in terms of the Old Testament roots. Let's take a look at 1 Corinthians 15, which is written as a result of some people feeling that the resurrection never really occurred. And the Apostle Paul is writing to straighten them out about this. And this is what he says in 1 Corinthians 15:3-4: "For I delivered to you as of first importance what I also received, that Christ died for our sins according to the Scriptures, and that He was buried, and that He was raised on the third day according to the Scriptures."[2] First, note that he said, "I delivered what I received." There is a sense in which Paul is saying, "Okay, something was handed down to me. What was handed down to me I delivered." He talks about them holding fast in verse 2, for example, "Now I make known to you, brethren, the gospel which I preached to you, which you also received, in which you also stand, by which also you are saved, if you hold fast the word which I preached to you, unless you believed in vain."[3] In other words, there is a threefold development that we always need to keep in mind: I received it. When I received, I delivered. You hold it. While he does not say it here, what is going to come out in the pastoral epistles is the fourth development, which is to pass it on, hand it down. . . . This is the theology of the early church. . . . See what is happening?

The second thing that I want you to notice about 1 Corinthians 15 is really very interesting. I have already read it, but I want to comment on it again. Note what he received, what he delivered, what he is asking

---

2. 1 Corinthians 15:3-4, NASB.
3. 1 Corinthians 15:1-2, NASB.

them to hold, and what he later asks them to pass down. Christ died for our sins. He was buried. He was raised on the third day in accordance with the Scriptures. The death, the burial, and the resurrection of Christ. What do we have here? We have the basic content of Christ. If we say, as some people say, "No creed but Christ. No law but love." Ever heard that? Take that idea in your hand and throw it down on the floor and stomp on it, because it is a lousy idea. Why is it a lousy idea? Not because if you say I believe Christ, that it is a meaningless statement, unless you also talk about the content. . . . I believe Christ, who is the second person of the Godhead, fully God, fully human. Died. Buried. Rose again. Ascended into heaven. Sitteth on the right hand of the Father. He will come again for our salvation. In other words, there is content through the tradition. So when we talked about passing down Christ, we talk about passing down the content. It is interesting that immediately in the early church you begin to see this content form. The interesting thing about this in the content, in the death, burial, and resurrection, is that this content forms the basis for later creeds. In particular I am thinking about the rule of faith or later the Apostles' Creed.

I believe in God, the Father Almighty, creator of heaven and earth; and in Jesus Christ, His only Son Our Lord, who was conceived by the Holy Spirit, born of the Virgin Mary, suffered under Pontius Pilate, was crucified, died, and was buried. He descended into hell; the third day He rose again from the dead . . . etc., etc.

What is happening is that there is a summary taking place. So you can get into all your stories about how Jesus raised Lazarus from the dead and how Jesus walked on the water, conversations that Jesus had with Peter, all the things that happened during the Passion. You are receiving a voluminous amount of material. What do you do with all of that? What do you do with the epistles that are written to particular churches with particular problems? All that is part of the tradition, but the tradition is growing. It is becoming vast. How do you take that vast body of tradition and begin to hone in to some kind of a summary?

Student: Reduce it?

Webber: Yeah. It is a kind of reduction. It is not the reductionism of the twentieth century, but it is a reduction which seeks to discover the framework of historic Christianity. And the framework of historic Christianity develops out of this particular model that Paul sets forth in 1 Corinthians

15 and grows into what we call the Apostles' Creed. So that the Apostles' Creed is an authoritative summary. It is an authoritative summary of the truth of the New Testament. It is not the whole thing. It is not all the tradition, but it is the summary statement of the tradition. If that is the case, it is important for us to recognize that at the very bottom level of the idea of Scripture, tradition, and authority in the Protestant, the Orthodox, or Catholic world, there is this deposit which I have described up here. And the summary of that deposit in the creedal statement, particularly the Apostles' Creed. Now it is a lot more complicated than that. I am going through an awful lot of bypassing, an awful lot of developments in the early church, to get you to this point, but I can guarantee you that I could, you know, work through a lot. . . . One other thing before we take a break. . . . I think I will erase all this because I am going to draw some nice little circles for you. In the context of tradition, we start like this. We put Christ at the center. Then, immediately after Christ, we put the apostles, because Christ handed himself over to the apostles. Now in the apostles we want to develop this so that you have oral preaching. You would have the offices immediately. Then the gifts. And you would also have the sacrament. Beyond that, as the church begins to develop, you have the written records. I want to put the written records out here because they are extremely important, next to the apostles. Beyond the written records, then you begin to get the summaries of faith, such as the early creeds, and you could include the Apostles' Creed. Beyond the summaries, you are now getting into ecumenical creeds. And here we include the two creeds that we talked about, the Nicene Creed and the Chalcedonian Definition, both of which define for us the Trinity and Christology. Beyond that, we are getting into the interpretations of the Fathers.

As you can see, you could have an Eastern interpretation or you could have a Western interpretation. . . . Beyond the interpretations of the Fathers, you could start getting into what we will call systematic theologies. Now in the systematic theologies you could have Aquinas, Luther, Calvin, Arminius, etc., etc. Beyond that, because of the Reformation, you get into confessional statements. These confessional statements could be something like the Augsburg Confession of Faith, or the Heidelberg Confession of Faith, or the Westminster Confession of Faith. All of these are confessions that develop during the time of the Reformation. Beyond that, you can get into a variety of Protestant movements. You could get into Pietism. Revivalism. Out of that arises denominationalism. Beyond that, you get into specific local interpretations like dispensationalism or a host of other possibilities.

Student: That's good, but again that entire interpretation of tradition is from a Protestant Evangelical perspective. The Catholic Church, at least up until Vatican II, would not see it that way at all.

Webber: See it which way?

Student: They wouldn't see it as a series of concentric circles. They would see it more as a tree. The Catholic church is at the bottom going up and so forth, and the branches being Protestantism or something like that splitting off from the true mother church. . . . There is no way that I can conceive the old diehards as interpreting the Christian church's experience as concentric circles.

Webber: I do not mean to offer the concentric circles at this point as a principle of interpretation, but as a chronology of development.

Student: What I'm saying is that this is looking down the tunnel of 2,000 years of Christianity from a purely Christian or a purely Protestant Evangelical telescope. I don't think a Catholic would look at it this way at all. . . .

Webber: I am not setting it up as a method of interpretation. I am setting it up as a means by which we can come back after the break and start talking about how the Protestant, the Catholic, or the Orthodox would view those circles. You are right in what you have said, but I did not mean to convey that particular point of view at this moment. Are you ready for a break? It's hot in here. It's always hot in here. Can we open the doors or something?

***

Webber: We are going to talk about the Protestant, Catholic, and Orthodox interpretation of these concentric circles. . . . What would a Catholic say? Who wants to start? What is the Catholic view of Scripture, tradition, and authority . . . ? The church, which receives the Scripture, wrote the Scripture, has the right to interpret the Scripture, so that the interpretation is dynamic to this whole process. As a matter of fact, it is the church that was immediately interpreting the Scripture. The Scripture is already itself an interpretation of the tradition because the Scripture is an interpretation of Christ, which was handed down to the apostles and passed down in the life of the church. As you move through history, then, it is the responsibility of the church to continually interpret the Scripture. That could be rule one, which is a very good point. Let's call it the original tradition. The thing that I want to emphasize, from the Catholic point of view, is that the tradition which develops is always interpreted in coinherence—here comes that word again—with the original deposit. The Catholic would insist that they are not developing a new tradition, but that the traditions that they developed grow from the Scripture itself, from the original deposit.

Student: Could not the Protestants also say that the church interprets the original tradition? What I'm trying to get at is who is the church? From the Catholic viewpoint, would this be the hierarchy from the pope down?

Webber: The church in this respect would be the official interpreters of the tradition.

Student: So it wouldn't be the whole church. It would be just the official interpreters in the church.

Webber: See, that is where we get ourselves involved in the complexity of this thing. I want to take you back to AD 450 for a moment and give you the Canon of Vincent of Lérins. It is called the Vincentian Canon. Any of you ever heard of the Vincentian Canon? Vincent of Lérins in 450 said something that goes like this: "Don't be greedy. I look around and see so many interpretations. Augustine says this. St. John Chrysostom says that. Gregory of Nazianzus says this. St. Basil says that. Then there are all these crazy heresies. You've got the Montanists and the Arians and all of these others. Valentinas and Nestorius and all of these other guys. My head is splitting. I'm going nuts." What does he do? He came up with three very interesting approaches to this thing. He says there are three rules which we apply in the life of the church to the interpretation: 1) antiquity; 2) consensus; and 3) universality. He expressed it like this, "That which is believed always, everywhere, and by all." In other words, this "always, everywhere, and by all," really is not a top-down authority. It is not the magisterium[4] standing up, saying, "Thou shalt all believe the following." But rather, that which is believed is like a grassroots emergence. This is

---

4. Magisterium means teaching authority, especially of the Roman Catholic Church.

the original idea. It is a grassroots consensus and emergence which hangs into what everybody has always believed in reference to antiquity and is affirmed by the teaching office of the church and declared to be the truth.

Student: Are you saying that no people who have believed the orthodox truth of the Church were ever condemned by the Church? Was what had been believed by all, always and everywhere, ever been condemned by the Church? I'm talking about the Catholic Church community.

Webber: I do not know all the details of the history of the Church to be able to say yes or no to that. There are points at which the Catholic Church in history has itself gone apostate and was then corrected. Maybe there was an apostate bishop or an apostate pope or something like that. But there is always a kind of self-correcting that is going on in the context of the church. Let's apply it to some specific questions and see what we come up with. Is Jesus Christ God? That is a very simple one, but it is a good place to start. *That which has been believed always.* Antiquity. The church has always believed that Jesus Christ is God. *Everywhere.* All the way around the world, wherever you go in the Roman Empire, people are saying Jesus is God, confessing to this Jesus. *And by all.* Everybody agrees to that. And then the Nicene Creed, the Chalcedonian Definition. . . .

Let's take a more difficult problem, the Immaculate Conception. Of course, that is affirmed in the twentieth century by [Pope] Pius back in 1930 or so. If you want to have a truly ecumenical belief, you would have to say that that is not believed by all, everywhere, always. For a Catholic position, all Catholics, always, everywhere, and all, have believed that. The argument of Pius at this particular point would be that the concept of Immaculate Conception is not a concept that emerged in the twentieth century, where all of a sudden the twentieth century realized, "Oh! The Immaculate Conception of the Virgin Mary!" The argument would be that somehow that is rooted in apostolic teaching. That the church never, ever, never, ever, never, never affirmed something that is not rooted in apostolic teaching and therefore in Scripture. The problem is that the Catholic Church has in fact at times not followed that point of view. But neither has the Protestant church. For example, when you come up to the sixteenth century, you have written in the in the Council of Trent that the authority of the Church is *partum* scripture and *partum* tradition. That is like partly Scripture and partly tradition, so that you would have Scripture and tradition. This is the way it appears. Now tradition becomes something other than Scripture. It is in addition to Scripture from that point of view.

The Catholic Church has sometimes slipped into that, but in the Vatican II decrees, they are trying to get back to a more original conception of the relationship between tradition and Scripture, and that is to say, that only those traditions which are rooted ultimately in Scripture are acceptable to the Catholic [Church]. I have not followed this in great detail. I simply happen to know that a lot of the traditions with a small "t"—I want to make a distinction between tradition with a capital T and lower case t—that the Catholic Church has rolled back and erased and declared not to be traditions many of their traditions since Vatican II. A lot of Protestants do not realize that. They are checking out the traditions by Scripture, because they regard Scripture to be the source of tradition.

Student: They are also considering the Apocrypha as Scripture.

Webber: That is true. They are also considering the Apocrypha as part of Scripture. So there are different traditions with the lower case in the Protestant and Catholic and Orthodox world. There are several different points of view that have occurred in the history of the Catholic church, so it is difficult to pinpoint. If you are talking about Counter-Reformation Catholicism, tradition is added to Scripture. If you are talking about ancient Catholicism, tradition is coinherent with Scripture and only that which is taught in Scripture is to become part of the tradition. If you are talking about contemporary Vatican II Catholicism, there is an attempt to get back to the patristic notion. But in the process of that there is an unevenness in the Catholic point of view. Attend one church, and the tradition is over Scripture. Another church the Scripture is over tradition. Another church is going to be coinherence of Scripture with the tradition of the church.

Let's talk about the differences. Let's take a look at the Orthodox position. Who cares to venture a point of view in regard to the Orthodox in regard to tradition? Maybe the best thing for me to do in reference to the Orthodox is to read a statement from Georges Florovsky, because it is such an integrated approach. Florovsky writes in his article, "Scripture and Tradition: An Orthodox Point of View,"

> Now, tradition is described in the following sentence, "The true believers transmit to each other—and one generation to the

> other—by word and example, the teaching of faith, the law of God, sacraments and holy rites."[5]

Here is an idea that the church hands down the church. Let me read another statement.

> The term tradition is used in the *Catechism* only in order to clarify the manner of propagating and preserving divine revelation.[6]

See the difference? Tradition is not therefore "a body of material," additional material, but rather it is the manner of passing it down.

> It is the *paradosis*, the handing down of what God chose to disclose and communicate to men. It is not a particular source of truth and doctrine. Revelation is adequately recorded in scripture. But scripture is, as it were, "stored" or "deposited" in the church. On the other hand, tradition is equated with the mind and continuous memory of the church. And in this sense it is the guiding principle and criterion of scriptural interpretation. Accordingly, tradition does not and cannot add anything to Scripture, but only elicits what is contained in Holy Writ and puts it in the right perspective. The Scriptures "belong" to the church, are committed to her and not to individual leaders. A faithful guide is required for true exegesis. The church catholic is that guide. Or in other words, Scripture is given and preserved *in* tradition. Tradition and scripture are inseparable.[7]

What Florovsky is doing here—and incidentally, the Catholics tend to do this too—is that they see the church, and within it is Scripture and tradition, so that you want to talk in terms of a dynamic relationship existing between Scripture, church, and tradition, that there is a kind of dynamic interrelationship between these three that as the life of the church flows forth in history as the church hands over the church, the church is always handing over the interpretation of the Scripture to the world in which it finds itself. There is more ambivalence here, because it is a dynamic conception rather than a static conception. A static conception would say something like, "There is the Scripture. Here is tradition. Here is the church."

---

5. Florovsky, "Scripture and Tradition," 288.
6. Florovsky, "Scripture and Tradition," 289.
7. Florovsky, "Scripture and Tradition," 289.

Student: Is that because the view is that the church is Christ, and you cannot separate them?

Webber: Right. If you do not have any understanding of the church—and this is why I discussed the theology of the church last week prior to discussing Scripture, tradition, and authority from the ancient perspective. The Catholic and Orthodox Churches have tried to maintain this ancient perspective. Maybe it has gotten lost along the way, because sometimes it becomes clouded over. But in the ancient conception, you always think of the integrated understanding of the church and Scripture tradition. You do not pull them apart. In Counter-Reformation Catholicism, they were pulled apart. So you have the Scripture here, the tradition as another source of truth here, and the Church which hangs over both the Scripture and the tradition, giving it its straight interpretation. See what I mean? Now they are trying to correct that. Let's put it this way. Scripture is in a box. Tradition is in another box. This is bad Roman Catholicism at this point. And the church is up here, sort of over both. Now in the Orthodox. . . . Let's go to our circular position. When we were talking about authority last week in terms of circular position, you would have church, Scripture, and tradition. I am trying to present a dynamic interrelatedness of it, so that church and Scripture and tradition are always properly working together. Again, when Orthodoxy goes bad, so to speak, you get this schema too. In the Protestant point of view, what you have is Scripture, tradition, and church. Again, a sort of breaking apart of these things. For example, you have Luther's concept of *sola scriptura*, the Scripture alone as the final touchstone of authority. The point that I want us to keep in mind is that when Orthodoxy and Catholicism are working right, they also have a strong emphasis on Scripture. But it is always Scripture in the church, understood through the interpretation of the church, which becomes her tradition. But the tradition is never apart from Scripture in the church, for they exist coherently, and that is what both the Catholic and the Orthodox church are trying to recapture now in the twentieth century.

Let's take a closer look at the Protestant point of view and Luther's view. Try to understand Luther's view in context. First of all, in understanding the original Protestant point of view, I think it is necessary for us to understand that by the time you get to the late medieval period, you have something that looks like this: the church, tradition, and Scripture. This is a fourteenth- and fifteenth-century concept. Scripture is really far in the background. The caricature that we seem to have today of Roman Catholicism is the caricature of a Roman Catholicism gone wrong in the fourteenth and fifteenth centuries. Somehow the Protestant memory will never get beyond that. We have locked all the poor Protestants and Catholics in the fourteenth and fifteenth centuries, and that is a terribly wrong thing to do. What occurred is that Luther could not find in his own experience of the gospel in either church or tradition. He found it in the Scripture. Now there is one thing that I want us to keep in mind. You did not have the press. You did not have a local Tyndale House who was able to publish millions of *Living Bibles*[8] or $3 million for somebody to publish the New International Version of the Holy Bible, the King James, or the American Standard, all the numerous translations that were just not available. The Scripture was only available in the monastery, and then maybe only one copy, because they had to copy the whole thing by hand. The moment the Gutenberg press makes print available, and they are able to print the Scripture, all of a sudden people become verbally oriented. They can read. They can look at it, they can study it. It is not just hearing it or occasionally hearing about the epistles of Paul, or this epistle or that epistle, which people lived and died and never saw. At best the church would have only one Scripture and maybe not even the whole Scripture, incidentally bolted, not chained, to its pulpit so that nobody could steal it.

Student: A couple of years back we were going through a town and we wanted to find a French Bible. We asked and asked, and some people told us they had never seen one. And finally somebody said, "Well, if you go ask in this local Catholic church, they might have one." So we went there, and the priest went back in the back room for like forty-five minutes, and they finally found this Bible and brought it out. I see the same thing happening today. Where's the big change that everybody is talking about taking place?

Webber: Well, it has certainly taken place in the States. And it is also taking place in other parts of the world, and there are many agitators for this within the Catholic reform movement. The Bible is becoming gradually circulated to the people. For example, *The Living Bible* has a Catholic edition, and they sold millions of copies. You are right. A lot of this is still witnessed today in Europe and particularly the Third World.

---

8. Tyndale House Publishers first published *The Living Bible* paraphrase in 1971, almost eight years before Dr. Webber taught this class.

At any rate, going back to the sixteenth century, [what] I am trying to do is put the Protestant notion into perspective and help us understand why the Protestants went the way they did.

When Luther discovered the Scripture and was able to read it in the original languages, all of a sudden, he saw how the Scripture was very much different than the church and the tradition, because there had been a lot of accumulated traditions that were bogus in the fourteenth and fifteenth centuries. So Luther went to the extreme—no, I should not say that it is an extreme within that context. I think it was necessary within that context. He simply saw the Scripture as being so much against what he had been taught, that the Scripture kind of cancelled out everything that he had been taught. And thus he raised the Scripture up here, and put church and tradition down here as being basically meaningless. Out of that came this concept of *sola scriptura*, which put a cleavage between that coherent relationship—Scripture, tradition, and authority—and set the Protestant movement off in a direction in which it did not see the relationship between church and tradition but saw only Scripture.

Now one more comment here that I want to get some feedback on this. As a result, let's move down now into the twentieth century. We have had our individual interpreters of scripture come along. And so you have Calvinistic interpretation, the Arminian interpretation, the dispensational interpretation, the covenantal interpretation, the Evangelical interpretation, the Baptist interpretation, Webber's interpretation, etc. So what have we got now? Let me tell you what we have got. We are back in the same bag again. Amen? We are back in the bag of having a new set of traditions that hide the Word of God. We have to break down those new sets of traditions (with a small "t"), because they are misinformed. They are not traditions that care about what has the church always taught. Where is consensus, universality, and antiquity? It is ME. Graduate of such-and-such a seminary, holder of all these PhDs and ThDs and blah, blah, blah, telling all you people how you are to interpret scripture. And believe you me, you had better believe what I am telling you. Well, sir, how long has this been believed? I stand in continuity with St. Paul and St. John. It is the leap. What we do is we leap back through 2,000 years of church history and development of Scripture. We leap, we read the Scripture with our own grid, and we accuse poor Paul of believing or teaching exactly what we believe today, without any continuity, without any care for the Holy Spirit in the life of the church. It is a pneumatological problem. If I bathe myself in the Holy Spirit, he will give ME the answer. This is what he said to ME. You see this going on in the little coffee klatches. Have you ever gone to a coffee klatch where you sit around so-and-so's living room and balance the Evangelical teacup on your knee? "Shall we all turn to 1 John chapter 3, verses 1–5? What does it say to you? What does it say to you? What does it say to you?" They pool their ignorance for an hour, then everybody leaves without one care about how the church interprets the passage. Existential, subjectivistic, privatistic, individualistic religion run wild. And the strongest person, the one holding the most degrees and the greatest amount of wisdom, acquires his following and has his heyday, because he becomes the tradition. I will stop at that point. Let's see what you have to say.

Student: Getting back to Luther. I think your interpretation, frankly, doesn't account for the fact that he did not want to leave the Catholic Church, and up to a certain point he sought for reform within, so you know this total new version of church, tradition, and Scripture in the basement. . . . I don't know if that is totally valid. . . .

Webber: I agree with you, and what you are doing is you are asking me to give a little bit more information there, which I should give because I am lumping together Luther and what came after Luther, because I really see a lot of these things occurring, not so much in the sixteenth [century], but in the seventeenth century, but that they are somewhat initiated by the necessary Protestant rejection of the kind of tradition that grew in the fourteenth and fifteenth centuries. So you are right in that. It is what Luther initiated more than what Luther himself created.

Student: What you were saying about people getting together for coffee and spreading all sorts of different opinions that often are very contrary. . . . Well, not necessarily in such an informal manner, but many times in such a diversified manner I have heard in the Protestant perspective, I have heard people giving all these documentations of not just Paul and John, the apostles jumping back to Scriptures like you said, but traditional people, back through the years, given people out of each century that had held the opinion, whatever that may be. I am saying that if all these different various opinions can be supported by certain men, and even Calvin and the Catholic Church, they both quoted Augustine and they would come out with pretty diversified opinions about different things. I do not see how you can say that just the Protestants are jumping tradition, any more than you can say that just the Catholics in the fourteenth and fifteenth centuries were jumping Scripture. I do not see where you are coming from with that.

Webber: I guess what I am trying to say is that, and I am not sure if this is exactly what you're saying or not, but that as Protestants we have in fact created our own tradition, and that we do have as much a tradition as anybody else, except that we refuse to admit it. And that tradition for many of us is, in fact, over Scripture, that we do read the Scripture with the eyes of tradition. I am speaking to some extent out of my own experience as well. Having attended a Calvinistic school, a dispensational school, a Lutheran school, or a fundamentalist school like "Joe Bones,"[9] every one of those schools does have its tradition. And you better believe that you've got to interpret it through that particular tradition. I went to Philadelphia College of the Bible, for example, and that is a strong dispensational-oriented school. And you do not interpret something apart from the dispensational interpretation. I remember challenging several teachers, who just got furious with me. The point was, this is what dispensationalism says. I mean, who are you as a student to sit there and challenge this notion? Oh yes, sir. It was a system superimposed on the Scripture. We can do that as a Calvinist or we can do that as an Arminian. When John Owen[10] says, "How do you interpret 'for God so loved the world that he gave his only begotten son, that whosoever believeth in him should not perish'? How do you interpret the word *world*?" And [then] he says, "Well, it means the world of the elect." Because he has got to hang on to predestination and election, it seems to me that he is interpreting through a system. Let it say what it says. It is the same with the Arminian when he comes along and dismisses the teaching of election and predestination. Let it say what it says. And the fact is that it appears to say some very ambivalent things.

So I guess what I am saying is that we beat up the Catholic and we beat up the Orthodox for their view of tradition, but goodness, we have got the same thing in our system. We have set ourselves up for it, so that we are all heretics, really. And we all need to take a good look at what has happened in history and go back to that original deposit, and make Christ our tradition. But that is not a contentless Christ.

---

9. "Joe Bones" was Dr. Webber's nickname for Bob Jones University, where he earned his bachelor's degree.

10. John Owen was an English Puritan theologian who lived 1616–1683.

We do have to recognize that there is such a thing as tradition and traditions. This is what chapter 7 in *Common Roots*[11] is all about. I do not know if you are reading that stuff or not, but if you are bothering to read the material that you are supposed to read for this class, it affirms and expands the kind of stuff that I am talking about. In chapter 7 of *Common Roots* is a very, very important principle that helps us to break down this business of setting ourselves up as being the only persons who really follow the scripture. We begin to see that we impose on the Scripture a tradition.

Student: One of the difficulties I have with the reading and understanding of it is that your explanation of tradition did not come across to me in the same way as it does here, and that left me with a kind of a bad taste in my mouth after reading the book. But as I understand it here, I take my Evangelical stand and say "amen" to it.

Webber: Verbal communication is always more easily understood than written communication. Maybe if you went back and read chapter 7 again you would see it a little bit differently. You could see it in the light of what I'm saying here. But it is compressed over against some expansion here. What do you think of this? Do you think that we are going down the wrong path here? I am trying to beat up the Protestants.

Again, what I am trying to do is to help us to see that there really is not much difference, that the basis of our view of tradition, except that we do not use the word *tradition*, is really back here in this New Testament concept.... And if anything, we need to rediscover the tradition of the church, which is Jesus Christ. And that the way in which he is handed down to us in the life of the church is in the worship of the church, which constitutes preaching and sacraments and offices and gifts and ministry....

---

11. See Webber, *Common Roots*.

13

Orthodoxy, Catholicism, Protestantism

SESSION #10, FEBRUARY 8, 1979

Webber: Discussing the subject of the sacraments, the first thing that we ask is why do we use that word? Why not use the more traditional Protestant word *ordinance*? The word *ordinance* of course comes from the word "to order." And the idea is that Jesus ordered baptism and the Lord's Supper, therefore these are called ordinances. It is something that we are ordered to do in the church. But I want to take a look at this word "sacrament" and try to break down some of the caricatures that we have in our mind about it. Let's get back to the original meaning.

So let's begin our class today by looking at the word *sacramentum* and try to find the meaning. The Latin word comes from two words. *Sacra*, of course, is the word from which we derive our word "sacred," which is literally translated as "holy." And the suffix, *mentum*, means "to make." So it is "to make holy." The word itself, *sacramentum*, or sacrament, is not a bad word. It is not an evil word. It is not pagan or Roman or anything of that sort. It just happens to be a nice, good Latin word, which means "to make holy." I do not think any of us have any problems with that, do we? All of us realize that part of the whole Christian pilgrimage is becoming holy. So a sacrament is that which makes you holy. In order to expand on the idea of this word, let's take a second step and see it in the Latin Vulgate. The interesting thing is that in the Latin Vulgate, the New Testament word *mystery*, the Greek *musterion*, is always translated as the word *sacrament*. Wherever that appears, the mystery is called the sacrament. When we think about the mystery of Christ, we think about the sacrament of Christ. One of the ways in which we can get a handle on the early concept of the word *sacrament* and its usage is to take a look, for example, in the New Testament at the way in which the word *mystery* is used. I do not intend to go through the entire [New] Testament, but the book of Ephesians uses the word *sacrament*, or *mystery*, more than any other book. So what I want to do is turn to the book of Ephesians and simply quote from those sections that use the word *mystery*, and that will give us an idea of how it is used in the early church.

First of all, starting with Ephesians 1:9, "He made known to us the mystery of His will, according to His kind intention which He purposed in Him."[1] Let's write "mystery of his will." This is a slow way of getting at the meaning of this, but I think it is quite important for us. The mystery of his will.

Secondly, let's look at Ephesians 3:3, ". . . that by revelation there was made known to me the mystery, as I wrote before in brief."[2] In that context, it is basically the mystery of Christ as known to the Gentiles. So we will write "mystery of Christ."

Let's jump over to Ephesians 5:32, "This mystery is great; but I am speaking with reference to Christ and the church."[3] So in 5:32 it is the mystery of Christ and the church. Since we have written Christ down, we will add the word *church*.

Then in chapter 6:19, ". . . and pray on my behalf, that utterance may be given to me in the opening of my mouth, to make known with boldness the mystery of the gospel."[4] The "mystery of the gospel" is generally referring to the mystery of proclamation, or the mystery of preaching. What we see in front of us is a rather expansive notion of the idea of sacrament. When we look at this from the perspective of the early church, as is translated in the Latin Vulgate, we would think in terms of the sacrament of God's will or the sacrament of Christ or the sacrament of the church, the church as sacrament, the gospel as sacrament, preaching as sacrament. It is a rather expansive notion, much, much larger than what we originally caricaturized sacrament to mean because even in a Catholic or Orthodox sense, we normally think in terms of seven sacraments. But here we have a much more expansive use in the early church. Reading the early Church Fathers, you find that there is an even more

---

1. Ephesians 1:9, NASB.
2. Ephesians 3:3, NASB.
3. Ephesians 5:32, NASB.
4. Ephesians, 6:19, NASB.

expanded concept. Believe it or not, the study of theology or doctrine is called the sacramental mystery. So what we have been engaged in over the past quarter is a sacramental exercise. The Christian life is a second good example. Prayer is a sacrament. So there is just simply an expansive notion of sacrament in the early church, and not just rather exclusive understanding that we seem to have today.

Student: Does the Greek word *mystery* really convey all of that, or were the translators of the Vulgate communicating something through their cultural grid?

Webber: You are picking up my language! That is a debatable question. First, let's go back to the meaning of the word *mystery* and try to delve into that. I realize that in today's theological world, the word *mystery*, particularly in the Evangelical Protestant church, is as much a no-no words as the word *sacrament*, because we think in terms of mystery cults, or the mysterious and ethereal. And of course, we are so rationally attuned, there are no mysteries. The mystery is gone, because our mind has figured it out. God gave us a mind. He gave you your mind, and he expects you to use it. You are created in the image of God. God has a mind, therefore you have a mind. Use it. That is the approach taken by rationalistic Protestantism. Well, I do not think very much of that idea.

But let's go back to the original concept of mystery. What does it mean? In the New Testament mystery means the event of Christ, and everything that entails what is related to Christ, the coming of God in Christ, the incarnation, the death, the resurrection, the expression and expansion of God's work beyond Israel into the Gentile world. It is all a great mystery, the mystery of God. Now connect that with this question. . . . Looking at this, how many sacraments are there? Did I see a hand back there, or are you scratching your eye?

Student: The Protestant church has two, and the Catholic Church has seven?

Webber: Nine sacraments! That is a quick way to come to it. How many sacraments do you think there are? How many think there are two, baptism and the Eucharist or the Lord's Supper?

Student: Is that two and more, or only two?

Webber: Two. I think that nobody is willing to put their neck on the line today. Listen, I didn't bring my axe, I don't have my matches.... Nobody thinks there are two. How many think that there are seven? How many think there aren't any?

Student: There are seven that are recognized by the Church, and I think there are more than that.

Webber: Okay, there are more than seven. How many want to say there are more than seven? How many of you are just afraid to say anything at all? One honest person.

Student: The whole idea here of sacrament is a problem for me, because we are taking it to mean "to make holy." Christ makes us holy positionally, as we learn in the Scriptures. He declares us to be holy.... I realize there is also the progressive holiness in which we become in this life more and more like Christ, so it is hard for me to understand, to try to accept a certain number on it or an infinite number, because I am not really sure what we are trying to say what the sacrament does. Because if I am already holy, I do not need to be made holy. There isn't anything I can do to make myself holier in that sense.... I sound very Protestant, don't I?

Webber: A real, budding theologian here! The question: how many sacraments are there?

Student: How many? There is one sacrament.

Webber: Let's work on this idea for just a moment. Remember what we did last week? Does anybody have any idea, from one week to another? Remember, we talked about tradition with a capital T. Christ. And that does not mean that we have reduced him to a nebulous figure, because when we talk about Christ, we are talking about a cosmic redeemer, and therefore there are many things that are understood when we mention the word *Christ* that includes a number of theological insights. So he is the tradition of the church, which is passed down in the church as Jesus Christ. Sacrament is the means by which one is made holy, and you were right when you said, "Hey, wait a minute, there is only one way that we are made holy, and that is through Jesus Christ." Baptism does not make you holy. Eucharist does not make you holy. Christ makes you holy. Not confession, not penance, not confirmation, not marriage, not holy orders, not unction. None of those make us holy. Only Jesus Christ. That is a very Evangelical, gospel-oriented point of view. Right? But that is a New Testament and early church notion. Only Christ makes us holy right now. Let me comment on that a little bit in terms of Tertullian before we begin expanding that idea. That definitely is the place at which we must begin, because it gives us the best meaning of this word, *sacramentum*, to make holy—only Christ makes holy—and it gives us the meaning of all of this, this is to say the Christocentric understanding of the will of God, of the church, the essence of the church, which is an extension of the incarnation. Christ and the church. Christ is the church. The gospel preaching. The essence of all of that is Christ.

Now Tertullian in the late second century argues for this concept. There is only one sacrament, so we can put Sacrament here with the capital "s." And he looks, for example, at the whole history of the world in terms of Christ, and I think all of us would agree that a Christocentric understanding of the universe puts Christ at the center of time, the center of space, the center of reality. He is the cosmic center of the universe, and therefore everything leads into Christ. Christ is the one who gives meaning and significance to life itself, and therefore we must not perceive anything outside of Jesus Christ. Rather, we perceive all things through Jesus Christ. This is what Paul is saying in Colossians 1. Christ is the creator of all things, whether things visible or invisible.[5] The second thing he says is "by him all things consist."[6] That is a very difficult notion for us to get a hold of, because we have no experience in terms of a cosmic perception of things. We have no way of really perceiving that, except to say that Christ is that power, Christ is that energy. It is the presence of Christ in which all things exist, through which all things find their meaning. And then the third thing that Paul says is that he reconciles all things,[7] so therefore Christ stands at the center of creation, the center of meaning, and the center of redemption. All things flow through him and out of him by remaining in him. Very Evangelical persuasion. Our buddy Tertullian looks back at the Old Testament and therefore sees that the Old Testament has what is called a sacramental character, because the Old Testament finds its fulfilled meaning in Jesus Christ. For example, what about the offices of the Old Testament? Examples? Well, there is prophet, priest, and king. Who fulfills that? Jesus is the ultimate Word of God. Jesus is the only mediator between man and God. Jesus is the

---

5. See Colossians 1:16.
6. Colossians 1:17, KJV.
7. See Colossians 1:20.

King and Lord of the universe. Look now at events. The major event of the Old Testament is the exodus. What is the real meaning of the exodus? The real meaning of the exodus is to be found in the cross in Jesus. The fulfillment of the exodus. Look at the ceremony of the Old Testament. For example, the whole worship ceremony, the way in which God makes himself known to us through the high priest and the Levites, etc. The sacrifices, the burnt offerings, the ark of the presence of God, and the Holy of Holies, even down to the vestments and the things that the priests wear. What is all the meaning of this? Well, when we read Hebrews, which says that all the meaning of this is to be found in Jesus Christ, so there is a sacramental character, you might say, to the entire Old Testament. Everything leads into Jesus Christ. . . . Tertullian says when we move from Christ out into the world, the same thing takes place, except that it is a movement outward, so that Christ is made known to us sacramentally, say in preaching, the Scriptures. Because all of these are means by which we are made holy, that is to say, they are not ends in themselves. Preaching is not an end in itself. Scripture is not an end in itself, and that is why it is very important not to be involved in bibliolatry, the worship of the Bible. But rather the Bible and preaching and the sacraments are means through which the saving reality of Jesus Christ is made known to us. You might call them the sacraments of my encounter with Jesus. . . . Just as you have tangible, visible means in the Old Testament, so you have tangible and visible means in the New Testament through which Christ is made known to us. But it is always Christ. It is not something else. It is not a thing in itself. It is always Christ. In that respect, of course, the church is the context. Back here, Israel is the context in which the tangible, visible means of God is made known to us. And here the church is a kind of sacrament in which God is made known especially and uniquely to us. Let's get a couple of comments on that before we move on. Did I give you an expanding notion of the sacraments, I hope?

Student: It seems like the same way in the Old Testament that people got carried away with the ceremony and the objects to the point where they began worshipping that, and in many ways we have done the same with our New Testament objects, our Evangelical habits, where we worship the things.

Webber: Since you brought that up, let me give you a good example. It seems to me that we have developed a kind of *ex opere operatum* approach to our new sacramentalism in Evangelicalism. I must be careful what I say. In the medieval church, baptism became a means by which one is saved. Baptismal regeneration. In a few cases, it is still carried on in some communities. We look at that and say, "Wait a minute. Baptism doesn't save. It is Jesus Christ." That external form of baptism is the expression of the visible, tangible expression of our faith. . . . But it seems to me that what we have done today is we have shifted baptism and Eucharist into an altar call. Decision-making. What day were you saved? "Oh, May 3, 1923." That is just nasty. No one else here would be that vintage. But yeah, 9:30 in the evening at Madison Square Garden. Sunday, 7:30. A datable moment, and then you sort of say, "Yes, okay," and just sit back and relax as a Christian. . . . So it is a kind of getting tripped up on the external. On the other hand, we ought not deny the reality of the external. We are getting ourselves into the form-spirit problem, which we are going to be looking at a little more closely as we get into the whole subject. We are not gnostic. "Pinch me and I say ouch."

There is the reality of the body, the reality of the physical and the material, which we must always deal with, and God works through the physical and the material, as is indicated in the incarnation, because God came to us in the physical and material. So there is no reason why God would not continue to come to us, make himself known to us, encounter us, in the physical and the material as he does in baptism, the Eucharist, and the other sacraments of the church. Let me summarize this and we will talk about it for a minute. . . .

It is kind of warm in here again today, isn't it? No? I feel my head nodding. There is a professor at the college who fell asleep while he was giving a lecture. That is really true. Isn't that something? I had a professor in graduate school who fell asleep during class while [he] was giving the lecture. It was really embarrassing. . . .

Okay, what we see is one sacrament, Christ. However, the church has also talked of two dominical sacraments. You know what the word *dominical* means, don't you? It means "of Jesus Christ as the Lord." These are the two sacraments which Christ himself enjoined upon his church. I like that word "enjoined," very Elizabethan. Then there are five church sacraments. We will call them ecclesiastical sacraments, if you want. Then you have the general approach to sacraments. Let's call it a general approach to sacramental living. That is to say, that all of life is sacramental in the sense that when one lives out one's life in terms of Christ at the center, then all of life becomes a sacred reality and not a secular thing.

What I would like to do is go into a discussion of the two dominical sacraments and the five church sacraments, and then come to a general understanding of Catholic, the Orthodox, and the Protestant position. This seems to me an awkward time to get into that. . . . Let's take a break.

***

Webber: What I would like to talk about this hour is to try to take a look at the Catholic, Orthodox, and Protestant concept of the sacraments. For the Catholic and Orthodox in particular, I want to try to put them into context, because the Catholic and the Orthodox both have this incarnational concept of ecclesiology, the idea that the church is an extension of Jesus Christ. If the church is a kind of extension of Christ in the world, as it states in the documents of Vatican II, and also you will find this in Orthodox teaching, the church is therefore a kind of sacrament. And they call it a kind of sacrament because we have specifically in the Orthodox and Catholic communion seven sacraments, and the church is not one of the sacraments, but it is a kind of sacrament. That is to say, that the church is the context in which the sacraments of our encounter with Jesus Christ occur. It is easy to see that that would come from that point of view. If you look at Cyprian's notion of the church, "He who hath not the church for his mother, hath not God for his father." Where, then, does one meet Jesus Christ? In the church. The idea is that in the church there are—and I want to emphasize this very strongly—visible and tangible means by which or through which Jesus Christ meets us. Visible and tangible means through which Jesus Christ meets us. That is the idea of the incarnation being extended, isn't it? Because God did not meet us in an appearance. Jesus was not some sort of phantom. He was here, flesh and blood. He ate, slept, drank, spoke, and got angry. A real person. Therefore if God comes to us in a real person, we can expect that God will continue to meet us in the material. There is a favorite saying by Teilhard de Chardin from his book *The Divine Milieu*, in which he says, "By virtue of the Creation, and, still more, of the Incarnation, nothing here below is profane for those who know how to see."[8] See, somehow we profane [the] material. We make it secular. We say the material is not really good, and therefore we have a low view of the body, a low view of the world, a low view of nature in a lot of our communities, because somehow we see the spirit as being something higher than the body, as belonging to another

---

8. Teilhard de Chardin, *Divine Milieu*, 66.

realm. But that is an absolute denial of incarnational reality and a denial, from a Catholic and Orthodox point of view, of the sacramental presence, or encounter, through the sacraments. Let's look at the seven sacraments in the church and talk about each one of them and what they mean.

Baptism. We are dealing, of course, with one of the dominical sacraments. Baptism in the early church is understood as our passage rite into Jesus Christ now. Let me comment in general on baptism, because there is a lot of material, and I am not exactly sure what I should not give you, simply because we could talk on baptism for hours. There is a lot of interesting material in the early church. But let me begin by saying that nowhere in the early church is it thought that baptism saves us. There is not a notion of "baptismal regeneration." Only Jesus Christ saves. I remember over at St. Barnabas a couple of years ago, Father Monroe gave a sermon at a baptism, which is really very interesting, because he stood before the crowd and preached a quite Evangelical sermon. He said, "Look, baptism does not save. Water does not save. All these external elements that we are going to be doing today, they do not save. Only Jesus Christ saves." Now that is a true Catholic persuasion of the early church. It is a true Orthodox persuasion. It is a true Protestant persuasion. . . . I have heard Catholics say that. I have heard Orthodox say absolutely the same thing. And that is the early church, New Testament, patristic[9] understanding of this point of view. There are a couple of additional things here that I must say about baptism coming from the early church. First, in the early church, there were two requirements for baptism, that it be the right baptism in terms of the external. Remember, we are talking about the internal and external. The two requirements of this are that it must be in the name of the Father, the Son, and the Holy Spirit. And the second requirement is that it must be a living water. Let's talk about this living water for just a moment. As a matter of fact, the word that is used is "living water." Come with me for a little walk through the woods. We are strolling down the path by a log cabin, when all of a sudden we come to a pool of stagnant water. Yuck. Green gross junk all over the top, little bugs scurrying across that water. Would you want to be baptized in that? Absolutely not. And if you were on a baptism tour, so to speak, and I was to take you to a water where you would be baptized, you would instinctively say, "No!" Why would you intuitively not want to be baptized in that water?

---

9. *Patristic* means of or relating to the early church fathers or their writings.

Student: If the person who is being baptized is seeking God, he will not care about the water. I am not trying to be picky, but the heart must [be] there, no matter the water.... If you don't want to be baptized in that kind of water, isn't that a kind of denial of carrying the cross of Christ?

Webber: No, no. I did not finish my story, and therefore I did not really get the whole thing out, because that is really not the point. The point that I am trying to make is that nobody wants to be baptized in dead, stagnant water. See, the whole business about water is that it is living. If you look at the theology of the early church, Tertullian wrote a treatise called *On Baptism*, and he develops a theology of water. The theology of water is that water is the seat of God's creativity. Tertullian goes back to the Genesis account of creating the world. God had separated the land from the water through creativity. Tertullian goes into the business of our first birth. We are born in water, and therefore it is no wonder that we also are born anew in water. The early translation of the of Jesus' statement to Nicodemus, "Except being born of water and the spirit," uses water in the physical sense. Protestants tend to interpret that as, "Well, you must first be born physically before you can be born anew spiritually." It refers to your water birth in the womb. But the early church understanding was that you bring in external and the internal together, even as Christ [did] in the incarnation, the external and the internal, the form and the spirit, the form and the divine, the human and the divine. The material and spiritual are brought together in Jesus Christ. Physical water, running water, living water, is the symbol of creativity in the Scripture, and therefore to be born of water and the spirit means to bring together form in spirit, that is to say, it brings together the external act and faith. Both are to be brought together.

Student: I would have a problem with being baptized in dirty water. Water symbolizes being buried with him in baptism, raised up into newness of life. If I were raised up out of the water, which is supposed to be a symbol of cleansing, with more dirt on me than before, this sort of defeats the symbol.

Webber: Yes, that is right. It is a symbol. It is the symbol of water, and nobody wants to be washed in filthy, dead, stagnant water. You want to be washed in clean water, because it is a symbol of the newness of life. In the early church baptism is always in the nude, and when you were baptized in this running water. You came up out of the water and you put on a new robe, which indicates when you take your clothes off, it is putting off the old man. Entering into the water of baptism is entering into our cleansing, and then the stepping out and putting on the new robe is taking upon ourselves the robe of righteousness in Jesus Christ. There was a lot of symbolism in the early church that we do not practice today, because we are more rationalistic, and we have gotten away from it. But the early church brings baptism together with faith and insists that both the external and the internal must be there. So to disregard baptism is really to disregard Jesus Christ. It is not just a matter of obedience, as we sometimes say, but in the early church it is a matter of a true identification with Jesus Christ by baptism in the water and faith in receiving the Holy Spirit.

An interesting thing happened to me a couple of years ago, which I think I would like to share with you about the subject of baptism. I had a very close friend who was saved as a Jewish boy and was immediately made a prize in the eastern area in which he lived. He was shuffled from church to church and became the Chuck Colson in that area, so to speak. Look at our prize convert. He spoke to all the youth groups and the churches, telling them how he had to suffer, etc., etc., as a Jewish boy becoming a Christian. When he came out to Wheaton for some reason or another, he lost his faith, and we used to spend lots and lots of time talking about the Christian faith. And I think he was genuinely trying to restore his Christian faith, although he is now an atheist. About two years ago he was at my house, and we were sitting in front of my fireplace talking, and I told him the story which I am now going to tell you. This is another story to which he responded. So there are two stories going here. Are you following? The story that I told him was this, that the previous week I had been asked by some students to celebrate the Eucharist with them, the Lord's Supper. So I took with me the later Christian Fathers and I quoted the early church's concept of the Eucharist and the importance of it. One of the things I quoted was that it was a hard-line rule in the early church that you could never take the Eucharist unless you had been baptized. As I was passing the bread and wine, I noticed that one girl did not receive the bread or the wine. She looked very troubled. She came up to me immediately after the eucharistic liturgy and said, "May I speak to you?" I said, "Sure." She said, "You noticed that I did not take the bread and wine. I didn't because I am not baptized. I never knew that one had to be baptized into Christ before one could receive the body and blood of Christ." I said, "That is the practice of the early church, and the practice of most churches today, except where there is a complete loss of historic Christianity." She said, "Well, I want to be baptized." And I said, "You should talk with your pastor at church about being baptized." She said, "No, I want to be baptized *now*." I said, "Okay." By this time most of the students were gone. I said, "Well, get your roommates," because in the early church you never baptized anybody without having a testimony as to that person's credibility. Does she believe? Does she live the life of orthodoxy and orthopraxis? So she zipped upstairs, brought down four or five girls with curlers in their hair, wearing their bathrobes. It was a sight to behold. So we went into a little room there, and they got some water. I said to her roommates, "Joy says she wants to be baptized. Can you confirm that she is indeed a believer in Jesus Christ?" They did. "Can you confirm that she does indeed follow after Jesus Christ and seek to live the Christian life?" So I baptized her in water in the name of the Father, Son, and Holy Spirit, and was desperately sorry that I did not have the bread and the wine lined up to serve the Eucharist immediately after, which is the proper thing to do from the early church perspective. Anyway, I told Steve, now back in my living room. He thought for a moment and said, "I want to tell you something now that I've never told you before about myself." I said, "Oh, what's that?" He said, "I never got baptized." I said, "Oh, that's interesting. Why is that?" He said, "Somehow I knew that if I were physically baptized, then that meant it was real. And I knew, from the very beginning, that it wasn't real." That really struck me, because this is what the early church is saying. Okay, you can make all of your external commitments, your spiritual pilgrimages and spiritual experiences, but unless you are willing to put it on the line and become baptized by water, through which one becomes identified with Jesus Christ and enters into the church, you have suppressed your relationship to Jesus Christ. I lecture on this up at the college every year, and there are a lot of students that end up getting baptized, because our churches somehow do not teach this. See the Protestant expression about baptism for just a moment. We are kind of gnostic when it comes to the external. We divorce the spiritual from the physical. But boy, if we did that with our Christology, what would we have? You would have a *whoo-whoo* Jesus, and nobody in the Evangelical world wants to do that. People bleed and die for the historic Jesus. Flesh and blood. Pinch him and he says, "Ouch." But we deny the significance of the physical and material and the visible in the other dimensions of the church, which is the body of Christ. How can you talk about anything without talking about the physical? How can you talk about love, for example, if any of you here happen to be in love, except by saying that love is expressed in physical terms? It affects the body. How can you talk about any kind of emotion—anger, for example? What happens when you get angry? The stomach knots up and the face reddens. Fists clench. All human emotions, all human reality, is almost as a spirit thing, love or anger or any of those expressions. Take the fruit of Spirit, love, joy, peace, long-suffering. They all have physical manifestation. Everything in life has a physical manifestation. The point about our identification with Jesus Christ, it has a physical manifestation in its baptism. I remember discussing this—today is story day—I remember discussing this with some people from the Bible Church. The Bible Church is split between those who believe in infant baptism, adult baptism, and no baptism at all. I remember how absolutely furious one woman got with me—I cannot believe *anybody* could get furious with me—for saying that the physical was important. She said, "I have never been baptized, and I want you to know that I do have Jesus Christ." What do you say to that? The early church says, unless you are willing to go through with water baptism, you do not really know Jesus Christ. I am not denying that they have Jesus Christ. I would not do that. But there was a sense. . . . And then I went on to talk about how we have split the secular from the sacred, the physical from the spiritual, in our world today, and we tend not to see the relationship between the two. Well, a couple of other things about baptism in the early church. For those of you who are Baptists, a word. There is concrete evidence to show that immersion was the preferable form. There is also no concrete indication of infant baptism until AD 220. So those are two things that we need to keep in mind while studying the early church. I cannot go into all the documents, obviously we do not have the time. Let me speak for a moment to the form in terms of immersion, sprinkling, and pouring. The earliest non-canonical document on the subject of baptism is found in *The Didache*, chapter 7, and it reads something like this:

> And concerning baptism, baptize this way: Having first said all these things, baptize into the name of the Father, and of the Son, and of the Holy Spirit, [Matthew 28:19] in living water. But if you have not living water, baptize into other water; and if you cannot in cold, in warm. But if you have not either, pour out water thrice upon the head into the name of Father and Son and Holy Spirit. But before the baptism let the baptizer fast, and

the baptized, and whatever others can; but you shall order the baptized to fast one or two days before.[10]

The important thing seems to accent the water and the triune, not the form of immersion or sprinkling. Why is that so? Well, the reason is because this is a document written in the East. If you have ever traveled East, Palestine or those parts, you realize that the East just does not have very much water. And you can live in places where there is no such thing as a running stream, and you have to get your water from wells. Well, in those kinds of situations, the best you can do is sprinkle or pour water on the head three times, because you do not have [much] water. However, again and again the early church documents say, if there is running water, which is usually a stream, then that is preferable. Generally, the scholars agree, even Roman Catholic scholars, by the way, that immersion is the preferable form. I think you know that Orthodox Christianity does immerse. It is the only form of baptism that is used in the Orthodox Church. They immerse children. They have a fountain. It is kind of deep, a couple of feet. They pick the kid up, take them by the hands, head under, and bring him up. Father, bring him up; Son, bring him up; Spirit, bring him up. Threefold baptism. If you ever have an opportunity to see an Orthodox baptism, it is really kind of a weird thing. Any questions about baptism from an Orthodox, Catholic, Protestant point of view?

Student: I would like to ask about the time between the profession of faith and the act of baptism itself. The Catholic Church says there must be fruit, or a confession or profession of faith in Christ prior to baptism. How would that hold with New Testament passages where baptism follows almost immediately after the conversion?

Webber: That is one significant difference between the New Testament and the early church, and we find that practice already explained in *The Didache*. On the Day of Pentecost, 3,000 were saved. They were immediately baptized and brought into the church. The Ethiopian eunuch was saved with Phillip baptizing him—*zip*—just like that. By the time you get to *The Didache*, let me read the beginning sentence again, "And concerning baptism, baptize this way: Having first said all these things, baptize into the name of the Father, and of the Son, and of the Holy Spirit, in living water."

10. *Didache*, chapter 7.

So there is a time sequence between conversion and baptism. Why? There are probably several reasons. One is very practical. In the early church, they baptized people without having any understanding of what they were getting into, and the early heretics were baptized Christians. So as the church grew and developed, she shifted her point of view to instruct them in both orthodoxy and orthopraxis. That is what it is referring to in *The Didache*, especially in two ways. By the time you get up to AD 220 with Hippolytus, the period of instruction is a full three years. No six-week course, one night a week, two hours. Nay. Three solid years of baptismal education into the meaning of it, completed by the baptism, usually on Easter.

We used to perform baptism on one Sunday out of the year, and that was on Easter Sunday. Of course, they could do it when they have had three years of education. Prior to that baptism, they always check them out in terms of what they understood and in terms of the way in which they live. So orthodoxy is correct doctrine, orthopraxis is correct living, the two things they looked for. Just to give you a little more history, they were able to do this quite well up until AD 311, because at 311 you have a tremendous shift. This is the persecuted church—and this is the Constantinian church. At the time of the Constantinian church, everybody was a Christian. Not really, but it looked that way. So there were lots and lots of infants that were baptized, and infants were brought into the church almost indiscriminately. As a result, the wholesale infant baptism created lots of problems with them because they had these adults who did not know beans about the Christian faith . . . and did not care much less. So a kind of worldliness crept into the church after the Constantinian era. That helps to explain the second thing that I am going to talk about, and that is confirmation.

I will talk about confirmation before I talk about Eucharist. Confirmation is the sacrament of receiving the Holy Spirit. In today's church confirmation usually takes place at age twelve or whatever. But in the early church, confirmation took place immediately after baptism. Baptism and confirmation were really a single rite. We are talking in the main, it appears, about adult baptism in the early church. Once one comes into Christ, obviously one receives the Holy Spirit. So confirmation is the signing with oil. Actually, in some cases at least, we know at Rome in AD 220 from the apostolic documents of Hippolytus that people washed their whole body with oil, then stood out of the baptismal font. Before putting on the white robe, signifying the new being, one would take oil and wash the entire body. See, the oil signifies the coming of the Holy Spirit. So this signifies the coming of the Holy Spirit into one's whole being. Usually there was special signification with the thumb, in the name of the Father, and the Son, and the Holy Spirit on the forehead, and the eyes and the ears and maybe the breast bone, as indication of the total permeation of the Spirit of God into one's entire life. It is probably not true that everybody would wash their entire body with oil, but some did as indicated by Hippolytus. What occurred in confirmation is by the time you get over into this period where you have infant baptism, a gap came between baptism and confirmation. This really did not occur in the fourth century, but by the time you get up into the ninth, tenth, and eleventh centuries, we have recognition of this, that you have infant baptism, and then about age twelve or so, because this was often the case with the Hebrew tradition of bar mitzvah. So you would have catechetical study and then confirmation. So a gap was between baptism and confirmation by the time you get up into the medieval period, which is not the case in the early church.

The third thing in the early church that occurred was immediately after confirmation, one received the Eucharist. These three right here were all part of a single sacrament that later became separated. Because once one is baptized into the body of Christ, then one receives the body and blood of Christ. The Eucharist is the expression of the nourishment. What do we feed on? What gives us sustenance and strength in the Christian life?

Student: Prayer? Sanctification?

Webber: Let's not separate that from physical participation in the body and blood of Christ though. If we do, that's gnostic again, a rejection of the material. You follow?

Student: No, it's not that I disagree. . . .

Webber: Somebody have a match? Well, it is back to the incarnational thing again. God did not come to us in an appearance; he came to us in flesh and blood. Our nourishment in Christ consists of many things. It consists of doing his will, which has fleshed out. I mean, you have to *do* that. You cannot build a little tree house and hide there and do his will. It is fleshed out in the midst of life itself. Certainly feeding on Christ would be caring about Scripture reading, learning the Scripture, letting it become a part of our life. Prayer would certainly be a part. But the Eucharist is the most climactic moment of our encounter with Jesus Christ. To feed on Christ means to encounter him. It means to let him be present to us. Where is it that he is present to us? Uniquely and chiefly, it is in the sacrament of the Eucharist. Every time you walk forth or receive, I suppose in most cases here you would be having it passed out to you. I like the idea of walking forth, because every time you walk forth and kneel at that rail, you are saying yes to Jesus. You are hearing once again the proclamation that at the center of life stands the incarnation and redemption, that God came to man, lived, died, was raised again for our salvation, and to receive it is to say yes, to receive it by faith and be thankful and feed on him in our hearts by faith, that is to say yes to Jesus Christ. For example, St. Cyril of Jerusalem in his *Catechetical Lectures*, written at AD 315, speaks of us as being Christ bearers when we take the bread and wine into ourselves, and we feed on him and become more like him.[11] It is a tangible, visible means of communicating with Christ and having him communicate himself to us. It is the great meeting place. It is the meeting of man with God in the sacrament of the Eucharist.

We need to stop at this point on the Eucharist, since this is a very important point to talk about. We need to talk for just a moment about the early church's understanding, and the Orthodox and Catholic and Protestant understanding of the Eucharist. If the Eucharist is the unique presence of Christ by which we are nourished, the early church spoke of it in terms of real presence. That is to say, that Christ is really present under the species[12] of bread and wine. He is really there. It is really Jesus. We really encounter him. The problem is that I cannot explain that concept of real presence. There is no way I can explain. In the history of the church, however, theologians have tried to explain it. The medieval explanation, which comes into an Aristotelian approach, is transubstantiation. What does transubstantiation mean?

Student: The bread and wine are the actual body and blood of Christ.

Webber: There was a debate in the eleventh century as to whether or not if you bite the bread you have bitten the body. That is an extreme transubstantiation that would say, "Yeah, if you've bitten the bread, you've bitten

---

11. Cyril of Jerusalem, *Catechetical Lectures*.
12. *Species* means the consecrated eucharistic elements in Catholic and Eastern Orthodox churches.

the body." Do not chew. Let the bread dissolve. This is really an ancient Catholic point of view, and there are probably some Catholics who still explain real presence in that way. Please note that that is what they are doing. They are trying to explain real presence. I do not think you can explain real presence. When you do, you get yourself into some trouble. The Lutheran point of view is consubstantiation. What is consubstantiation?

Student: The presence is in, with, and around the bread and wine.

Webber: It is in, with, around, under, and through, is the meaning of consubstantiation. The best illustration of that would be taking a poker, put it in the fire, and what happens? It becomes red hot in the fire. The poker is not the fire, but the fire is in, with, around, under, and through the poker. And you certainly find that if you pull it out and just stick it in somebody's tummy. . . . But again, at the bottom of consubstantiation, or at bottom of transubstantiation, there is an attempt to explain that Christ is really there. In the sixteenth century, Zwingli came up with the view known as memorialism. Somebody define memorialism?

Student: It is just a memory.

Webber: Just the memory. I remember when I was a little kid, five years ago. You have probably done this yourself. I remember I would be sitting there in my church, and the elements would be passed out to us, and I would hold the bread in my hand. And I would think hard, because I thought that is what I should do. I would create through imagination. There is Golgotha. I can still see the scene that I created for myself. I see the three crosses. I see Jesus Christ. That is basically a memorial point of view, which, I want you to recognize, had never, ever been expressed until the sixteenth century. New, radical, innovative.

Student: Why did Christ say, as often as you do it, you do it in remembrance of me? I understand what you are saying . . . and agree that there is probably more to it than the Zwingli sort of memorialism. But if we skip that, we must ask ourselves, what did Christ mean by remembrance?

Webber: What does the word "remember" mean? What does the word actually mean? That is a good word, and I really think that we ought to focus on it. But what does it mean?

Student: Is it not self-explanatory?

Webber: I don't know. Self-explanatory to whom? I am not trying to put you on the spot. Well, yeah, I am.

Student: I just think you are creating a problem that does not really exist by asking what remembrance means.

Webber: Have you read *The Eucharistic Words of Jesus* by Jeremias?[13] What we are involved [in] here is not a simple little problem. Liturgical studies constitute a whole field of inquiry. The Greek word *anamnesis* is the word "to remember." For example, if you go into an Orthodox church, there is big emphasis on *anamnesis*. See, there are a couple of different ways in which we can use this word "remember." We must go back and find the Greek meaning and the original context. When I say, "I remember," it means that my memory has recalled at this particular time. See, that is a wholly different concept than what *anamnesis* means. The meaning of the word is "re-member." So there is a difference between remembering and re-member. To re-member is to bring it all together again. Let me show you something about the meaning of *anamnesis*. Let me put it this way. Here is the eucharistic moment of anamnesis. Are you following me? This is present. It is today. It is right now. We are in a worship service, let's say. And the celebrant is in the process of remembering. We remember. We are using the words, invoking the words of Christ over the bread and the wine, having prayer for the coming of the Holy Spirit. The eucharistic *anamnesis* in one sense may be said to go back to the Last Supper, which anticipates the actual death [of Jesus]. To remember means not so much that we remember back there, but that which was anticipated in the Last Supper and fulfilled in the death is brought to us.

See the whole difference, is it man going to God, or is it God coming to man? The *anamnesis* is God coming to man. It is re-membering. It is bringing together again the gospel story, the gospel pronouncement, and the presence of Jesus Christ in it. Beyond that, the eucharistic moment also looks to the future, because the eucharistic moment goes to the messianic banquet. Remember Jesus said, "I will not drink of this again with you until I drink with you in the kingdom." So that the eucharistic moment, the *anamnesis*, not only looks back to the Last Supper and death, which is brought to us, but it also looks forward to the second coming of Christ and the new heavens and the new earth, which is also brought to us. Do you see these actions? In other words, the eucharistic moment,

---

13. Jeremias, *Eucharistic Words of Jesus*.

the *anamnesis*, is that point in history in which we are brought into touch with the meaning of the whole cosmos, because we are brought in touch with the real presence of Jesus, who is at once Creator, the incarnate God, the death, the resurrection, and the coming of Christ with his second coming. All of that occurs in the Eucharist. It is a lot more than just a memory.

Student: Yeah, that is what I do not understand. How is Zwingli's memorialism such a departure from that?

Webber: Zwingli's memorialism is the introduction of a rational prism. I mean, there is no way in which this is rationalistic. A persuasion of what I have just talked about in terms of the *anamnesis* has to be based on revelation. And the perception of that, see, is symbolic. It is symbolic. And the perception of that is communicated to us by faith. It is the hope in which we live. How do we know? How do we know that Christ is going to come again? How do we even know that he ever died and was raised again? We believe in order to know. We do not have ultimate facts, either back from then or in the future, but we know that this is true because the Holy Spirit witnesses in us that this is true. We believe in order to know. This is what rationalism began to take away from the church. It began to take away the mystery. It takes us all the way back to the original meaning of sacramental mystery. It began to reduce things to the explainable.

Now I think you know it is a wrong move for the Catholics to have made to explain the real presence in terms of transubstantiation. A wrong move in terms of consubstantiation. Significantly worse, I think, to just simply call it memorialism. Maybe not significantly worse. I probably should not say this, because transubstantiation in particular has created a kind of sacerdotalism[14] or sacramentalism,[15] which has extraordinary dangers within it. But again, the early church concept focuses on Christ as Creator, Incarnate One, Redeemer. All of that. See, that is why the church is often called the eucharistic community, because the whole tradition, the whole truth, the whole gospel, everything that is true about the reality of the world itself is communicated to us in the Eucharist. It is that sense that we have lost as Protestants.

14. Sacerdotalism is a religious belief emphasizing the powers of priests as essential mediators between God and humans.

15. Sacramentalism here is the belief that the sacraments are inherently efficacious and essential for salvation.

Student: You talk about the real presence. I do not really understand how that differs from transubstantiation or consubstantiation. Protestants believe it is a symbol, while Catholics and Orthodox believe that it is the body and blood of Christ. Of course, that is an oversimplification, but what is that third option of it being the real presence?

Webber: Well, the option of real presence is that is the body and blood of Christ, but you cannot explain it.

Student: So is it just the fact that attempting to explain about transubstantiation or consubstantiation . . . ?

Webber: . . . or memorialism. That is a rational attempt to actually explain what cannot be explained. It is the same way with the Trinity. We can talk all around the Trinity. It is not this, it is not that. It is not this, it is not that. But in the end it is paradox that three should be one and one should be three. It is the same way with Christology. It is not this, it is not that. It is not this, it is not that. But it is the paradox of the fully human and the fully divine in one. See, in the modern world we are so rationalistic. We have to explain everything. There is no ambivalence. There is no mystery. There is no room for dynamic flexibility. There is no room for misunderstanding. I say to my college classes, and I do not know if I have ever said this to you or not, but if I have not, I will say it. The circumference of your knowledge is measured by the circumference of your ignorance. The purpose of my teaching is to increase your ignorance, and by doing that, increase your knowledge. But see, we have in the Western world such a concept of knowledge. Knowledge is the accumulation of data that exhausts a certain subject, and we act as though we have exhausted everything, the Trinity, Christology . . . and you know who has? The liberals. That is the main, fundamental problem of liberalism. It is rationalism gone to its logical conclusion. Thank God the Evangelicals have not gone that far—*yet*. But I am not, by any stretch of the imagination, persuaded that Evangelicals will not someday be there. I think present Evangelicalism is the harbinger of future liberalism, unless we can somehow recapture the notion that God is greater than our minds. We are going to destroy God by our minds, just as the liberals did. And you know, if I were teaching modern historical theology, I could just simply show you the steps through the seventeenth, eighteenth, and nineteenth centuries.

Student: Do you suppose that is why there is no conservative or Evangelical seminary in this country that is more than fifty years old?

Webber: Yeah. Give them time, and you can already see.... If I went to most Evangelical seminaries today and gave these lectures, they would run me out. They do not run me out of Wheaton, because they pay stipendiary! The place is a little too big. Fortunately, they do not hang over our class notes.

Student: Was Harvard not once a place where you sent your son to be an Evangelical preacher? How did it fail?

Webber: I don't really know. Some people have made studies at Harvard and Yale and other institutions like that. I could say off the top of my head that it became supra-rationalistic, and it did. But I have never made a study of the decline of an institution in that respect, so it would be very hard for me to answer.

Student: Is there a coupling of our spirit with the Holy Spirit, where we are almost taken out?

Webber: I am glad you asked that question, because the epiclesis, which is a part of the ancient approach to Eucharist—and is now being restored, incidentally, in the Roman Church, which the Anglican church also has—is using the coming of the Holy Spirit. It is the prayer for the coming of the Holy Spirit. If I had a liturgy here, I could give it to you exactly. But it reads something like, "Come, Holy Spirit. Sanctify these elements that they may be to us the body of Christ. And sanctify us as we receive these elements that they may be to us the body and blood of Christ. Amen." In other words, the *anamnesis* occurs as a result of the epiclesis. That is to say, that remembrance is a gift of the Holy Spirit. And you can think of the alpha and the omega, the beginning and the end, all being brought together in that one moment. This is why there is such care given to the Eucharist in your ancient liturgical churches, Catholic, Anglican, etc. The less importance that we attribute to the Eucharist as the expression of the cosmic redemption, the less care we give to it. So now we have the Eucharist, you know, a lot of bread left over, and a lot of grape juice, whatever. Throw it away. Gulp it down. Pour it down the sink. They would never, ever do that in the ancient church. Why? Because it is consecrated. What does that mean? Set apart. We consecrate something and say, "Hey, don't abuse your body. You are consecrated. You are set apart. So be careful what you do." Yet we consecrate bread and wine and just treat it like it is [common] bread and wine. It is not bread and wine. It is the consecrated body and blood.

Student: I have a hard time reconciling that with the very act in which Christ did himself, in which it does not appear to me from the Scripture that he made a big to-do about it, like he was saying that this is going to be a holy cup and this bread is going to be holy bread, and be careful and do not let any of it drop on the ground. . . . I do not see him making a big to-do out of the actual things that he had in his hands as he did the spiritual significance of what was going to be happening.

Webber: Okay, if we are going to make a big to-do out of it and lose the spiritual significance, it is meaningless. I agree. Again, that is bringing form and spirit together in the same way as if we have no form at all, but actually I think most Evangelicals have a lot for him. There is quite a bit of form there. There is quite a bit of reverence directed towards the Eucharist. We have maintained the reverential attitude, but not the understanding, because I am not sure that we know what it is all about. And yet we tread softly, and it is almost a thing that a lot of people fear. Therefore, a lot of our churches at best observe it only every three months. Baptist churches, once a month. The early church celebrated at least every Sunday, because of this culminating point of worship itself.

Student: Was the Word celebrated as well?

Webber: Oh, absolutely. That was the practice of the early church. I think when you get into worship, the central theme of worship was the Word. Evangelicals are right about that. But we are wrong about one thing, and that is in our worship, which is supposed to be a reenactment of the history of God's action in saving us, we do not go all the way. We have the spoken Word, the written Word, but not the incarnate Word. See, the Eucharist represents the incarnate Word. And we leave our worship services at Malachi. We need to bring it into Matthew, and allow the incarnate, enfleshed Word in our midst, because that is what redeems us. That is what saves us. Therefore, this is the center from which the whole meaning of life itself derives. The eucharistic community. Christians are eucharistically centered. Christ is present now. He is not just someone who walked the earth 2,000 years ago and zipped up into the heavens. He is present now, and is uniquely present to us in our worship, made real in the celebration of the Eucharist. . . .

Student: I don't know if I got you wrong a few minutes back, but you said that he is made real to us in our worship. What about someone who comes to the service with faulty faith or understanding? If it is through their worship, it seems like it would not matter. . . . So there must be something beyond the person partaking.

Webber: Well, yes. The meaning of it is resident within the sacrament itself. Therefore, if you take it without faith, it works condemnation. If you take it in faith, it works for our sanctification. The Reformed community has a very high sense of sacramental consciousness for the Eucharist.

Bibliography

Blackmore, R. W., trans. *The Doctrine of the Russian Church*. Edinburgh: Russian Orthodox Church, 1845.

Brink, Emily R., and Robert E. Webber. "Don't Get Hung Up on Style: A Conversation." *Reformed Worship*, Calvin Institute of Christian Worship 38 (March 1996). https://www.reformedworship.org/article/march-1996/dont-get-hung-style-conversation.

The Council of Trent, Decree Concerning Justification and Decree Concerning Reform. https://www.ewtn.com/catholicism/library/decree-concerning-justification-decree-concerning-reform-1496.

Cyril of Jerusalem. *The Catechetical Lectures*. https://www.newadvent.org/fathers/310122.htm.

The Didache. Chapter 7. https://www.newadvent.org/fathers/0714.htm.

Florovsky, Georges. "Scripture and Tradition: An Orthodox Point of View." *Dialog: A Journal of Theology* 2, no. 3 (Autumn 1963) 288–93. https://doi.org/10.1111/j.1540-6385.1963.tb00083.x

Jeremias, Joachim. *The Eucharistic Words of Jesus*. Translated by Norman Perrin from the German 3rd ed. New York: Scribner, 1966.

Neff, David. "Together in the Jesus Story: Bob Webber's fingerprints are all over a new call to live the narrative that really matters. *Christianity Today* 50, no. 9 (September 2006) 54–56. https://www.christianitytoday.com/ct/2006/september/10.54.html

Rupp, Gordon. *Luther's Progress to the Diet of Worms*. Chicago: Wilcox and Follett, 1951.

Stedman, Ray. *Body Life: The Church Comes Alive!* Glendale, CA: Gospel Light, 1972.

Teilhard de Chardin, Pierre. *The Divine Milieu*. New York: Harper Torchbooks, 1960.

Wax, Trevin. "In Honor of Robert Webber: An Interview." *The Gospel Coalition*, April 28, 2007. https://www.thegospelcoalition.org/blogs/trevin-wax/in-honor-of-robert-web.er-an-interview.

Webber, Robert E. *Blended Worship: Achieving Substance and Relevance in Worship*. Peabody, MA: Hendrickson, 1996.

———. *The Book of Daily Prayer*. Grand Rapids: Eerdmans, 1993.

———. *Common Roots: The Original Call to an Ancient-Future Faith*. Foreword by David Neff. Reprint, Grand Rapids: Zondervan, 2009.

———. *The Complete Library of Christian Worship*. 7 vols. Peabody, MA: Hendrickson, 1993–1995.

———. *Learning to Worship with All Your Heart: A Study in the Biblical Foundations of Christian Worship*. Peabody, MA: Hendrickson, 1994.

———. *Liturgical Evangelism: Worship as Outreach and Nurture.* Ridgefield, CT: Morehouse, 1992.

———. "Orthodoxy, Catholicism, Protestantism," class lecture for the Institute of Slavic Studies, transcript from audio recording, Wheaton, IL: Buswell Library Archives & Special Collections, class session #1, December 5, 1978.

———. "Orthodoxy, Catholicism, Protestantism," class session #2, December 7, 1978.

———. "Orthodoxy, Catholicism, Protestantism," class session #3, December 14, 1978.

———. "Orthodoxy, Catholicism, Protestantism," class session #4, December 21, 1978.

———. "Orthodoxy, Catholicism, Protestantism," class session #5, January 4, 1979.

———. "Orthodoxy, Catholicism, Protestantism," class session #6, January 11, 1979.

———. "Orthodoxy, Catholicism, Protestantism," class session #7, January 18, 1979.

———. "Orthodoxy, Catholicism, Protestantism," class session #8, January 25, 1979.

———. "Orthodoxy, Catholicism, Protestantism," class session #9, February 1, 1979.

———. "Orthodoxy, Catholicism, Protestantism," class session #10, February 8, 1979.

———. *Renew! Songs and Hymns for Blended Worship.* Carol Stream, IL: Hope, 1995.

———. *Worship is a Verb: Celebrating God's Mighty Deeds of Salvation.* Rev. ed. Peabody, MA: Hendrickson, 1993.

———. *Worship Old & New.* Rev. ed. Grand Rapids: Zondervan, 1994.

Webber, Robert E., and Rodney Clapp. *People of the Truth: A Christian Challenge to Contemporary Culture.* Reprint, Eugene, OR: Wipf and Stock, 2001.

"What Younger Evangelicals Want—and Are Getting!" *Homiletics Online* (January–February 2004). https://www.homileticsonline.com/.

www.ingramcontent.com/pod-product-compliance
Lightning Source LLC
Chambersburg PA
CBHW031401230426
43670CB00006B/609